Thoughts often ran across his mind—what would life have been like if he had NOT taken that small step out of the ordinary? Mike played multiple team sports at reasonable levels, but his inner-self searched for adventure out of his comfort zone. Coming close to joining the armed forces as a reservist, he chose climbing and Mountaineering.

Instead of games dictated by multiple rules, he chose a game climbers play with rules made only by themselves.

Adventures on rock, snow and ice took him and a band of brothers to the edge. His own rules however, insisted he returned to a beloved family.

Credit for all the photographs included goes to Mike Hope/Martin Scrowston collection unless otherwise stated. A huge thank you to Martin Scrowston for the front cover picture.

For my Mother who inspired me to be humble and a kind human being. Her life and her love were for 'her three boys' a legacy which has continued for us all too.

For Lynne, Gary and Nicky who have inspired me directly and indirectly, each in their own special way, to write this book.

For Chester who had a battle from birth, will have battles throughout his life, but I know will grow to be a remarkable and kind person.

Mike Hope

STEPPING OUT OF THE ORDINARY

AUSTIN MACAULEY PUBLISHERS™
LONDON • CAMBRIDGE • NEW YORK • SHARJAH

Copyright © Mike Hope 2023

The right of Mike Hope to be identified as author of this work has been asserted by the author in accordance with sections 77 and 78 of the Copyright, Designs and Patents Act 1988.

All rights reserved. No part of this publication may be reproduced, stored in a retrieval system, or transmitted in any form or by any means, electronic, mechanical, photocopying, recording, or otherwise, without the prior permission of the publishers.

Any person who commits any unauthorised act in relation to this publication may be liable to criminal prosecution and civil claims for damages.

All of the events in this memoir are true to the best of the author's memory. The views expressed in this memoir are solely those of the author

A CIP catalogue record for this title is available from the British Library.

ISBN 9781398487574 (Paperback)
ISBN 9781398487581 (Hardback)
ISBN 9781398487598 (ePub e-book)

www.austinmacauley.com

First Published 2023
Austin Macauley Publishers Ltd®
1 Canada Square
Canary Wharf
London
E14 5AA

To Lynne, Gary and Nicky for everything, particularly their support writing this book in the first place. Their suggestions and corrections at various stages were invaluable.

To Martin and Carole Scrowston for sharing many adventures without which, there would not be this book to write.
The same goes for the rest of family and friends who also have a mutual passion for life and adventure.

Thanks to Audrey Salkeld (General Editor of World Mountaineering) for inspiration and allowing me to use a few words from 'unwritten codes'

Thanks to Corrie Jeffery (Digital conversions specialist) for her excellent digitising work on my photographs and slides.

To the UK's Air, Land and Sea rescue services who without them, people like me may not have been around to write a book.

Finally, I am grateful to Austin Macauley for taking me on and giving me the opportunity to publish my memoir.

Table of Contents

Introduction	11
Part 1: Early Years	17
Chapter One: My Childhood	19
Chapter Two: Mid-Teens to Our Marriage	25
Chapter Three: No Looking Back	36
Chapter Four: Proudest Moments	45
Part 2: Life-Changing Moments	57
Chapter Five: Direction Choices	59
Chapter Six: Sudden Epiphany	73
Chapter Seven: Alpine Initiation	86
Chapter Eight: Alps Revisited	96
Part 3: Early Expeditions	107
Chapter Nine: A Taste of Alaska	109
Chapter Ten: Running Wild	114
Chapter Eleven: Defeat in South America	117
Chapter Twelve: Mount Robson and Edith Cavell	123
Part 4: Short Stories/Long Journeys	129
Chapter Thirteen: Fun Together	131
Chapter Fourteen: Along the John Muir Trail	135
Chapter Fifteen: 1998	141

Chapter Sixteen: Rewards of a Bivvy or Wild Camp	*145*
Chapter Seventeen: The Corsican Traverse	*150*
Part 5: Further Expeditions	**165**
Chapter Eighteen: Mount Asgard, Baffin Island	*168*
Chapter Nineteen: Cutting it Loose on the Moose's Tooth, Alaska	*178*
Chapter Twenty: The Old Man of Hoy	*187*
Chapter Twenty-One: Jebel Toubkal and Moroccan High Atlas	*193*
Chapter Twenty-Two: Christmas in Patagonia	*200*
Chapter Twenty-Three: Korichuma, Bolivian Success	*221*
Part 6: Alpine Adventures	**241**
Chapter Twenty-Four: Winter Icefalls, Canada and Europe	*243*
Chapter Twenty-Five: Piz Badile, North East Face	*250*
Chapter Twenty-Six: Cycling in the Alps and Andalusia	*253*
Chapter Twenty-Seven: The Beautiful Lofoten Isles	*259*
ChapterTwenty-Eight: Les Courtes—North Face	*263*
Part 7: UK Playground	**271**
Chapter Twenty-Nine: Circuit of the Lairig Ghru	*273*
Chapter Thirty: Three Ridges	*277*
Chapter Thirty-One: The West Highland Way	*285*
Chapter Thirty-Two: Maesglasau Falls	*290*
Chapter Thirty-Three: Land's End to John O'groats (LEJOG)	*293*
Part 8: Epilogue	**301**
Chapter Thirty-Four: Past and Present	*303*
First Ascents	**311**
Adventures & Climbing Record – Mike Hope	**313**
Bibliography	**321**

Introduction

Twenty years from now, you will be more disappointed by the things that you didn't do than by the ones you did. So throw off the bowlines, sail away from the safe harbour.
Catch the trade winds in your sails, Explore, Dream, Discover.
Mark Twain

Why am I writing this autobiography? I'm not famous, nor am I at all wealthy, but thanks to the love and support of close family, and some special friends, I have had one heck of a life.

I am immensely proud of my wife, Lynne; my son, Gary; and my daughter, Nicky. Not only have they helped me accomplish my wonderful life, they too have made the most of their lives, and together we have shared some incredible journeys that I would love to share with others.

I guess there are two reasons I am writing this book, whilst being realistic and under no illusions, it's not likely to run off the shelves of Waterstones!

Firstly, just as it was for me wanting to know a little of my family history, this autobiography will be available in writing somewhere, should any of my progeny down the line want to know a tiny bit of 'Hope'.

Secondly, most of us don't inherit that rare DNA that helps one become an Olympian, a great musician, rocket scientist or micro surgeon. Like the majority, we settle for the lower divisions; but every single one of us can find that hidden talent waiting to be explored and do something special with the gift given to us, the gift of life. We only need to dare to dream, open our minds and work at it, bloody hard in most cases to have the same fulfilment.

I would like to think that this book may help encourage others, who like me, needed to seek adventure. To help make a life changing decision if necessary, into something that will consume mind, body and soul positively with great enjoyment, instead of a journey down depression, drugs or alcohol. In my opinion, it doesn't matter a toss to compare oneself to others.

It matters so much more to know in your heart that you have contentment and self-satisfaction in life. I could probably have achieved more in mountaineering terms, but it would have been too much at the sacrifice of my family. For me, it was that balanced combination that has given me the utmost pleasure and belief, to encourage others!

I did not think for one moment in my youth as an urban layabout that I was going to join a group of hard-core loonies and become a rock climber, alpinist and mountaineer at the ripe old age of thirty…not in a million years!

Although I wish I had found the sport in my teens. I couldn't have joined it at more dynamic period than in the early 1980s. 'British Traditional' climbing, known more commonly as 'Trad climbing'[1], had got to a level where E5 (E for Extreme) perhaps E6 was the pinnacle of the sport.

Along came the likes of John Redhead, Johnny Dawes, Gerry Moffat, Ron Fawcett, Andy Pollitt, and of course Catherine Destivelle, to name a few, who took Trad climbing and the new found love of 'Sport climbing'[2] into a different dimension. The legends that were Joe Brown and Hamish MacInnes had already taken rock climbing well into the E grades and Scottish winter climbing into the V/5 grades.

Very soon, Trad grades of E7, E8 and E9 were appearing along with F8a, F8b Sport routes. These guys were inspirational to me and others climbing in the lower leagues. Over the years, I was inspired by them and their training regimes, eventually managing a few E4s of my own, which gave me enormous pleasure.

There is no doubt that rock climbing and eventually alpinism/mountaineering changed my way of life. It has nurtured my soul, helped improve self-confidence, given extreme pleasure in the natural world, bonded family and friends and given me such a wonderful life. Unfortunately, it has left me with a legacy of fear; fear that as I grow old, and then *so* old, I will not be able to climb or walk in the

---

[1] 'Trad climbing' is a specific form of climbing in the UK where only the natural features of the rock are used for protecting the climber from a fall. Pitons or pegs are the only form of 'fixed gear' permitted and must not be used to 'aid' progression upwards. It also has very specific codes of practice relating to types of ascent.

[2] 'Sport climbing' has found its way from the continent onto selected crags or types of rock. The grading follows that of the French 'F' grading system. More to the point it has 'fixed gear' protection in place in the rock with the use of 'Bolts' or 'Staples' making for a safer, less 'adventurous' form of climbing.

mountains anymore. However, should that be the case, I will eventually depart this amazing world with a huge smile on my face.

Cross country running, football and badminton had been my main sporting interests until well into my late twenties. I was a husband and father but something was missing. Whether it was the desire to test myself out of my comfort zone or just 'explore', I'm not sure.

I was not academically strong at school, preferring to participate in any form of sport instead of knuckling down to secure 'O' and 'A' level qualifications like my peers. I was often punished for gazing out of the classroom window at others on the sports field.

My only degree was one of 'common sense', gained after leaving school, and in my opinion, it deserves much more appreciation than it gets in society today. I suppose there was one other degree I claimed which was 'bluff and bollocks' but I dared not include that in any of my CVs.

I believe today's youngsters are universally pushed into and judged by their 'A' grade achievements, what degree course they are signing up for and the university they will be going to. This, for many kids, is unnecessary pressure at an age when there is far more scope to seek other opportunities in life. Just as important is the understanding that we mature academically at different ages, often gaining our academic strengths in education outside of the norm.

Don't get me wrong, I recognise the need for many to focus on their education and career sooner rather than later, but for others, there is ample time for erudition.

As I write this, I hear on the news that Culham Science Centre (formerly Culham Laboratory) in Oxfordshire—where I worked for 4 years, is looking to take on numerous apprentices in a brand-new facility. This has been necessary to rebuild the huge gap in skilled craftspeople lost because of the trend towards 'must have degrees' and the stigma of learning a trade. If we don't take this seriously, we will lose the ability to compete worldwide in the technologies.

Great Britain has been so good at it, like the Aerospace, Nuclear, Automotive and Pharmaceutical industries to name a few. The UK remains one of the most attractive countries in the world for direct foreign industrial investment; we must not lose the skills that make it so vibrant.

Looking back, I was probably inspired by my mother, who was a good athlete in her day, before WW2 and 'the Blitz' buggered that up for her. She was also a very positive and lovely person.

I represented the county at cross country running and football, always hoping that someday I was going to be a professional footballer. A very short trial at Queens Park Rangers FC soon put paid to that, when they told me to come back when I was bigger; thank goodness I never went back!

My sporting prowess certainly outweighed my academic ability, none more so than poor English language and English literature grades from school. I hope I have at least been able to get the following history and stories in some sort of readable quality…so stick with it!

Mountaineers are quite often asked the question "why?"

It is difficult to explain and even more difficult not to quote the classic answer given by George Mallory[3]: "Because it's there."

Whatever answers we give, must wash over the heads of many who see mountains from an armchair, TV screen or windows of their cars. This is completely understandable, as unless climbing is experienced for oneself by applying the precise and calculated movements up a rock face, or the technical requirements and knowledge to scale vertical ice with axes and crampons in big mountains, it is impossible to comprehend the thrill and sense of achievement it gives to those who play the game.

Climbing also involves expression, action and a demonstration of what is possible. Above all else, it involves the recognition and acceptance of risk. As each generation evolves, this acceptance of risk deviates from society's convention.

Mountaineering has also opened my eyes to our planet's global pollution problem. Whether that be the glaciers in the Alps or further afield from Alaska to South America, without doubt it has shown me it is happening, and happening fast.

It has given me first-hand knowledge and observations of the absolute abomination and seemingly disregard of what pollution is doing to countries around the world in the atmosphere, in our oceans and on the land.

Small pockets of people are trying to bring it to world's attention, but the problem is now so huge because the greater percentage of countries and their populations cannot give a toss, consumed by greed of self-prosperity and wants of their own—at any cost.

---

[3] George Herbert Mallory was an English Mountaineer who took part in the first three British expeditions to Mount Everest in the early 1920s.

If we really are going to resolve this behemoth and help future generations enjoy the planet as we have, it must be led 'from the top' by every government, in every country in the world…and **force change without delay!**

Changes need to happen with great thought, not knee-jerk reactions, however if we take the case of plastics as an example, let us not forget that it was introduced and developed mid-twentieth century, primarily by a family who wanted an alternative to cutting down trees.

There are many organisations trying to help where they can.

The John Muir Trust is one such organisation that has inspired me. They are a conservation charity dedicated to protecting and enhancing wild places across the UK. Their work naturally fits alongside my heart, and is why I have been a member for nearly twenty years.

I shall close this introduction with a short piece by Audrey Salkeld[4]—a famous female Mountaineering author, who wrote an article in a book published in the 1990s called 'World Mountaineering'. It had a profound influence on me in my early days as a mountaineer.

Primitive people were geared to facing danger in almost everything they did. We have evolved a society that seeks to eliminate risk almost entirely—even to hold someone else accountable when anything goes wrong. In providing this expectation of safety, we fail to encourage the acquisition of skills, experience, and above all the common sense which would help us, if not to manage it, at least to react to risk constructively.

We lose the empowering sense of our own judgement. This is what climbing is mostly about—taking back the responsibility for one's own existence, and climbers react dramatically when they perceive this essence is being threatened or compromised.

---

[4] Audrey Salkeld was born in 1936 in Cumbria, England. She is known and respected for her work on Adventure (1987), National Geographic Explorer (1985) and Everest: The Mystery of Mallory and Irvine (1992).

Part 1: Early Years

*Life does not owe you anything,
because life has already given you everything.*

Mark Twain

Chapter One
My Childhood

I was born in Queen Charlotte's Hospital in the Metropolitan Borough of Hammersmith on the 22 March 1951 to John Richard Arthur Hope (b. 1/3/1924) and Lillian May Hope (formerly Lincoln; b. 19/10/1923).

Evidently, I was a bit of a porker, having popped out at nine pounds three ounces, and was the first of three boys for Mum and Dad. We lived in a flat above Grand Garages at Richmond upon Thames where my father worked as a motor mechanic, having completed National Service in the Navy up to the rank of Petty Officer.

It was a stone's throw from Richmond Bridge, the river Thames and Richmond Park, and judging by some early photographs they were obviously the places to walk and show off their new born. At fifteen months old, my one claim to fame was winning a baby competition. I'm unsure of the number in the contest or what the requirements were, but who cares, it remains the only competition I've ever won!

My mum also worked, often holding down a couple of part-time jobs which was the main reason us kids seldom went short of basic needs. To help her do that, I had an exceptional godparent called 'Nan' Philipson. She looked after me at certain times while Mum worked, remaining a close friend to her up until Mum's passing away due to cancer in 1985 at sixty-two years old.

'Nan' was a petite woman but had one hell of a constitution. She outlived her husband Roy and many friends younger than herself until her own passing in 2018, at the ripe old age of hundred and four years old. Not one single year went by without her remembering my birthday, always sending a card with cash enclosed.

She looked after herself and her house at Okehampton on the edge of Dartmoor right up to the last few months of her life. She made herself three meals a day and hardly missed seeing an evening out with a tipple of red wine whilst listening to the BBC news—a truly remarkable woman.

Memories and photographs show there were frequent visits from grandparents. On my father's side, I had a grandad who I often thought was rather hen pecked by my grandma, but he remained a jovial and kind bloke. He worked on the railways as a signalman. I remember being taken to his signal box now and again, and being awestruck by the mass of levers and bells, and with the whistles of the steam trains that came thundering through.

My grandma, on the other hand, was not the sort of person I warmed to, as she appeared to me to be a stern and grumpy old dear.

My nan on my mum's side was the complete opposite. She was quite a bit older than the other two grandparents, but was just a friendly, quiet person who was always around. My nan lived with us up to my early teens. I have always thought it a shame I never got to know my grandpops.

He was one of the first London cabbies, and by all accounts a bit of a lad. Sadly, he died during the Second World War.

I was around the age of three years old when we moved from Richmond to Goffs Road, Ashford in Middlesex. It was a new three bedroomed house and one of the first to be built on a 'new estate'; vague memories still pop into my head of the muddy, unmade road we travelled down to get to it.

I look back now with admiration at my parents for the nerve and risk it must have taken to acquire their mortgage at that time, especially on the salaries they were earning and the uncertainty of a country that was still coming to terms with the devastation that the Second World War had brought, nine years previously.

Pretty soon after moving in, my brother Chris was born (6/1/1955) and four years following that, my youngest brother Pete (1/6/1959). There were now six of us in the house as our nan occupied the smallest third bedroom, while us, three boys, shared the second bedroom.

Our nan lived with us for a few years, always being around for us when both our parents were out working.

The estate was pretty much full of housing by the time Pete was born, which enabled us to build friendships with neighbouring kids of respective ages as we grew up. We all had a happy life at home well into our teens and each of us brothers lived there until either getting married or going to university.

However, there were a couple of dark moments in our lives, one of which affected Chris and myself more than Pete due to our age; and one that affected us all, which I will bring up later.

My father never really got on with my nan and he was a bit of a shit really. I suppose space could be tight at times, but she did contribute to the house in many ways. Eventually Mum found her an 'old folk's home' near Streatham Common, London, but not once did the old man take my mum to visit her.

For years she relied on public transport, friendly neighbours or much later, by us brothers. It set the scene for what was going to happen later.

We all went to the same Spelthorne infant school followed by their primary school. Thereafter, it was Kenyngton Manor Secondary school at Sunbury-on-Thames for myself and Pete, whilst Chris, the academic of us three, went to Ashford Grammar school.

For me, there was always plenty to occupy me after school hours. At one end of Goffs Road, there was a recreation ground with a pond. It had an enormous oak tree which I was very fond of climbing, and a large grassy area ideal for playing football.

For years it attracted many like-minded kids to come home from school and go straight to the 'rec' for a game of footy until it got dark, often up to 15-a-side in the summer. Very often the old man would have to come over and shout at me to 'get home'.

Another attraction for me were the local gravel pits, not for swimming, as I knew how dangerous they could be, but they offered a sense of wildness and dare-devilness for roaming around, lighting fires, firing catapults, pea shooters and other boys' stuff.

Not quite into my teens, the pits were a great place to ride old wrecks of motorbikes. Inevitably if the old man caught me, I would get one hell of a bollocking. I know my mum worried terribly over that, encouraging me to stay out of trouble, but I didn't see the fun in that. I honestly believe it was a heuristic period of my childhood that gave me early self-confidence and self-belief.

Failing my 'eleven-plus' and starting senior school were two memories that are still very vivid for me. Most of my mates had passed the exam and were going to either Ashford Grammar or Sunbury-on-Thames Grammar schools, whilst I was on my way to Kenyngton Manor Secondary School. I was gutted; it was the end of the world, but of course that only lasted the short time it took to make new mates.

Worse than that, I had to endure the first day going to my new 'big lads' school in shorts. I swear I was the only one in the school, let alone the class, that wore shorts. I knew times were hard at home, but made it very clear to my mum that I was not going back the next day unless I had long trousers!

In those days, one could not just nip out to the local shops to get a pair. Fortunately, there happened to be a good friend up the road about the same age and size as me, so I was able to borrow a pair. It mattered not that I had to roll up the waist band a couple of turns, I was just so relieved not to be associated as the new kid in school, which had been so bloody obvious the day before.

This was especially important as all the new girls the school had to offer looked much more mature and grown up for their age; they were not about to be chatted up by a short arse in shorts.

It didn't take long to feel part of the school and make some good friends. I believe my participation in as much sport the school could offer helped support me with the lack of interest I had in most of the lessons, although I did just manage to hold my own in subjects that kept me in the first stream throughout the five years.

I represented the school and the county of South West Middlesex in cross country running and football. Basketball and gymnastics were also where I made the school team. These activities required a certain amount of time after school for training and certainly for competition, so there was little time for homework—my excuse anyway!

I did not regard myself as a trouble maker, just full of energy and inquisitiveness, although I did get attached to a couple of groups, loosely called gangs, made up of girls as well as lads.

Smoking was the indulgence in those days, not drugs or heavy alcohol. I think I tried a couple of packets of cigarettes to keep up with them, but found no appeal in it whatsoever. I was more concerned of the impact it might have on my sporting activities.

That's not to say I stayed completely out of trouble. One of my gangs had a fascination for pipe bombs. Jimmy G, Christine G (no relation, just boyfriend/girlfriend) and others would get a short length of metal pipe, close off one end and drill a small hole one third up the tube. We filled it with a mix of weed-killer and sugar, then carefully sealed the other end.

The pipe was usually placed on the ground in a local field with a short length of the mixture making a trail up to the hole. The other end of the trail would be lit and we would run like shit and hide. Most of the time the bang was loud but not excessive, about as loud as some fireworks, but of course the pipe bomb making practice had to end in tears sometime.

It was inevitable we would ramp up the scale of the thing. Goodness knows where the bits of pipe ended up, but having blue lights and sirens looking for us all over the place certainly put an end to all that larking about. It was made a little more concerning knowing that Jimmy and Christine's fathers were policemen. I was a lot older when I realised our innocent larking about was surpassed by the violence of IRA terrorists using similar materials.

That's how it was for a year or so, right up to the point where I nicked Christine from Jim while he was away on holiday. Didn't go down too well obviously, but at the time I thought I was in love and as I was learning a lot, an amazing amount in fact about the birds and bees, I didn't really care. Not surprising it fizzled out, Chrissy went back to Jim, and I went back to other sports!

As a family we all got on well together, and to this day, us three brothers have remained very close. Holidays were spent together mainly on caravan sites in Cornwall or at Holiday camps such as Warners on Hayling Island. One memory my brother Chris and I remember very clearly (Pete was too young) was when our father decided he wanted to buy his own caravan. He paid about £35 as I remember, certainly not a lot more, for a four berth 'Eccles Alert' caravan, sited on the Isle of Sheppey.

Looking back, as we have done on many occasions, it was a pile of junk. I think we had to make two visits with the old man to pick it up, as our first visit was met with ankle deep snow and everything frozen solid. Extra tools were obviously needed to get this monstrosity back home.

I remember very clearly us having to hammer seven barrels out the towing hitch with a lump hammer to free the thing off so it could operate the brakes. The same effort was needed thereafter to release the corroded drum brakes. He obviously saw this as an interesting project, as not only were the mechanics in a bad way, the front body work was rotten and so was the roof. A shed load of TLC was needed to get it on the road.

Effort on Chris's and my behalf didn't stop at just getting it back home. For two or three weeks after school, we spent most evenings underneath the damn thing, wire brushing rust off the main under-body metal chassis, then painting it with red oxide—a rust proofing.

Wind whipped under that bloody van continually. It kicked off a spate of sinus for me, giving me headaches the likes of which I never want to experience again. I needed two weeks off school with head buried in a Friars Balsam inhalant three times a day. I wasn't happy.

In fairness to him, the skill and knowledge gained as a motor mechanic certainly showed through in transforming that heap into something fit for many holidays to follow. All of us, apart from the old man, did wonder however, why he only went for a four-berth van when very clearly there were five of us. Pete must have been tucked in somewhere, although I struggle to remember where.

Chapter Two
Mid-Teens to Our Marriage

Involvement in sports gave me the opportunity to make many genuine friends, and it was football for a decade and a half that gave me the most.

One of my best mates at the time was a lad called Nigel H. He had a touch of class, in football terms anyhow, and went on to play senior amateur football in the paid ranks. We also had another sport in common, which was an emerging passion for golf.

Nigel and I had the same enthusiasm and attitude to something new and challenging. At around the age of fifteen, we would catch a bus or cadge a lift from his dad, who ran a taxi service, to Sandown race course which also had a driving range on the site. We hired a couple of clubs and hit endless numbers of balls until we were either knackered or skint.

One Saturday, we went over to Wentworth Golf Course, a very prestigious course near Virginia Water, Surrey. Nigel had heard somewhere that they were advertising for caddies, so went on our way to find the Caddy Master. We expected to be turned away due to our age, but obviously bluffed him sufficiently, as we both got a round each with a course member to see how we fared.

We never looked back, in fact, we were hooked. Not only did we thoroughly enjoy the caddying, we revelled in the banter and craic with members and other caddies. We were quite well paid by the caddy master, and if we aided 'our golfer', typically on the run of the greens or helped with club selection, a handsome tip came our way too. Caddying was certainly the most single thing that helped improve my own game.

We got to know some older caddy hands, who gave us many tips and tricks of the trade. To look at them, you could easily mistake them for tramps or dirt bags[5]. They would arrive at the caddy house in the morning looking as though they had spent the night in a ditch.

It probably wasn't a million miles from the truth, as most of them had spent their considerable earnings of the day on the horses or pissed it up at a local pub. They saved just enough to buy the famous caddy house fry up the following morning before venturing out for another two rounds on the course.

Nigel and I pissed ourselves with laughter on a regular basis watching one or two of them trying to walk a straight line, let alone having to carry a client's bag weighing up to 15kgs. However, those old boys were amazing, they knew their stuff even half cut. When one considered how heavy the betting could be in a 'four-ball', it mattered not so long as they were delivering the goods to their golfer.

Nigel and I continued to play golf and caddy when we could for a few years. I joined Laleham Golf Club as a junior member during my Engineering apprenticeship years, managing to get my handicap down to eleven.

One claim to fame on the caddy front was working two rounds with Peter Oosterhuis who at the time was an amateur. He turned Professional not long after at the end of 1968. Peter went on to play on the European circuit from 1969 to 1974, and played in Great Britain's Ryder cup squad from 1971 to 1977.

Lynne bought me my first set of decent clubs as a first wedding anniversary present which I still have in the loft today. Unfortunately, golf took a bit of a back seat for me when Lynne and I moved to South Oxfordshire in 1974. There were, and still are, top class courses in the region, but even back in those days, annual memberships and course fees were exceptionally high for me.

Nigel and I played football for the county of South West Middlesex for two or three years. It was a great band of brothers, although we were a mediocre team compared to a few other counties. We travelled south as far as Dover and north as far as Warwickshire.

A good few of the county team players stayed together into our late teens, early twenties playing Saturday football for Ashford Town (Middlesex) FC and Sunday football for Matthew Arnold FC. Great friends such as Pat Munns, Alan Constable, Jimmy Bedford, Nigel Howard, Johnny Marshall, and of course Bob Parker, a great friend and manager of Ashford Town.

---

[5] I came across the term 'dirtbag' when I started climbing, a person who dedicates their existence to the pursuit of climbing. Making ends meet using creative means. Obtaining food and clothes from any source, living in a vehicle, ditch or tent to save money.

I started to knuckle down academically around fifteen, much too late to get reasonable grades at GCE 'O' level and certainly no point in pursuing any studies at 'A' level. However, I was encouraged to stay on a year, the fifth year, by both my parents and teachers as I was reasonably competent at certain aspects of Maths and Physics. There was no way I wanted to go to university even if I could, and it was obvious I was not going to make it as a professional footballer.

The time was approaching to start thinking about what I should do as a career. I had always enjoyed metalwork, woodwork and technical drawing lessons, delivering a pretty good standard in all three. Amongst my close mates, there were a few that could see themselves going to university, but others were talking of apprenticeships.

I remember my mum continually encouraging me to look at one or other of those trades. Time was on my side as I was always going to see the fifth year out and at least try and get a couple of 'O's.

It was around this period that a bombshell hit us. Mum told us she had been diagnosed with breast cancer. It sure came as a shock to Chris and I, Pete was still only around eight, so affected him not quite as much. I always felt Mum was fit and healthy for her age; she was certainly full of life.

She enjoyed a few fags a day and a little glass of wine now again, but very few vices. She was still fit enough to chase us lively kids around the house with a cane that used to sit behind a picture of 'Charlie'[6] over the mantelpiece. Most of the time it was all in great fun after we had taken the piss about something.

Little was known about breast cancer in 1967 and likewise the treatment of it. We were told by Mum a form of radiotherapy and surgical treatment was available, and so assumed everything would turn out okay. It was many years later unfortunately, that new methods of combination chemotherapy could have a much greater effect in curing patients.

I suppose the initial shock to us was offset by our lack of understanding and/or that Mum played it down. She overcame the initial cancer scare by having a mastectomy and radiotherapy, but the cancer was to reappear a decade and half later.

After the treatment was successful and family life started to return to normal, I became aware how little the old man had helped Chris, Pete and myself overcome the worrying time. I remember nothing about him giving any support

---

[6] 'Charlie' was a nick name we gave to a framed print of a portrait of *The Laughing Cavalier* by the Dutch painter Frans Hals.

or understanding to any of us during that worrying period, which said it all to me really. It felt very much like we were left to get on and over it ourselves.

I know now of course, it was to set the scene for the following years to come. It showed with his lack of interest in anything my brothers and I did, coupled with fuck-all affection.

I became closer to Mum, whether that was because of the cancer scare or the way the old man was behaving I'm not sure. I always cycled the 3 miles to and from school each day, no mums taking us to school in those days, and started to cycle home most lunchtimes just to have lunch together and chat. It kind of coincided with me taking studies a little more seriously too. I was still heavily involved in any sporting activities, but also paid more attention to the shortened 'options programme' of fifth year academia.

Towards the end of my school years, I had decided on an apprenticeship in toolmaking. I went for a couple of interviews at a toolmakers and precision engineering firm called Gay's (of Hampton) Ltd, based in Hampton, Middlesex. I had gained 'O' level passes in woodwork and technical drawing and was lucky to be accepted on a five-year contract as a Toolmaking Apprentice at the age of sixteen.

23 March 2020—Covid 19: *We are now on the infamous 'lock down' for 3 weeks or more. Coronavirus has hit the country badly. Lynne and others at Brett's pharmacy remain at work, potentially risking their lives supplying prescriptions for the public.*
A lot more on this will follow…

And so, it was in September 1967 that I left school and started life in a man's world of engineering at the tender and rather immature age of sixteen.

It was to be a great adventure for four years, apprenticeships were reduced from five to four years not long after I started. I revelled in being accepted as 'one of the blokes' by most of my work colleagues in what was quite a large production environment. I had also been accepted on to a Mechanical Engineering Technicians course at Twickenham College of Further Education for one day and one evening a week.

The first year sorted out the men from the boys. There were twelve that had been accepted into the apprentice school that year. By the end of it, about half had drifted off, either because it wasn't for them, or because they could earn more money 'on the buses', building sites, or other better paid short-term contracts.

I stuck with it and enjoyed it. I learned a great deal from the skills we were taught and practical engineering test pieces we were given throughout the year. It certainly wasn't all serious stuff, as on many occasions we led the poor old apprentice master up the wall.

A classic trick was to sneak into his office and coat the ear piece of his telephone with 'engineer's blue'[7]. He would walk around the factory departments clueless until eventually realising why everyone was smiling at him. "Those little bastards have been at it again, haven't they?" he would shout.

The company had some extremely high-profile projects, two of which I can remember.

One was for 'The Metal Box Company' building, some of their first automated canning machines. The other was for the military, building small 'submarine auto pilot' units with an overall size of about a cubic metre. They were extremely technical, precision made pieces of equipment. I can still remember being mightily impressed by the guys that built them.

There were certainly a lot of characters in the factory. One guy was the factory namesake; he had salmon pink hair and was as gay as they come. His nickname was 'Snatch' and worked as a skilled operator in the grinding section. Every now and again there would be a raucous in the workshop and everyone tried to get a look in, Snatch had been wound up by someone.

He would chase them down and grab them by the balls, lifting them bodily with one arm. Hilarity broke out around the factory, bringing smiles even to the foremen who were powerless to stop it. It was all in great fun and friendship, alas I guess, wouldn't be tolerated today. I considered myself lucky not to be 'snatched', but maybe he thought I just wasn't worth it!

I regarded my apprenticeship as one of the best I could have hoped for, and with the accompanying academic HNC qualification, it has given me career opportunities I have been exceedingly grateful for. Throughout my working life, home maintenance life and later, my mountaineering life, I have drawn on those skills to get me through complex, technical situations. I can also say in over forty-five years in an engineering environment, I had never been made redundant.

---

[7] Engineer's blue is a highly pigmented paste used to assist in the mating of two or more components. Also used for scribing a line that stands out for machining purposes. It was very difficult to remove without the correct solvent.

I was nineteen years old when I collected my Toolmaking Indentures, or 'papers' as we called them, to confirm I had successfully completed my apprenticeship. I was really chuffed knowing I had the skills that could now command a huge salary…or so I thought.

It was common in the industry where one had done an apprenticeship, not to be recognised as a skilled tradesman and be rewarded as such. Most, therefore, left to seek employment and their fortune elsewhere. I was one of those, I also needed a change from a factory environment, if only for a while.

I landed a job in central London working for a company called Premaberg Pipelines who were market leaders at the time in 'Hot Tap and Stopple techniques'[8].

Travelling to Regents Street head office on the tube was certainly an experience, an experience I soon learned was not going to be the long-term future for me. In fact, just about every job I have had has been a great mix of experiences. The best remembered at this job was coming home one evening just before Christmas, when our packed tube train suddenly ground to a halt.

Lighting and air conditioning immediately went off, and it was a good two hours before we started to shuffle along the length of the train and vacate at the very front and down onto the track. A short walk later along the de-electrified track, we entered the rear of a stationary train that had been in front of ours and then further exited via open carriage doors onto the platform. Extremely hot, sweaty, disorientated and pissed off, we were later informed that someone had committed suicide by jumping in front of the train.

The job lasted nine months before I found myself needing to return to my previously acquired engineering roots, as well as needing to get the hell out of London commuting. Don't get me wrong here, I love London, the greatest city in the world. I personally think however, one needs to dearly love a job or career in London to endure the punishment and unsociable 'grind' of that daily city commute.

I landed a job as an Instrument Maker with Hawker Siddeley[9] avionics at their factory in Hammersmith, London. True to form, it wasn't long before

---

[8] 'Hot tap and Stopple' is a neat way of bypassing an industrial pipeline supply safely, without disrupting flow, enabling the pipework in between the bypass to be worked on.

[9] Hawker Siddeley are now defunct having been taken over by British Aerospace Corporation (BAe) as one of their founding counterparts.

another experience confronted me when I was asked to join the union. 'Asked' is too courteous, forced was more the approach from the shop steward.

"Nah it's alright, mate, I don't want to join your union thanks," did not go down very well. Cutting a long story short, I was given the ultimatum of joining the union or paying into a charity box. I reluctantly paid into 'the charity box' but have always wondered where that charity money ended up!

It wasn't long before looking around for another job. An Instrument Maker role came up in Slough, Berkshire, at a Radio and Space Research Station, manufacturing one offs or small batch telemetry components. I was edging further and further out of the city, and this role looked very interesting, as well as being in a much more relaxed environment.

The workshop was small compared to Hawker Siddeleys, but very well equipped. The lads I worked with were a great bunch, every one of them a piss taker.

For some reason the boss came in for most it, behind his back of course, due to travelling into work from Didcot, Oxfordshire. The taunting was due to their weird perception or reasoning that the railway towns of Swindon and Didcot were way out 'in the sticks' and akin to 'hillbilly country'. 'Didcot Diesel Depot' or 'The Swindon Swine' seemed to tickle their fancy with regular monotony. Little did I know at the time that a few years later, Didcot was going to be virtually on our doorstep, when Lynne and I moved to Wantage.

During all the changes with work and travel, I was still heavily involved with golf and football. I found little time for anything else in the week other than, football training, golf practice, then playing Saturday and Sunday football.

I started to follow my mate, Johnny Marshall, around on his county badminton matches. It was John who made me realise what a wonderful sport it was. He was a natural, had so much talent that given more opportunity, could easily have made the national squad.

When I could, I used to watch his training (he had a personal trainer) and tricks he could pull off with lightning reactions. It was great fun having a knock about after his serious side of training, but inevitably I was left floundering in the bastards wake with very few points to show for it.

It did however, inspire me a great deal for improving my own game later.

Around this period a momentous occasion had come into my life. I met Lynne (1/3/1952).

We met at an Ashford Town FC dance. I had plucked up the courage to ask Lynne for a dance and we pretty much hit it off straight away, although there was a bit of competition from another lad called Mick. It turned out that Lynne didn't have to buy a drink all night as unbeknown to me, Mick and I had been feeding them to her all night. At least, I managed to win the last battle by being the first to ask her out the following night.

It was the era of the mini skirt and hot pants, and what a period it was! Each time I went to take her out, a different higher, tighter, sexier pair of hot pants or skirt greeted me.

We were very soon a couple enjoying weekends at dances all over the place with other friends from the football club. We spent lots of time with each other's families. I know my mum really warmed to Lynne from the off, not just because she made a female companion amongst a house full of men, but because Lynne had, and still has, a warm, honest personality.

I had been driving for a year or so, having been taught by my father. We certainly made use of my access to his Hillman Minx whilst being on his insurance, especially as both of us were not earning a great deal. Lynne had just completed her hairdressing apprenticeship and I was still not earning top end rates in my trade.

I found Lynne incredibly sexy. It was as much as I could do to do the respectful thing. We did that sort of thing in those days, some of us, anyway! That was until we got engaged, then everything went out the window…literally.

I was lucky to have Lynne as both a love and closest friend. My brothers warmed to her as well, which when I look back, helped to break the ice at home. Things were clearly on the slide between Mum and the old man.

It did not take Lynne and myself long in deciding to get married. We were very happy together, with a similar outlook on life, and if we were to have children, we would both like to have them while we were young. We gave ourselves a year and set about saving as hard as we could, our plan was to try and buy rather than rent, which meant requiring a 10% deposit and a mortgage. Both of us worked extra hours when we could and I helped a mate at weekends with his window cleaning business in between football of course! I also took a temporary job for two weeks at a soap making factory during the holiday shut down period of my main job at the Radio and Space Station.

Now, for anyone who has worked in a soap factory, they will certainly be able to confirm that you never walk out of one of those places without smelling of roses! All very well if you can jump in your car and drive home, but let me say, when you're reliant on public transport it wasn't fun. I would end up waiting to hear for some smart-arse comment, so I could show them I wasn't as camp as I may have smelt.

We both knew it was going to be impossible to buy a house in our local areas around Greater London, Middlesex or Surrey, so looking outside these counties as far as Wiltshire, Somerset and Worcester at weekends became the norm. Affordability still seemed a daunting proposition even then. For some reason, we neglected Oxfordshire and as things turned out, a year or so after getting married we found ourselves living there, fate, I guess.

Lynne's family name was Cayley. She had two brothers, Lawrence (Lol for short) and Brian, plus two sisters, Helen and Jackie. Lol was the eldest and was an ex-Naval electrician; he was married with two children living in Wolverhampton. The family was quite close at the time and we often met up. It occurred to us when visiting Lol and family that it was an area we could afford to buy property.

It was a huge decision for me to leave my roots, particularly my mum and brothers under the climate at home. Mum was very happy for us, although I knew deep down she wasn't looking forward to us being so far away. It was also a huge wrench for both of us to leave a great bunch of mates.

Our decision was made swiftly, as it always has done in 47 years of marriage. A deposit was going to be within our budget, I just needed to work out how to obtain a mortgage. My old man worked for Duckhams Oils (now part of BP) and was site manager at their canning factory in Hounslow, Middlesex. He had a variety of contacts, one being in the West Midlands.

Somehow, with luck or by cunning we managed to secure a mortgage with the Abbey National by convincing them I was moving into the area and to be employed by Duckhams Oils Walsall Division, which of course was a complete bluff.

We had set a date of the 31st March 1973 for the wedding, and it came very quickly. A short one-week honeymoon on the Island of Jersey followed immediately after, which stretched the purse strings a bit, but was an invaluable break after a tough year of saving.

Having reached our ten percent deposit target and secured a Mortgage with the Abbey National, we purchased a two-bedroom semi-detached house, coincidently in the same street as Lol, on the outskirts of Wolverhampton. All that was left to do was find a job!

Time was on our side, as signing the deeds, obtaining keys and moving in was going to take at least two months. Lol and his wife kindly offered to put us up until then, which we gratefully accepted. I knew when the time came it was going to be a huge change and challenge to make the break from our respective lives at home where we had been since childhood.

We were young, I was twenty-two, Lynne was twenty-one. But I knew we shared beliefs, and with combined confidence we would make a great team and not look back.

One event I hadn't seen coming was when my Sunday football squad suddenly looked like it was going to reach a Cup Final the day after our wedding, Sunday, 1 April 1973 (first day of the honeymoon). Cup Finals didn't come our way very often, there was pressure coming from every angle from players to parents each pulling in different directions with me in the frigging middle. Bob Parker, our Manager and good friend, didn't help the situation when he offered to pay for both Lynne and my flights on the Monday after the game.

It was all good fun really and although I 'played to the audience', I knew deep down I wasn't going to let Lynne think she came second to football. She may have felt she came second to Mountaineering, but that's another story for later.

Our day came upon us very quickly. Mums and friends did a brilliant job decorating the reception hall and setting it up for wining and dining. The Church and reception hall was situated close to where Lynne had lived all her life, which made it easy and convenient for the various visits that had to be made.

I'd like to think I was in control on the day, but it was a struggle. My brother Chris, who was best man, didn't do a very good job of keeping me sober at the stag night. Fortunately, it was the Thursday before big day and not the Friday, I doubt I would have been able crawl up the aisle, let alone walk up on it, on the Saturday.

It was thanks to everyone who came that helped make it a great and memorable time for us.

We stayed the night at The Runnymede Hotel beside the Thames, too knackered for all things passionate, but that mattered not as hot passionate things was nothing new to us by then. A flight the next morning, Sunday, 1 April, to Jersey was followed by a great relaxing week. Only one bad memory that could have been extremely embarrassing and dangerous was on a round of golf Lynne treated me to.

I played on my own, with Lynne walking round the course beside me. On a certain dog-leg hole, I needed her to walk 100 yards or so to a marker pole indicating where the fairway turned sharply left. I let fly with a great and unusually straight drive…suddenly and in great haste, I bellowed "Foorrrre!" as the ball hurtled towards her.

Lynne had no chance of seeing it coming as she hunkered down by the pole. It missed her by a smidgen, and saved me from a likely call for an ambulance on the very first day of the honeymoon.

The same evening, I took a phone call to tell me the boys had lost the Cup Final. All in all it had been a day to forget!

Chapter Three
No Looking Back

And so, we arrived back from Jersey ready for a new life together and an adventure neither of us knowing its direction.

We packed an old battered Morris 1100 to the brim, mostly with clothes, and bid farewell to family and friends. We had little money; the only other items to our name were presents from the wedding and engagement, which had to be left behind for another day. It could have easily gone pear shaped but I think we were pretty determined to make it work.

Lol and Marlene were extremely kind in putting us up considering they also had two young children, Sean and Louise, in a not too spacious three-bedroom house.

Within the first week, I found a toolmaking job at a small lock manufacturer in nearby Willenhall. It was a classic 'spit and sawdust' machine shop, making jigs and fixtures for the production line knocking out lock parts for a variety of security locks. It was mid-April, bitterly cold, with three inches of snow on the ground. For a moment, I did wonder if I'd made the right move.

Lynne found a stylist's position at a hairdressing salon in nearby Wednesfield in much the same time, so at least we had income coming in. The salon was next door to a sex shop which, with the comings and goings, caused a few tales. (*Why don't we see sex shops anymore? I guess with the Internet there's more choice, more discreetness.*)

Before long, we had keys to our three-bedroom semi-detached home. All we needed was something to put in it. Over a short period, we manage to acquire some second-hand bits and pieces, a settee from Marlene's father, a dining table from our new neighbours and a couple of dining chairs from the local second-hand shop.

The only new item to our name was a double bed my parents had bought us as a wedding present. It wasn't long before we travelled south to visit family and pick up our presents from the wedding, all in all it didn't take long to have our basic needs and feel happily independent.

We were okay financially, but had no desire to spend lots of money on new items for our house at that time. It was time however, for me to look for a better job. I went for an interview for a position as an Instrument Artificer at Summerfield Research Station, 20 miles from home near Kidderminster, Worcestershire.

I was offered the job and exceedingly grateful, as for one thing, it was a far cry from the not so glamorous environment of the lock manufactures. Travelling to and from Kidderminster would take considerably longer, but I was prepared to see how it panned out.

The Research Centres main line of business was producing solid fuel rocket propellant for the Ministry of Defence. Soon after starting, I realised why all the buildings on site were single storey!

The solid fuel manufacturing process had several processes before it was transformed into small solid pellets. The pellets were then packed in cases and stored in silos with strict temperature and humidity environments until needed for further assembly.

It was my first taste of a Government owned establishment, and of signing the Official Secrets Act.

The strictest Health and Safety codes of practice were adhered to. It was paramount workshop tooling in the assembly areas *had* to be of a 'no spark' generating nature; this typically meant all spanners, hammers, screw-drivers and other tooling needed to be made from brass or copper, or any other non-ignition material.

One role for me was a twice daily check of the environmental conditions in the silos. Walking into these vast bunkers on my own waving a hygrometer around was to say the least, very spooky if not fucking scary.

I missed not playing football in my new life, but soon met up with a couple of lads at work who played for Cookley FC, a local village side. They invited me down to their training session and before long I was playing in their first team. A great bunch of lads, serious about their football but humorous along with it. We even won a league cup medal.

Approximately nine months had passed from when Lynne and I had first moved to Wolverhampton and the Black Country. We were very happy in ourselves but were looking to move out of the city suburbs. By pure chance at work one lunchtime, I borrowed a friend's newspaper and spotted a recruitment advert for Instrument makers at Culham Laboratory, near Abingdon in Oxfordshire.

Culham, along with Harwell Laboratory, operated under the United Kingdom Atomic Energy Authority (UKAEA). The role sounded right up my alley, it was in a lovely rural part of the country, closer to our families, offered a good salary and came with a tied house. Too good to be true, I thought, but we both didn't want to build our hopes up.

The biggest decision was giving up owing our own home, but funnily enough our thoughts were the same as our synergy. We had done it once, we would do it again, only this time it would be where we wanted to live.

Two or three weeks later, I was invited down for an interview, excitement had started to build! I did the round trip and interview in a day. It was a wonderful location, large modern sprawling site in great countryside, and one of the reasons it's remained in my memory to this day. I felt the interview went well and couldn't wait to get back to reveal all to Lynne, still not getting too excited for fear of being unsuccessful.

I wasn't, I got the job, and we were heading to Oxfordshire! I was to start around the middle of the year 1974.

It gave Lynne and myself a month or so to get organised, sell the house, which obviously wasn't going to make any money, and hand in respective notices to our employers. One downside to the new job was the fact that I could not commute daily to Culham. The transition meant living in hostel accommodation (Rushcommon Hostel, Abingdon) during the week and travelling back up to Lynne for the weekend until the tied house became available.

We eventually sold up in Wolverhampton before the tied house was ready. Lynne moved back in with her parents for a while and I joined her at weekends. We were given the choice of four towns where a tied house would become available to us, so using a couple of weekends we had a good look around Abingdon-on-Thames, Wallingford-on-Thames, Didcot (aka-Diesel Depot fame) and Wantage.

The two towns on the Thames sounded very attractive, but the housing estates did not appeal to us. Didcot was out of the equation (although over the years it has greatly improved), which left Wantage.[10] It was a town that had immediate ambience and has given us immense enjoyment ever since.

It took a frustrating three months from the point of starting in the role and moving into our semi-detached house in Foliat Drive. It was a semi-prefabricated structure, which was different and not quite what we had expected, however, waiting for a full brick version to turn up, which was primarily given to new starters with a family, could have taken a lot, lot longer.

Our house had been freshly painted throughout with magnolia, but still needed a good clean. There was quite a large rear garden that had plenty of opportunity for a range of ideas, once the waist high grass had been cut.

We had no complaints. We set about making it our home and knew straight away we were in an area we would enjoy.

By now, I had been working at Culham[11] in the 'Special Purpose Workshop' for over three months, alongside two other guys called Charlie Birks and Steve H. Charlie was from Yorkshire, and as with all Yorkshiremen I've come across, was a brash, confident and perpetual piss taking loveable bastard. One soon learns to give as much as one gets in return to win respect, and Charlie remains a very dear and close friend to this day.

All three of us worked on small scientific projects for furthering the progress of nuclear fusion energy, either as individual projects or combined efforts on bigger ones. The exotic materials we used in the workshop were new to us all, especially the likes of Titanium, Tantalum, Molybdenum and Carbon to name a few. Our small but very accurate machine shop equipment of lathes, milling machines, micro drilling machines, etc. were very interesting to work on and a far cry from the large machinery in the adjacent D6 workshop.

---

[10] Wantage is a market town full of ancient history, nestling at the foot of the North Wessex Downs. It is famous for being the birth place of King Alfred the Great, the Uffington White Horse and the Ridgeway long distance path, described as Britain's oldest road. It had a population of around 17,500 in 2017.

[11] UKAEA Culham was established in 1965 as the centre for fusion energy. It had an organisational change in 2009 and was renamed Culham Centre for Fusion Energy (CCFE). It is the site of the Joint European Torus (JET) and the Mega Ampere Spherical Tokamak (MAST).

Our foreman was a guy called Jim Fox MBE, a great character who lost his voice due to cancer of the larynx. Jim learnt to gulp and burp his words out, like the actor Jack Hawkins. It must have taken huge practice and energy, nevertheless, we all understood him very clearly. He gained his MBE through teaching others the art of speech again after similar operations.

April 15 2020: The legend that is Joe Brown has passed away, aged 89.

It seemed an appropriate point in writing this book, to remind myself and to mention an account of one of Joe's routes that I had always wanted to do. Ironically, it didn't turn out as expected and could have ended my climbing career if not my life.

There were countless first ascents that Joe was famous for and that climbers like myself wanted in their portfolio. Cenotaph Corner, Cemetery Gates, Right Unconquerable is to name a microcosm of his climbing legacy.

One trip of a couple of days to Llanberis around the year 2000, was with three keen mates, Martin, Dave and Nick. We had done a route or two in the slate quarries and decided it was appropriate to head to a bigger crag in the mountains. Crag of choice for us was Clogwyn Du'r Arduu, 'Cloggy' or 'the black crag' for short, a huge crag lying below the North West shoulder of Snowdon and adjacent to lake Llyn D'ur Arddu.

It was Dave's and my turn to climb together and the two-pitch route of 'Shrike', one of Joe's 3-star classics at E2 5c, 5b, would certainly give us that sense of adventure climbing we were seeking.

Scrambling up to the ramparts of the route with its massive, brooding exposure with two hundred feet of climbing above was intimidating. However, full of confidence I started up the crack of the first pitch, followed by a short traverse left. This led to the thin crack and crux of the pitch.

After moment's hesitation, I gathered myself together, placed some good protection and made it, not too gainly, to the belay ledge, sixty-five feet up from Dave. I placed two good pieces of belay protection and brought him up without much trouble.

Dave took the lead gear from me and set about the next hundred and twenty-five feet of the second pitch. The initial overhang directly above us was tricky and strenuous but he eventually overcame it. An arête followed by a crack just to the right led to an exposed wall, from what I was able to see, Dave was placing frequent gear, but then moves back left to the arête and up the tricky wall to the right and top, were mostly out of my vision.

It looked like Dave had pretty much reached the top, when in that classic slow-motion moment, I saw Dave fall and keep falling. There wasn't time to count the number of bits of gear that ripped from the rock, only time to think 'shit' before being launched from my ledge and thumped into the overhang. Dave and I met eyeball to eyeball. I had only travelled ten or twelve feet from the belay; Dave had travelled more than a hundred feet.

I knew instantly I had cracked ribs with the force of hitting the overhang, but couldn't work out why I was struggling to breathe. I still held Dave on my belay device and lowered us both down to the ledge. I gave myself a sound bollocking for only arranging my belay on the ledge for a downward pull and not an opposing upward pull.

Clearly Dave was shaken, but had no injuries. I, on the other hand, was gasping for air.

With no possibility of finishing the route, we decided to rap off (abseil). I made one pathetic attempt but realised I wasn't going anywhere in a hurry.

Although most of us who operate in the mountains prefer the choice of self-rescue, it was looking more than likely I was going to need a hand. We decided Dave should rap down and get to the other guys, call the rescue team and leave me on the ledge. I remember nothing other than trying to keep calm and trying to breathe.

I suppose it was around and hour to an hour and a half when I heard Martin calling me from above; he had set up a rappel from the top and was heading my way. On his way down, he collected any remaining gear that Dave had placed which included a sling that was still in position around a rock spike. The frightening news hit us both when Martin showed me the state of the sling. It had been cut halfway through by the force of Dave's fall. It was the only piece of gear that saved him from hitting my belay ledge. Furthermore, if that sling had failed it was very likely we would have both ended up at the bottom of the crag.

Encouraged by the fact that we had both survived and that the rescue team had been alerted, I drew confidence that my condition whilst dire, wasn't getting worse. Soon the blades of a Sea King helicopter were whacking above us. A 'winchman' was on his way down, but it was going to be a tricky swing in to the ledge.

With marvellous precision from the pilot, the persistence of the 'winchman' and a pull from Martin, he was onto the ledge. I still had my harness on with a screw gate karabiner attached. In no time at all, I was hooked up using it and we were away from the austere position. Dangling two hundred feet below the helicopter above Snowdon summit was a massive experience, probably not fully appreciated at the time. In a couple of minutes, we were reeled in and positioned inside the chopper as it headed for Bangor Hospital.

I could not thank everyone enough for their help and bravery. Our rescue teams throughout the country are second to none. Once in hospital, I was seen quickly for an X-ray and by a doctor who explained that I had cracked four ribs, one of which had penetrated the lining of the chest wall and caused a pneumothorax;[12] fortunately the lung had not fully collapsed.

The procedure for fixing the lung was simply having a local anaesthetic, followed by one end of a tube inserted between the ribs (which is a weird feeling) into the cavity to drain the air, whilst the other end of the tube dangled in a glass jar full of fluid. Martin, Dave and Nick had finally got off the hill and visited; as expected there was little sympathy, just plenty of piss take.

I forgot the doctor had told me not to eat before morning. The boys and I were famished, so they wandered off into town to the local fish and chip shop soon returning with a portion for me. I hadn't eaten more than a couple of mouthfuls when the doc returned, making it very clear I was not to eat anymore. With very little sympathy, one of the boys, I forget who, promptly took my package and proceeded to share it with the others, with grins all round.

Lynne and I had been staying at my brother and sister-in-law's house on Anglesey. She had been informed of the accident and was brought over to see me. Between the boys and Lynne there had been a bit of a laugh.

My personal gear was left at the bottom of the crag and had been collected by Martin. He came across my mobile phone and to inform Lynne, had looked through the contacts list. No contact number for Lynne was in there, only 'my lover' which left him hesitating somewhat. In the end, he dialled the number and found that it was indeed Lynne.

Lynne drove home by herself the following day and I eventually caught the train to Oxford a few days later. So many experiences happen in a lifetime of

---

[12] A pneumothorax is a collapsed lung. It occurs when air leaks into the space between your lung and chest wall. This air pushes on the outside of your lung and makes it collapse. It can be a complete lung collapse or a partial collapse.

climbing and so many lessons are learnt. Needless to say this experience reminded me to question myself on correct anchors.

Another of Jim's marvellous feats was his hobby of repairing watches, particularly with his huge hands. He would shut his door and we knew instantly he was onto a watch repair. That was further backed up by the sudden loud burping expletives of 'fuck' or 'bollocks' as his giant sausage like fingers dropped the tiniest of screws on the floor. Through life one meets inspirational people, he was certainly one of them.

Charlie and I got to know each other quite well as we both had rooms at Rushcommon and met for beers at the local pub now and again to break the week up. I quickly found he had a profound knowledge of history and a remarkable memory. He was also into motor cycle racing, big style! He had a particular passion for sidecar racing, known as 'outfits'.

Charlie was passenger in the outfit, with Mick Boddice as the driver; they raced around various European circuits competing at a high level. I think the proudest moment for them was when he and Mick won their first TT race.

If you're a road racer, the ultimate road racing circuit has got to be the Isle of Man TT circuit, and on one occasion it very nearly cost Charlie his life. Anyone who has witnessed this insanely dangerous sport, hanging over the edge of the outfit with one's arse and elbow a few millimetres from the ground at speeds of 150mph plus, will know there is huge potential for accidents.

It was on one such occasion I visited Charlie in hospital with Gary (he was about ten at the time). Charlie was laid flat out, face down with a framework over the middle half of his body with a sheet covering the frame. Inquisitively, we lifted the sheet to reveal his arse a bloodied pulp completely devoid of skin.

He had been thrown from the outfit breaking several bones and sliding goodness knows how far on his backside. His racing leathers were ripped clean from his arse with the excruciating result. He was a very lucky guy and still carries scars and metal pieces to remind him…nutter!

Lynne and I soon had the house cleaned up, with bits brought down from Wolverhampton and a couple of second-hand pieces from another set of new neighbours, it was soon in a liveable and comfortable condition. Living in Wantage made it easier for my mum to visit and likewise for Lynne and myself to re-visit home. It was certainly a difficult time for Mum and my brothers with divorce from the old man looking imminent, although she hated the thought and discussed it with us very little.

Lynne and I were far more settled mentally with our lives in Oxfordshire, and we both knew it was time to give enlarging the numbers in our little house a go. Lynne fell pregnant very quickly. Around the same time, we both joined Wantage badminton club and I also joined Wantage Town FC. Both clubs had a friendly atmosphere, and enjoyable social scene. I played first team Badminton with the club who were competing at quite a high standard and made the reserve squad for the town's football squad.

It was around three months of being pregnant, Lynne started having trouble carrying the baby. One very distressing evening, she quietly went to the bathroom where I soon found her distraught. I knew instantly what had just happened. A picture that will live in my memory for ever, is of a tiny, almost fully formed foetus, laying in the bottom of the loo. It felt, at the time, that life was indeed a bitch.

I couldn't help feel it was the badminton that was to blame, but our great doctor at the time, Dr Teare, told us differently. Lynne was soon to find out that a 'tilted womb' was the likely cause. The fix for her was to have a ring inserted in her womb. No sooner had that been done, we were keener than ever to try once more. It was, however, under the condition Lynne stopped playing badminton for a while!

Chapter Four
Proudest Moments

DAD...A short title for a very big job.

1976 was a year of the endless summer. It led to the second hottest summer average temperature in the UK since records began. It was one of the driest, sunniest and warmest summers in the twentieth century and the country suffered a severe drought. Although official records show the dates as being from 23 June to 27 August (66 days), I can assure you it was shorts and not much else from early April.

Lynne had been carrying since September 1975. We had arranged for her to get to hospital by ambulance when the time came, where I would meet her from work. It must have been incredible relief come May 16th 1976 when Gary was delivered in the Maternity unit of Oxford's John Radcliffe Hospital. Even Gary looked like he had been cooking in the womb as he came out as brown as a berry!

I say came out; he was stubborn even at birth and needed forceps to encourage his delivery. We were assured his elongated head was only temporary and would soon go. Both Lynne and Gary were kept at the Radcliffe hospital for a couple of days, then transferred to Wantage cottage hospital just to be sure they were both ok. It was amazing being beside Lynne at the birth, another one of life's experiences.

Little did I realise how much joy it would bring into our lives having another member of the family. It released a huge amount of tension following the miscarriage of the previous year.

It was also such a wonderful moment for my mum to be a nanna for the first time, especially when times were tough in her personal life at home.

For the next couple of years, Lynne and I indulged ourselves in parenthood. I could not wait to get home from work, strip off and get into shorts. As I have said, it was one of the hottest years and to come home and be outside in the garden as a threesome was fantastic.

Lynne joined a baby-sitting circle which operated using tokens. If tokens started running low, it meant having to do some sitting for other parents in the club. Money was tight for us, so it was an ideal way of going out for an occasional social evening up the pub or to a dance. That's how it was for those couple of years—work, family fun, a little socialising and of course badminton and football.

Playing football for a good number of years and badminton a lot more frequently inevitably led to a few niggly knee problems. In the end, I gave up playing football, but started a FA refereeing course to keep in touch with the game. I qualified as a class three ref and for a few years enjoyed refereeing and running the line for divisions in the North Berks league.

Meanwhile, Lynne started playing club netball for a local village team. Now and again, I would take Gary along to watch his mum in games that were far from tame!

Work at Culham was interesting; it was a laid-back affair with very little stress. Prototype work was beginning to filter through for the new JET project, although it was to be many years later that the project took shape on the grounds outside our workshop window as it was still a potato field.

The years between 1978 and 1982 encompassed many events; there were also a couple of life's paths which, had I chosen the wrong one, could have gone really tits up for myself and the family. I have tried to precis the events in the following paragraphs.

By late 1978, I was getting itchy feet on the work front again; I was looking more towards making a career in management and could not see much coming my way at Culham. I remember reflecting on a few individuals who gave a rather lifeless and apathetic appearance, almost zombie like, and feared I would end up the same way.

A small advert for a 'chain maker' in the Oxford mail caught my eye. I was interested to know a little more, as I hadn't a clue why such a position would require a toolmaking background.

I attended an interview at P Friman and Co Ltd in Oxford and was astounded by the precision of the processes and even more by the extraordinary attention to detail and precision for setting a chain making machine.

It was a small set up of around fifteen production operators working in a building that can only be described as a three-storey brick barn. It reminded me of a Victorian work house.

All the floors had original wooden floorboards, and the noise coming from the machines was tremendous. I felt it needed a frigging good clear out or preferably a bulldozing. However, it had to be a Grade 1 or 2 listed structure.

The Production Director interviewed me. He was the only skilled man setting the machines, and was honest enough to admit it was stressful keeping the machines running. It was obvious to me he needed assistance.

I also met Paul Friman, the owner, an elderly, seemingly pleasant mannered guy. They intimated that they were looking to expand the business and a role for a Production Manager was looking possible.

The whole place seemed a challenge. I should have said no, but for some strange reason it seemed a challenge worth taking. I accepted the role as a chain making technician. I knew Culham would not throw us out of the tied house, but we would need a plan sooner or later.

April 25 2020—Covid 19: UK still on 'lockdown' Coronavirus deaths exceed 20,000.

May 6 2020—Covid 19: Still on lockdown with UK deaths now exceeding 30,000.

Back in Ashford during 1978, my brothers left the family home. Pete was about to leave home for the Polytechnic of Wales. The Poly was a merger between Glamorgan Polytechnic and Glamorgan College of Education a few years earlier in 1975.

It was later to be awarded university status as the University of Glamorgan in 1992. Meanwhile, Chris and my sister-in-law, Lesley, (Lez to us all) married in July and bought their first house in Bracknell.

Our mum had been resolute in keeping them together even though the strain of her marriage to the old man must have been incredibly difficult. Perhaps a lesser person would have preferred to sit back with what they had both worked hard for and gone about lives comfortably, albeit separately, under one roof. Mum was wise enough to know the mental, if not physical abuse, would have meant a life of unhappiness for the years ahead.

The irretrievable breakdown and trust had long gone, and she had been determined to enjoy a personal life once more. Divorce and the going of their own ways happened quickly as I recall. Mum moved out to a flat in Marleycroft, Staines, Middlesex, whilst the old man bought a flat in Feltham, Middlesex.

It was great to see Mum with independence, laughter and a twinkle in her eye once more. She enjoyed having us bros and family all visit the flat at times. Pete would often stay over when on holiday from the Poly. Mum would also catch a train to come and stay with us in Wantage quite often, relishing being a nanna and doting on her grandson.

It was quite a big break for me too in leaving the security of Culham. It was work, if not a career, as close as it came to a job for life. And so, I launched out once more into the uncertainty of working life, this time with the responsibility of being a father as well as a husband.

I walked into Friman and Co certainly wondering if I had made the right decision. It was without doubt a complete contrast to the cleanliness, tidiness and professional workshops of Culham; it was nothing short of a shit hole. Weirdly, I saw it as a challenge, not only a challenge in getting to grips with the machines and processes, but proving to myself and others that workshops, no matter what is manufactured, can operate more efficiently and productively in a clean, organised environment.

I guess nearly every one of us has worn either a neck chain or bracelet at some point in our lives, but very seldom do we see how they are produced. The skill sets required in the hand-built manufacture of chain making machines and/or the making of huge ranges of chains, lies somewhere between the combined skills of toolmaking, instrument making and horology.

I'll attempt to give a precis of chain manufacture at P. Friman and Co.

There were approximately 18 chain making machines, each of which occupied a space on a work top of no more than a cubic metre each, one or two exceptions being larger machines capable of producing men's chunky bracelet chains. Each machine was 99% mechanical, the only electrical features were the power switch and a micro switch that knocked the power off if the chain making process failed whilst unattended.

Each operation of the chain making process was driven by a cam on a camshaft, there could be up to twenty cams per machine.

A typical sterling silver trace chain started from wire off a spool containing a hundred metres or more, the wire was fed through a guide and cut to a length to make one link, the smallest length was 4mm long with a diameter of 0.25mm. The short length of wire would then be formed round a mandrel producing a teardrop link.

The link would be held in small jaws, turned through 90 degrees to have another piece of wire fed into it where the process would start over again. The result being very similar to making children's Christmas paper chains.

This was achieved in the first instance using a hand-wheel on the camshaft rotated very slowly by hand, to ensure every single movement of the operation was precise enough to make the following link. The precise detail behind the various movements and the continuity could only be achieved with the aid of x5 and x10 eyeglasses.

Once the machine looked setup and a metre or so had been run off by hand, it was time to set the thing running automatically.

If it was your lucky day, chain would be flowing at the rate of several links per second and collected in a pot situated below via the centre of the machine. If the movements had not been set accurately enough, one's whole world would come crashing down with fucking links and bits of wire scattered everywhere.

Stress was instant, particularly as one chain making operator was expected to run six machines, and exacerbated when the machines were running precious metal. It's not hard to imagine the stress factor building with each failing machine suddenly spitting links out every which way, and escalating scrap costs of sterling silver, 9ct gold or 18ct gold mounting by the second!

The top of each link formed a vee between the mating ends of the wire, the bottom of which needed to be touching with a slight opening at the top. This allowed a tiny piece of silver solder from the pre-soldering process to remain trapped in the vee. A single link 'trace chain' as described above, was the simplest to produce. There would have been several thousand of these teardrops interlinked to form a length of chain of thirty metres or more, coiled and known as a 'hank'.

The pre-soldering process was quite labour intensive and intricate which I won't go into here, but suffice to say it was a skill that took a while to master, with more scrap potential!

Thereafter, the soldered 'hank' of chain would have been unwound, cut into individual lengths of neck chain and assembled with a bolt ring and jump ring ready to be packed for the customer.

In the early days of working at the factory, the biggest contract was for Woolworths high street shop's when the fashion and demand in base metal chain jewellery[13] in the late 1970s to early 1980s was quite strong. However, to make even a modest profit it required hundreds of metres of chain to be produced very cheaply. This in turn led to quick wear and tear on the tooling, which was time consuming and costly to replace.

It wasn't long before the business realised there was a consumer move away from base metal chains and into precious metal. It meant competing with the bigger boys in the UK as well as the renowned quality and competitive prices coming out of Spain and Italy. It was certainly going to lead to further challenges.

Within the first few months of starting, I was sent over to Stuggart, Germany for two weeks, where the chain machines were manufactured. It was an invaluable experience as I quickly realised that the transition from producing base metal chains to precious metal chain back in the UK workshop required a whole new level of tooling accuracy and production practices across every discipline.

It was all very well producing a relatively straight forward single trace chain, but a double rope or triple rope with diamond cutting was a whole new ball game.

By the middle of 1979, the Production Director had left for a sales job with the competition somewhere. I had been promoted to Production Manager, we had just recruited another chain technician and Lynne was into her ninth month of pregnancy with our second child. I was still playing club and county badminton, but had given up football and refereeing due to the increased time spent at work.

Lynne was a week or two away from giving birth when we had a major scare at home in Foliat Drive. Our car battery was playing up and needed replacing, but before I got to fitting it, I had put it on charge in the kitchen with a borrowed charger from a neighbour.

At some point in the early hours of the morning, I awoke to a black mist in the bedroom. At first, I thought I was dreaming then it suddenly dawned on me what it was. I ran downstairs to see the whole fucking lot on fire, charger, battery and table top. Black mist and soot were everywhere, fortunately in my panic, I

---

[13] Base metal chain was made from mild steel wire which was generally chrome or brass plated, or aluminium wire which was anodised in various colours of red, blue, yellow, green etc.

remembered to turn the electric off before wrenching the sizzled cable out of the socket and chucking the whole lot outside.

I shouted to Lynne, who by now had already realised what was happening. She had grabbed poor little G from bed and was half way out the front door with blankets wrapped round them.

All three of us were blackened as we gathered our thoughts and senses on the front lawn around 2 am that morning.

Lynne and I were a bit hesitant knocking on the door of our immediate neighbours Keith and Diane at that time in the morning, but they were marvellous and couldn't help enough as usual. They looked after Gary for the next twenty-four hours, enabling us to start the massive clean-up.

We soon realised that a damp cloth only made matters worse, it was necessary to vacuum every room, every nook and cranny first before wiping over with soap and water. My brother Chris and Lez came over from Bracknell in the morning, which was a tremendous help and it was well into the following night before we could all relax a little.

Another lesson learnt, and I haven't charged a battery overnight, or without one of us being around, ever since.

As if that wasn't enough excitement for a month, the following week on July 2 1979 Lynne was taken by ambulance, once again, to the John Radcliffe Hospital. I met her from work and was there by the skin of my teeth to see Nicola Jane arrive. Lynne had confessed to me that between her and Diane next door they had waited until her contractions were well underway before phoning for the ambulance.

Nicola's birth was straightforward compared to Gary's. It was wonderful yet again to be at her birth, and a great feeling to now have both a son and daughter.

Life was full on at work and at home with our new family, once things had settled down after the excitement of Nicky's birth and the trauma of the fire. We were so very fortunate with the outcome of the fire and so very, very grateful to all our immediate neighbours for the help they gave us.

Gary was becoming an artful little bugger from an earlier age, and formed a great relationship with the lad next door who was a year older and went by the name of Coggy. How Gary managed to find the name Coggy from his real name Simon is a mystery still to this day; together they were a lively little pair to say the least.

Lynne and I still found time to enjoy our respective moments of independence, Lynne with her netball and myself with badminton. There were many happy occasions on the beaches together, particularly at Bournemouth and down in Cornwall. My mum would join us occasionally down at Cornwall, which always had fond memories for her.

I needed to consider our plans for moving out of the Culham house in Foliat Drive. With the help of my mum and my father, we managed to scrape a deposit together for our own house again in the village of Grove just 2 miles to the north of Wantage. It was a three-bedroom end-terrace, quite small in comparison to Foliat Drive, but it did come with an attached garage, and it was ours!

Back in 1974 when we first moved to Wantage, those houses were selling for around £9,500. When we eventually bought ours in 1980 prices had increased quickly, as it then cost us £21,500. We settled in the village of Grove very quickly at Colne Close and although making one more move twenty odd years later, we still live in Grove to this day.

Grove was and still is a lovely village surrounded by farmland and a disused World War II airfield. It has a stream known as Letcombe brook running through its entirety, having its source rising at the foot of the Berkshire Downs in the village of Letcombe Bassett. It didn't take long to find new friends in the close for the kids and in the village for us all.

The following winter came with quite a lot of snow, total contrast from the record-breaking heatwave in the year Gary was born. Great fun was had that winter on the sledge I knocked up in the garage.

Work at the factory was exceedingly busy, giving little time for mind to wander or ponder on leisure outside of it. However, I started to feel the desire to seek an adventurous activity once a year, something that was becoming a popular thing to do, I guess as it was outside of every day comfort zones. Marathon running had become the newly found fashion. That was going to be for the following year, as I felt six months training would be the minimum I needed.

Until then, I would do a parachute jump! God knows why, but I had seen it advertised somewhere and it seemed like a fun thing to try. I rang the telephone number on the advert and was pretty much sold the idea straight away. The training and jump would take place at Thruxton airfield in Hampshire and run by ex-military personnel.

A bonus was that if I could muster a dozen mutually interested nutters, the price would drop and the training could take place locally at a gym, rather than all having to trundle down for a full weekend.

Not much effort was needed to find the twelve and the training went ahead on two evenings at Wantage leisure centre. It was to be a 'Static Line Parachute' jump.[14] A specific Saturday was set for the jumps, the first couple of hours of which would be for final prep and elements that couldn't be carried out in the gym.

The weather was a little iffy on the day and the possibility of getting all twelve of us up and jumping in a day was looking unlikely. However, we were all suited and booted with a jump suit and parachute, all looking a little sheepish! The plane used for the jumps was a single engine aircraft with a fixed wing above the cockpit.

A wing strut on the underside of the wing on both sides came down about forty-five degrees and fixed to the fuselage. The jumps door was opposite the pilot and permanently open. Attached to the fuselage just below the jump door was a foot-plate. The plane carried one pilot, one jump master and three trainees, all static-line cords were hooked up to the aircraft.

Our instruction was clear: on the jump masters call we would shuffle forward, making our way to the door. Thereupon, our LEFT foot had to be placed on the footplate whilst both arms and hands reached out to clutch the wing strut while uttering gibbering nonsense.

The RIGHT leg had to be thrust outwards into thin air, it was at this point, everyone knew there was no turning back, no "sorry Sir I don't want to do this," as we also knew it would just end with a hefty push from the instructor into oblivion. All this preciseness had to be achieved with a 60mph 'prop wash'[15] before letting go and pushing away from the aircraft, counting;

a thousand and one…a thousand and two…a thousand and three…to a thousand and six. It's probably fair to say, that if one got to 'a thousand and six' looked up to find the canopy hadn't opened, it would have been too late anyway.

---

[14] Static-Line Parachuting differs from an Accelerated Freefall course.as your parachute opens automatically by a 'static-line' which is attached to the aircraft (there is no freefall element involved).You can then fly and land the canopy yourself.

[15] A 'prop wash' is the term given to the rush of air behind the propeller as it is throttled back from full speed, just before jumping.

I swear that if that had happened to me, I would not have had the wherewithal to pull the reserve chute. It is why I had always wanted to do a second jump, to justify to myself I could be more aware.

As it was, the chute opened almost straight away. I reached up to grab the toggles, and floated unceremoniously down not too far from the landing point. My underwear was still dry as I gathered up the canopy. The other two had landed and were doing the same.

We all marched back to the Nissen hut with huge grins on our faces. Some of the lads did not get to jump that day due to the weather, but came back the following weekend and completed theirs. It was without doubt, a tremendous experience for us all.

Mum and my Godmother (picture by Roy Philipson)

Mum (picture by her sister)

My Nan (picture by Mum)

Engaged at Lands End 1972

A Wantage winter

Part 2: Life-Changing Moments

The two most important days of your life are
The day you are born and the day you find out why.

Mark Twain

Chapter Five
Direction Choices

The years between 1980 and 1982 seemed to be the turning point in Lynne's and my lifestyle.

We were being more adventurous together and as a family. Adventurous walks together both coastal and hills with Nicola in the back pack and Gary managing to keep up under his own steam. Perhaps this was the foundation for both as they grew older, that was to give Lynne and myself immense pride and satisfaction.

Gary was to perform well at judo and football, eventually going through the Army's Royal Military College Sandhurst. He joined the Parachute Regiment as a Lieutenant, until furthering his forces career in the reserves, whilst founding his own businesses in security and skydiving.

Nicola also found her strengths in judo and football, often having to compete against lads nearly twice as big as her; she eventually grew into a strong triathlete and women's rugby player.

Life in the chain making factory during those years was particularly stressful and hard. I found it necessary to employ another technician to keep up with developing business in precious metal chains, and help cover me when travelling abroad to exhibit our jewellery chain manufacturing at the annual Basle show in Switzerland.

Fortunately, I managed to persuade Chas Birks, who had remained a close friend after I left Culham, to come across to Friman's and learn the art of chain making. It was indeed one of my better recruitment moves!

I had just about managed to do a sufficient amount of training to compete and finish the—1st Abingdon Peoples Marathon on May 6 1982, in a reasonably respectable time of 3hrs 22mins. I wanted to beat 3hrs, and was on target around the 21-mile marker, when all of a sudden I hit the infamous 'wall'. It came as quite a shock to feel how quickly one can become drained, it was as much as I could do to get to the finish line, completely and utterly drained not giving a toss what the time was.

The following summer was one of fun, but tinged with some sadness. Much fun was had on the beaches of Cornwall with the four of us and my mum. Nicky was around three years old and Gary six, so they were able to enjoy the sun and sand to the max.

One quiet moment whilst on the beach, my mum confided in me, that a small scaly rounded blemish on her upper chest looked suspiciously like a return of her cancer. I think I tried to play it down a little, but deep down had the sinking feeling that it was the awful frigging carcinoma making a return.

1982 was also the year I could have made a dreadful mistake. As it was, I believe fate played a part in turning it around to be the best outcome I could ever have wished for.

To this day, I cannot remember the reason for wanting to take up a chain making position in Ruthin, North Wales, and make yet another move, especially away from a town we were so very fond of. Not only that, I now had the title of Production Manager and a company vehicle. (OK, it was only an Austin Allegro, but so what!)

On one of the long trips to Basle, Switzerland to display the wares of P. Friman and Co, I was approached by a Director of another UK company called Ecco Jewellery. Discussions took place and I had given it a little, if not a great deal of thought, by the time I returned home. A week or so had passed, when a letter came out of the blue offering me a position at Ecco Jewellery and the potential of a better career with a much better salary.

Maybe it was the stressful nature of the job at Friman's; maybe it was the carrot of a boardroom position at Ecco Jewellers. I don't remember, but looking back now, I haven't a clue why I accepted the offer. It could very well have been the fact that I had given a tremendous amount of time and effort over nearly four years, in turning the factory round from being the shit hole it was to something more habitable and pleasant for all employees.

Also my technical input in turning the production output from base metal chains to precious metals, enabling Friman and Co to be competitive with the bigger boys in Europe. I suppose, to be honest, I felt under paid and under rewarded.

It meant putting our house up for sale quickly in Grove, followed by paying a second visit to Ruthin (the first was for a short interview) to seek appropriate accommodation for us all. It wasn't as if there was a house we liked at an affordable price; instead, we put our name down on a new build in the area that had only just had the 'footings' laid.

It would not become available for at least 4 months, and would need me to be in a temporary B and B until then, with Lynne, Gary and Nicola down in Oxfordshire. (What was I thinking!)

I agreed a notice date with Paul Friman and felt guilty leaving Charlie with the responsibility of maintaining production at the factory. I must admit though, I had little regret leaving on the final day. We had a very quick offer for our little house in Grove.

The sale went through extremely quickly, so much so, that the deeds came through the post just before I was due to start the first week up at Ruthin. Lynne and I were required to sign them as soon as possible, but I decided to take them with me, read through them thoroughly and then sign on my return the following weekend. (If there is one decision I've made in my life that has been for the best, it was that!)

There is little point in going into detail of the factory, other than it was a very modern workshop, with up to date Italian manufactured chain making equipment. The first day went okay, the second day not so well after discussions on salary and prospects, by the third day I had to make a big decision: go with my intuition or stick with the job.

I think I had already made up my mind before ringing Lynne and my mum. On one hand I was gutted that I had made a bad move and bad decision to give Ruthin a try. On the other, enormously pleased I had not signed the deeds to the house, even though it would piss the buyers off who were moving down from RAF Valley in North Wales.

I handed my notice in the very next day and probably pissed them off too, but I cared little. The whole episode had left our bank balance well in the red, and had it not been for Mum helping me out a little, finances would have been very difficult.

I was determined not to eat humble pie and see if my role back at Friman's was available, as I had enough of there too. I set about looking for other work and rang Alec W, a friend who I knew at the Badminton club. I had also met Alec whilst I was at Culham; he owned a cutter grinding business and had contracts both with Culham and UKAEA Harwell. He had great business acumen and now owned Oxford Engineering Ltd, one of Oxfordshire's largest CNC machining services.

Alec did not have any vacancies himself, but thought Oxford Instruments Ltd did and would put my CV through John P, the Production Director. I liked John instantly. He and Mike C interviewed me, and I was offered a role as an Instrument Technician.

It was a step down from my position at Friman's and a bigger step down from the prospects I thought I was heading for up at Ruthin. However, I was immensely pleased to accept the job and breathe a big sigh of relief.

I joined Oxford Instruments in 1982 at their Osney Mead factory beside the Thames at Oxford.

The company was founded by Sir Martin Wood in 1959 with the help from his wife Audrey (Lady Wood) to manufacture superconducting magnets for use in scientific research. It was started in his garden shed, then progressed to a boat house beside the lock on the Thames at Osney. It was further developed when the building that still exists today (no longer a factory) was built over the top of the boat house whilst production was maintained.

The business had a pioneering role in developing magnetic resonance imaging (MRI) and the first whole body scanner was manufactured in 1980 for use in Hammersmith Hospital, London. Further scientific innovations were developed and manufactured at that site and is where I started life as a Technician. It was the first day of which was to become 10 years with the company.

It was around 16 miles from home and I cycled it on the first day, as we were very skint following my not so sensible experience in Ruthin. I picked up a puncture on route and was embarrassingly late on my first day, but managed to get away with it very lightly because my manager Mike C, was terribly impressed I had cycled in from Wantage.

I cycled that journey along the A338, 3 days a week, not only until our bank balance had improved, but also as it helped maintain my fitness level. I would choose a time very carefully if I was to do it now, as the volume of traffic has increased tenfold. I also remember very vividly the prevailing head wind that always seemed to blow for my return home. It kept me fit, that's for sure!

The skills needed to produce some of the highly technical instruments were very different from the skills of chain making, but no less clever and dextrous.

Parts made from brass, copper and stainless steel were expertly assembled using very skilful silver and soft soldering[16] techniques which needed to withstand the rigours of testing in cryogenic[17] temperatures.

I was treated very well by the company from the start and learned a lot in a short space of time from the many colleagues I worked with. Oxford Instruments has always been close to my heart for the way it treated its employees, the benefits it provided including a good pension scheme, the working environment and the way it kept its staff up to date with business developments.

I regarded it way ahead of its time and its competition.

May 20 2020—Covid 19:

As I write the next few lines, England is slowly coming out of the Covid 19 lockdown, Wales, Scotland and N. Ireland will follow shortly.

It has been glorious weather for several weeks, tempting many thousands of people outside, on the whole the population has stuck to the rules.

Outdoor activity, including climbing, has had a slow release using sense and discretion. Pedro and I have been out twice to climb, today we agreed to meet at Wintours Leap on the Wye valley again. Each travelling separately and via Gloucester as we are restricted in crossing into Wales via the M4 and M48 Bridge.

I led the first pitch of a two pitch HVS 5a route, a route we thought was comfortably in our capability. Pedro struggled a little on that pitch, but wanted to lead the second shorter pitch. Towards the top he fell, the last piece of gear ripping out (reminiscent of Dave on Cloggy).

I got him to Gloucester hospital, they were fantastic but unfortunately severe damage to his replacement hip from two years ago and a break of the femur means he's probably not likely to be climbing anymore.

1983 through to 1984 was a period of consolidation for me at work and at home with family. I think it was a period that cured me of my wanderings on the

---

[16] Silver soldering is the process of permanently joining two or more pieces of metal using heat to melt silver solder at temperatures of around 655degC to 780degC which fills a prepared joint.
Soft soldering does much the same but at a much lower temperature, usually between 200degC and 300degC and uses a soft alloy of tin and lead.

[17] Cryogenics is the production and behaviour of materials at very low temperatures.

work front. Sporting life had taken a bit of a knocking with the various ordeals taking place (self-inflicted, of course), but I was still on the hunger trail for adventure. I had managed to fit in training for a second Abingdon marathon in 1983 and had taken myself off hiking and camping for the odd weekend.

At work, a new business group was formed called the Ion Beam Group. I was asked by JP to join the scientists as the build technician for the projects they had lined up and was obviously delighted. In short, the IB group designed and built large stainless steel, high vacuum chambers for Ion Beam Sputtering[18]. It was a highly technical venture, quite demanding for us all but always very interesting and rewarding.

By the middle of 1984, life was extremely busy; the Ion Beam Group was flying with heavy commitments on delivery that in turn put a lot of pressure on build workloads, late night finishing was quite frequent.

My mum was having to go through another set of chemotherapy treatment; it was important we met up as often as possible, as clearly it wasn't looking good. Quite often she would come and stay for a few days at Wantage or at my brothers at Bracknell. It was great for us all, particularly for Gary and Nicky to see their nan.

Gary was in his third year at primary school and growing up fast, forever active with out of school activities, such as football, swimming and judo. Nicky had just started at the same primary school and joined her brother at the swimming club. Lynne enjoyed playing club netball and was a very active swim coach and athletics coach at the respective kids' clubs.

Both Lynne and I had always promised to involve ourselves in the kids' sport and other activities, we in turn liked to involve them in ours. It was something we can proudly look back on, but heaven knows how we ever found time to eat!

A young guy I worked alongside at Oxford called Bob S, belonged to the Scouts group for many years and was also a member of the Oxford Mountaineering Club (OMC). He suggested I go along to one of the 'indoor meets' held on the first and third Wednesday of each month. I went along and met a lot of friendly and keen individuals whose activities ranged from climbing, skiing, hiking and general walking.

---

[18] Ion Beam Deposition (IBD) is a thin film deposition process that uses an ion source to deposit or sputter a target (material or dielectric) onto a substrate to create either a metallic or dielectric film.

The evening certainly impressed me. I was keen to return the following fortnight. Indoor meets were the precursor for 'outdoor meets' that were organised for the following weekend. I noted that the Lake District was arranged for the next event, and was keen to try and make it.

Two weeks came very quickly. Work was going well, and I felt I had settled down into a role that was going to last a while, much to Lynne's piece of mind. She had been incredibly stoical during the whole of our marriage and family life. Lynne was also very supportive of me exploring a potentially new dimension in adventure.

I must admit the weekend in the Lakes was very much on my mind. I gathered what little gear for the outdoors I had. Fortunately, no tents were needed (mine was a little embarrassing) as the club had hired the 'Langdale Hut' owned by Fylde Mountaineering Club and situated in the beautiful Langdale valley.

It was certainly a new adventure for me. I forget how many in the club went, not many I recall. We travelled up in two or three car loads after work on Friday night, mostly guys but a couple of girlfriends too, plenty of time to get acquainted before arriving around midnight.

Nearly everyone was keen on some easy rock climbing, which suited me as I owned no rock shoes, harness, chalk bag or possessed the foggiest idea. I remember picking up the essentials quickly, as I was dead keen to learn. A borrowed harness from the clubs kit helped me out.

I just needed to choose between my walking boots or running shoes which ever I felt suited the grade of climb. I managed to get up all the routes, albeit 'seconding' the leader. By Sunday, I shared the lead on 'Ledge and Groove', a 6-pitch route on Bowfell Buttress at the head of the Mickledon valley, graded V. Diff, it was my first real rock climb 'on the lead'.

All the routes were British Trad grades; there were very few bolted areas in the Lakes at that time. I was certainly hooked. It also dawned on me how wonderful, wild and free it felt, no rules or regulations other than one's own rules and decisions. It was something else that had a profound effect on me.

I had been to Snowdonia and the Isle of Anglesey because my brother Pete and his partner Siân had moved there, but I hadn't appreciated the scope for outdoor adventure in the hills until it poked me in the eye in the Lake District that weekend. Pete and Siân later married in 1988 and in 2012 (platinum jubilee), Siân received an OBE in recognition for her contribution to Computer Science and Innovation whilst working at Bangor University.

June 1 2020—Covid 19: *Coronavirus lockdown easing a little.*

Easing of the virus lockdown is moving to the next level, even though a few medical experts and scientists are advising against it, we will no doubt see.

Personally speaking, I have found the criticism of the government over the last few weeks totally mischievous and incorrect. From the press to social media, they have been besotted in slamming the government and individual MP's on their handling of the crisis. Fixation on the negatives instead of the supporting the positives given the enormity of the task. Unfortunately, I feel it influences many of us as individuals wrongly and turns discussions into political arguments.

Nothing in the last seventy-five years has come close for this country and the world to deal with on such a humanitarian and financial scale. Given to us by China and not helped by the WHO (World Health Organisation) as both are guilty of withholding vital information in its early stages.

Only 'Trump' (forgiving his bigoted manner for a moment) has slammed China and demanded they be held responsible! Tedros Adhannon Ghebreyesus of the WHO is hardly blameless too.

I am angered as to why our press including the BBC could not help the country more, not a thread of condemnation from them or demand for accountability.

The press could also help with 'positive propaganda' by helping to nail the thousands of 'tiny selfish minds' who are potentially destroying the opportunity we have been given at this point. A serious situation that could revert us back into lockdown due to a second wave.

The following two weeks came very quickly once again. I had been thinking of my first indoor and outdoor meets most days at work and was certainly looking forward to the second. The club's social scene was very friendly, a good mix of old'uns and young guns eager to listen, or tell tales of recent adventures. As with other club gatherings, it eventually lent itself to socialise more with like-minded people, be that for the passion of the activity itself or a combination of family commitment, age or available free time.

I found a lot in common with a few guys at the club. Dick P, Andy D and Sean surname forgotten were as keen as I was. We very often travelled to places like the sandstone outcrops of Cleeve Hill, near Cheltenham or the limestone cliffs of Symonds Yat on the river Wye after work from Oxford, not getting home until a little before midnight or even in the small hours of the morning. Looking back through my diary, I even cycled to work the next day, as if life wasn't busy enough already!

Dick was a very knowledgeable and capable climber. He was a few years older than me (ten, to be precise) but had obviously gained considerable skills not only in rock climbing, but winter snow and ice climbing and general mountaineering. I tagged on to him for his enthusiasm and his keenness, he saw me as his protégé. There were precious few bespoke indoor training walls like there are today, so it was a 'make do job' on anything that resembled a piece of rock.

Close to where Dick lived near Horsepath, Oxford, was a disused railway bridge built of large limestone blocks. It proved an ideal training spot as the side walls were plum vertical. It turned out to be a regular and ideal place for improving our finger strength, the bonus being it was free. We did, however, constantly cut back the damn nettles and brambles that seemed to grow with rapid intensity.

One other regular training venue for us was at the Oxford University climbing wall, just off the Iffley road and situated next to the athletics track where Roger Bannister broke the four-minute mile. It was a traversing wall, only about 10 feet high, with an imaginative design and interest for climbers in the early days, having various bits of rock, slate and pebbles cemented into place.

None of the holds were interchangeable like they are today; however, tough problems could be worked on. After a session on that wall, we certainly knew we had a good workout.

Two future world class climbers, Johnny Dawes and Sean Myles, were studying at the University and would regularly meet there to strut their stuff. It was inspiring to watch those two guys, two very different climbing styles and body shapes, go through their gymnastic routines. Sean was a top athlete in his own right, perhaps not so well recognised amongst the media as Johnny, but nevertheless a world class climber with shedloads of natural ability.

It was while bouldering at the University wall one evening that Dick and I were introduced to a new rock shoe. 'Firé' shoes (pronounced 'fear-ray') were coming out of Spain with a revolutionary 'sticky rubber' sole. Up until then, the

Mode De Rigueur were 'EB's or 'PA's[19] from France, which were an advancement on nailed boots and gym plimsolls, but did not have the smearing or friction capability that the new design of 'Fire' had.

I still had very little gear of my own and had been borrowing an old pair of 'EB's from Dick up to this point. I went out the very next weekend and bought my first pair of 'sticky' rock shoes. All that was needed now was to justify I needed them!

The new rock shoes were the start of my climbing gear that I was to purchase over the following months. I perish the thought on how much I've spent over the years.

I was commencing an apprenticeship all over again, or so I thought, as there was a tremendous amount of knowledge to take on board and experience to gain. I learnt a lot from Dick's initial coaching. It was excellent groundwork for what was to follow over the following three decades.

The second essential bit of kit I bought was a harness. Climbing gear was starting to go through some quite radical developments; unfortunately, harnesses had not got any further than the 'Whillans sit harness'. I say unfortunately, not to deride it, as it was certainly an advancement from tying a rope round one's waist.

Don Whillans[20] is credited with its design in conjunction with Tony Howard and his Troll Mountaineering Company, but it did have one minor draw back. The central crutch strap on the harness was said to have rendered several male climbers impotent and was not the most comfortable for an abseil. The harness certainly aided and abetted lead climbers from falling off the rock as the resultant damage to the tender regions was unthinkable!

A belay device was an essential bit of kit which was to go through some radical developments over the coming years. For the period I started climbing,

---

[19] Pierre Allain's passion to climb higher and harder, led him to design a shoe specific for climbing. He did so with a shoe maker called Edmond Bourdonneau. Eventually Bourdonneau bought out Allain's business, but the rock shoes were still recognised by either name around the climbing fraternity thereafter.

[20] Donald Desbrow Whillans (Don) was a blunt Northern rock climber and mountaineer, famous for his quick witted one-liners. Along with Joe brown they shook up the world of climbing with their hard 'first ascents'. Don loved the fags and the booze, ultimately leading to an early grave at 52 years young.

there was the old fashioned but effective body brake method. An improvement on that was a device called a 'figure of eight'.

This was essentially devised for abseil security, but was also used to belay. The most preferred method was using a Sticht plate, which is recognised as being the first mechanical rope brake, named after its designer Fritz Sticht in the 1970s.

Climbing venues that we frequently visited were all lead climbed using British traditional (trad) climbing methods, necessitating double ropes (two half ropes). This was as opposed to sport climbing with a single rope that was developing in the UK later in the decade.

The OMC owned a club hut called Cefn Gawr in North Wales at Pentrefoelas, not far from Betws-Y-Coed. It was open to club members and their families. It was an opportunity Lynne and I took full advantage of, with Gary and Nicky for a week in June 1984, especially as cash was still a little tight.

We made the most of the good weather with some easy climbing at the small Capel Curig rocks for a couple of days, then onto the beach at Penmaenmawr. There were no showers at the hut so body washes in the large sink were order of the day, Nicky actually fitted in it, before spending evenings at the nearby Geeler Arms for a beer and supper.

After midweek, we parked at Pen-y-pass car park at the bottom of Snowdon and walked up to Glaslyn via the miners track in beautiful weather. Gary was keen to continue to the summit with me, whilst Lynne headed back slowly with Nicky to the car.

We treated ourselves to a B and B in Llanberis for the following night, as it was my intention to meet up and cheer on some of the club members who were competing in the Welsh 3000's fell race the day after. Unfortunately, the weather turned foul, which put a few off the race, but it certainly opened my eyes to yet another sport I felt I could have a bash at.

It had been a great week for us all. It was tarnished a little for me after arriving home to hear that while Mum had received her fifth chemotherapy treatment, the outcome was not good.

As mentioned, Dick, Andy and I each had families to think about outside of climbing; Sean and Jill were younger and soon to get married. It meant we all had mutual commitments at home and like me, wanted to involve them in outdoor adventures as much as possible. It led to meeting up now and again as a group, either as part of the outdoor meets or just on our own.

One of the first family gatherings was camping in the Peak District at the Hathersage campsite.

It was an initiation for us as a family as well as being part of the climbing group. I had acquired an old three-man Vango tent from my brother Pete, fortunately Nicky was only around five years old and fitted quite snugly at the bottom of the tent at the foot of the three of us. Bless her, she never complained once; in fact we all saw it as a great weekend adventure of climbing and walking with rewards of coffee, cake and ice creams.

Waking up in the morning to the sound of the stove going for a brew was nothing new, as we had done that a few times on the beaches of Cornwall; however, when it was followed up by a cooked breakfast and a camp fire later in the evening after supper, the sense of adventure for the kids was evident.

Work at Oxford was full on but enjoyable, family life at home was full on too. Lynne worked a part time job which enabled us to have little pleasures, and although we struggled to make ends meet by the end of each month, we were very happy. It was hard sometimes to justify the evenings away climbing, but the desire to improve was increasing. I could feel improvement coming, as the grades were getting marginally more difficult but I was feeling comfortable on them.

Typically routes at Symonds Yat like 'The Russian'-VS 4c, 'Red Rose Speedway'-HVS 4c and 'Mango Highway'-HVS 5b (with pre-placed protection), were challenges I was now dealing with; even a top rope on 'The Wasteland'-E2 5c was not too far away for me.

The effects of regular training paid dividends, showing the gains you get from efforts put in. With climbing it's not about huge muscle gain, but about power to weight ratio, tuning muscles, ligaments and tendons together, gradually enabling them to work in unison to withstand greater loads without injury. Combined with sensible diet and exceptional consumptions of beer, results can be readily obtained!

At home, Lynne and the kids were all very active in their individual sporting activities; we supported one another, just as importantly, at every opportunity too. Gary was playing regular football for the village and The Vale of White Horse (VoWH), Judo and swimming; Lynne was heavily into Netball and swimming coaching, whilst Nicky at five was enthusiastic with her swimming.

Outside of our home life, my mum's life was dramatically changing. October to December 1984 was particularly important for the wider family to support

Mum too. It was clear the cancer was accelerating; all we could do was enjoy her company on the good days, wherever and whenever that might be.

Sometimes, Mum would come up to Wantage and stay with us, on other occasions staying with Chris and Lez or her flat in Staines. Pete and Siân would come down and stay to be together too. There were also visits to Middlesex hospital where different treatments for Mum were a possibility. Blood transfusion, cryogenic surgery, even plastic surgery were options to improve her condition, provided future scans showed it being possible.

She was on 30% morphine to stem the pain, but that needed to be a balanced pain relief as it made her feel quite sick. A week or so later it all hit home when, after speaking with her doctor following the result of the scan, he reluctantly concluded that the cancer was too deep for cryogenic or plastic surgery.

Mum knew time was short. She said a few words to me over the phone that live vividly in my memory: "I realise the chances of seeing my grand-children growing up are now slim." It wasn't long before she needed to be better cared for in a hospice.

Climbing was becoming a huge passion for me; it was also a release from my worries surrounding Mum. Short climbing visits at weekends to more distant venues like the gritstone edges of the Peak District and mountains of the Lake District may seem daft to many, but it fed an increasing passion for climbing.

Dick got to know a hill farming family in the Lakes by the name of Jean and Keith Rowan. They had three children and ran 'Stool End Farm' (owned by the National Trust) situated at the head of the Great Langdale valley. One weekend just before Christmas Dick drove his son Max, myself and Gary up to stay at Stool End.

It was a great eye opener to the inner workings of a Cumbrian sheep farming and livestock farming lifestyle. The small B and B they also ran was served with fantastic hospitality.

Unfortunately, the following morning's weather ended up being dire, but not to be outdone, we did have a wild, wet day walking on the fells and an evening in the 'Old Dungeon Ghyll' pub to make up for it.

Sunday was just as bad, so with little point in hanging around, we headed back to Oxford.

This was a typical weekend that was to follow for many years to come and to many parts of the country. Many of them became 'snatched opportunities of amazing adventures' with very few of them wasted journeys.

The following weekend was another one spent away, this time to Wales for the OMC annual Christmas dinner. It was my first with the club and a return to the club hut, Cefn Gawr, where Lynne and I had spent a week with the kids.

It was the familiar start after work on Friday with the team from Oxford, and a late arrival at the hut. Keen souls as they were then had alarms on for 05.00, breakfast by 05.30 and out the door by 06.00. Around six of us were keen to do an easy route up 'Tryfan' situated beside Lake Ogwen.

We 'geared up' at Tryfan car park and set off for First Pinnacle Rib, V. Diff by 07.30. Climbing as two teams of three, we all had an enjoyable climb arriving on the summit by 12.30.

After a quick lunch at the summit, we had a fast scramble down to the cars. An afternoon spent at Plas-y- Brenin climbing wall was followed by a shower and a return to the club hut.

The evening was spent at the Geeler Arms for the pre-arranged Christmas dinner and of course lots of Ale. It was also nice to catch up with Pete and Siân who had come across from Anglesey to join us.

Fortunately, there was not the rush to get up early the following morning as it was peeing down. The eventual play around on the Capel Curig slabs didn't aspire to us much, so after a brew in the local café we headed back home.

Christmas 1984 was very soon upon us, with frantic shopping for food and pressies on my part as I had been swanning around the country climbing beforehand. I think we all knew it was very likely to be Mum's last Christmas with us, so it was great the three families and Mum were all able to spend Christmas Day together at Chris and Lez's.

Boxing Day was spent at our house in Grove with Mum, Pete and Siân. A nurse from Wantage cottage hospital visited and treated Mum's wound each day until she returned to stay with Chris. Looking at my notes retrospectively, I'm thinking this was yet another marvellous feat of the NHS.

Chapter Six
Sudden Epiphany

After a boozy New Year it was back on the bike, cycling to work on the 2 January 1985, and bloody cold it was too!

The first two weeks into the New Year was centred round the kids' activities, and work with a new vacuum chamber construction for Litton Industries, based in Los Angeles, USA.

I found a little time of my own to throw in some training.

The OMC had arranged its first winter climbing trip of the season to the Lake District and I was keen to indulge. I knew very little about this mad idea of climbing snow and ice but I was certainly intrigued.

Four of us from the club stayed at Stool End Farm, and in the morning would meet up with three other guys. Two of the guys were New Zealanders, both called Rob, while the other guy called Martin, lived in the Langdale valley just up the road. Little did I know at the time that Martin was to become a very close friend and mountaineering partner, as was Rob Blackburne until he returned to New Zealand.

We all headed up Rossett Gill towards Hanging Knotts where winter climbing can sometimes form early, it hadn't, and further march up to Great End was required. Upon reaching the crag, it was clear to those with the knowledge (not me at this point) that something could be found.

The group split into different teams. Dick, Martin and I made our own version up the 600ft cliff of ice and frozen sods at around grade 2/3. That was followed by a run (rather than a walk, and still a bloody test of fitness to this day) back to Stool End Farm for a much-needed brew.

The morning after the night before proved a challenge to get the head and the body mobile; it was short lived though, sorted out with the plod up to 'Red Screes' at Kirkstone Pass. Ice was in pretty good nick and made for some good practice; all in all it was another short but valued weekend. Returning home after my initiation into winter climbing it had left me with the desire for much more.

Three weeks passed very quickly with the frequent pattern and involvement in the family's activities, along with regular visits to keep in touch with Mum. Oh, how nice it would have been to have had Skype or mobile phones in those days!

Another winter trip had been planned, this time a venture across the border into Scotland.

It was five days of adventure in mid-February and needed a few days off work. We set off from Dicks on a Tuesday evening bound for Lakes to pick up Martin, then leaving his house around 23.00 in a borrowed Land Rover heading for Fort William. By 04.30, we were knackered having arrived in Glencoe and needed to get our head down for a few hours. A bivvy (bivouac) in a Glencoe carpark was the first of many such experiences to follow in my climbing life.

We were up by 08.00 and in Fort William for 09.00, queueing for a hearty breakfast at Nevisports Outdoor Shop. A reliable forecast was obtainable in the shop and gave a poor weather report for the West Highland mountains, these days with improvement in clothing, equipment and avalanche awareness, there is a tendency to venture out winter climbing in most weathers, save for high-risk avalanche levels.

However, the report for the East Highland Mountains of the Cairngorms promised a better proposition for us. With little hesitation, we headed for Aviemore. A cheap self-catering apartment for the afternoon and night gave us time to sort ourselves out and catch up on some sleep.

Up again at the unearthly hour of 04.00 was followed by a breakfast of bacon and eggs (the last decent one for a couple of days). We parked at the Coire Cas car park by the ski centre and walked with heavy packs into the mountains bound for Jeans Hut[21]. I must point out at this point that I was a novice to this game and only had a cheap frame rucksack.

Clearly not enough volume inside the thing for everything needing to be carried, I was left with the only obvious solution, which was to have stuff

---

[21] Jean's Hut was first built in 1951 on a site in Coire Cas, only later removed to the site in Coire an Lochain. It was a prefabrication donated by Dr Alastair Smith in memory of his daughter Jean who died of a skiing accident in 1948. It offered refuge to the sub-arctic conditions of the Cairngorm Mountains. It was deemed inhabitable and subsequently demolished and removed in 1986.

attached on the outside. I looked and sounded like a tinker and suffered endless piss take the entire trip.

We made it to the ramshackle hut situated in the most amazing landscape of Coire an Lochain. Unloading our heavy sacks, we proceeded to clean up the hut as best we could; very clearly the hut, (it was nothing more than a large shed!), was on its last legs, as snow and mice were finding the way in through various gaps in its structure. There was probably a metre or more to the depth of snow outside, and with the use of a handy snow saw it was ideal for obtaining regular shaped blocks to build a structure.

To kill time and keep warm, we started on the front door and gave it a porch, Igloo style. This at least helped stop snow drifting in to the adjoining room. Then we started building an igloo behind the hut, building its circumference around a deep hole we had dug.

The luxurious abode would probably have been drier to sleep in than the hut, but alas, it was destined to end up with the title of 'The Loo' above the entrance. It suited our needs, but heaven knows what occurred after our stay. (I still have a few pictures somewhere of our workmanship, and unbeknown to us at the time, we were one of the last parties to use the hut before it was demolished.)

Jean's hut is situated a short distance from the infamous 'Great Slab' a notorious avalanche slope that has a full depth avalanche every spring. Our first venture out the next day was a gulley climb called 'The Vent' which is rather exposed above the Great Slab. Conditions were good and meant there was little danger of avalanche as we approached the climb via the slab.

The route was Scottish grade 2/3 and had variable difficulties around a 'chockstone' in the gully, once negotiated it opened out into a broader easier funnel. It had been a most enjoyable adventure as we made our way back to the hut for a brew and well-deserved scoff.

The overnight stay in the hut was not quite as enjoyable, with 'spindrift' coming through the cracks onto our sleeping bags and the noise of scurrying mice searching for remnants of our grub. However, looking back many times as I have, it was without doubt a great craic!

The following morning we had a welcome brew and warm porridge for breakfast, re-packed our sacks and out the door for around 08.30, bidding farewell to our slum and the arctic loo. We were heading for the remote Shelter Stone and Hell's Lum area via Coire Domhain. The scenery was amazing and the wild panorama, for me was awe inspiring.

The decision was to climb the fine route and namesake of the crag called Hell's Lum Chimney, another 3-star route of 150 metres and graded 2/3. The conditions were not brilliant but certainly good enough; we took turns in leading the four pitches without too much difficulty, and it was pleasing not to have the large cornice build up at the top, as it sometimes can be.

We eventually decided to leave the Cairngorm earlier than planned and head for yet another area called Creag Meagaidh in the hope conditions were as good there. Camping overnight was another new experience, as temperatures dropped to around minus 10degC. My buffalo sleeping bag(s) were not a match for the temperatures; inevitably it meant I woke up periodically and was forced to add yet another layer of clothing.

None of us were keen to get up early, but by the sound of activity outside the tent a lot were. We eventually got our acts together and walked the 6km into Coire Ardair, which lies east of the main summit of Meagaidh. We climbed the open corner of Eastern Corner, a grade 3, at around 300m in length, again taking turns to lead each pitch.

It had been the best climbing of the trip and had been enough for me for one day, especially as I now needed to be back home and to work.

Dick and Martin were to spend a couple more days in Scotland, while I headed home by train. The guys dropped me off at Fort William railway station, I caught the 17.40 train to Glasgow passing through wonderful scenery of Loch Linnie, Rannoch Moor and Loch Lomond. I then caught the train out of Glasgow at 23.55, arriving Birmingham at 07.15. Eventually leaving Birmingham after many brews at 09.45, arriving into Oxford at 11.15.

I then caught a bus to Dick's house to pick up my car, eventually getting home around 13.00 to lots of hugs and kisses, nineteen hours from leaving Fort William.

There was so much more detail to those few days I could have added. Nothing that was super dangerous or heroic, just simple pleasures whilst being in the mountains at that time of year.

Reflecting the trip on my journey home, it occurred to me that the last few days experience was not a transient moment in my life. It was a moment of sudden revelation, of realisation that my outlook on life had changed; it was indeed an epiphany for me.

I had experienced an adventure longing to be released from deep within, an experience that was so much a different way of life. It challenged me in a way I had not been challenged before. It enabled me to deal with potential danger, to touch the myths of the wilderness and began the craft of winter survival.

I learnt more about myself in those few days, of dealing with self-doubt, confidence and lack of experience. Not only had I dealt with it, I was passionate for more, a lot more.

Nothing meant more to me than my family. The new passion would sit alongside them and I knew we would have great fun and adventures together. The desire to build a career in industry was meaningless now. *I knew where I wanted to go!*

Never get so busy making a living, that you forget to make a life! – **Dolly Parton**

It was back to work with a crunch as the 'Litton chamber' was having problems pumping down a vacuum. It was great to be with Lynne and the kids again, involving myself in their activities as well as all of us making regular visits to see Mum.

By early March, the hospital doctor had recommended that Mum should be transferred to a hospice, as her condition was now terminal. Within a matter of days, she was admitted to the Sue Ryder hospice at Nettlebed, near Henley, South Oxfordshire. Both my brothers and I made as many visits as we could during the rest of the month and into April.

An unplanned opportunity came up in mid-April for a quick visit to 'The Ben' on the strength of a reasonable weather forecast. Dick and another OMC member Mike D, and again Martin were also keen. I managed to get the time off work for a couple of days the following week and so by that Thursday morning at 01.30 we were stepping out of the car in the pouring rain and into a 3-star hotel just outside Fort William.

This, to quickly add, was not for a comfy warm bed and a three-course breakfast, but a corner of the lounge floor that Dick had blagged his way into, all for the princely sum of nothing! One thing Dick hated was putting up a tent in the pouring rain or finding a dry bivvy spot for a few hour's kip.

I felt slightly guilty that the kind nightshift supervisor may have felt a wee bit intimidated by four hairy arse climbers seeking his floor for the night, but we assured him of our most honourable intentions of being out the door by 06.30, so the residents didn't see us. I doubt we would stand a chance of the same situation these days!

Forecasting weather for the Scottish hills in those days was about as accurate as 'a wet finger in the air', and of course, it was still raining as we left the hotel. We hung around Nevisport's, waiting for it to open, before tucking into one of their hearty breakfasts once again.

Eventually, the rain eased enough for us to make tracks up to the CIC hut[22] situated below Coire na Ciste. We hiked up to the hut along the rough track and bogs alongside the Allt a' Mhuilinn burn. It took a good two and a half hours from leaving the car fully laden with climbing gear, camping gear and food for a couple of days.

It was my first visit to the panoramic splendour of the North face of Ben Nevis and although the mist and gloom was down most of the time, it cleared on occasions to reveal an awe inspiring, jaw dropping spectacle of its northern flanks.

One could be excused from feeling a tiny bit of trepidation and dread at first sight, particularly with its raw winter coat and atmosphere from the iffy weather. However, given a good degree of preparation, sensible route choice for a first visit and a bucketful of nerve, a good day was always there to be had.

The CIC hut is owned and managed by the Scottish Mountaineering Club (SMC); it is open to mountaineering club members, provided bookings are done in advance. Unfortunately, our trip was a spur of the moment decision which meant the hut was fully booked. Not to be outdone, we decided to camp on a small flattish area adjacent to the hut.

It did mean, however, that we remained independent to the hut, as it is strictly out of bounds to all but those who book a bed and remains so to this day. The snow was quite deep as we pitched the tents and thick ice plastered the nearby rocks, conditions were looking favourable!

There was no running water inside the hut and no toilet facilities; gas stoves were fed from large propane bottles delivered by helicopter. Water for us campers as well as residents of the hut was via a small plastic pipe, one end of which was up the hillside in the Allt a' Mhuilinn, the other end tied to a stake a short distance from the hut entrance.

---

[22] The CIC memorial hut was erected in 1928/9 by Dr and Mrs Inglis Clark in memory of their son Charles Inglis Clark who was killed in action in the 1914–1918 war. The original building was extensively refurbished and extended between 2008 and 2012. It is arguably the only alpine-style hut in the UK and owned by the Scottish Mountaineering Club (SMC), its situation below the North Face has saved many lives.

The absence of loo facilities meant it was up to every individual to find a suitable large boulder to duck behind. It was also up to the conscience of all concerned to pack out what was necessary or at least dig a hole. Needless to say, that didn't happen very much!

All I can say is, it must have been wretched in the summer. It took until 2008 when the hut underwent modifications, to eventually supply it with a composting loo, obviating the need to drag and stumble across rocky ground to find an adequate spot. Why it took so long beats me, when one considers the world status of the climbing and its environmental footprint in such prestigious surroundings.

After nearly twelve hours sleep and a quick breakfast, we geared up to look at Point Five Gully, a classic climb on the Orion Face, graded V/5. At the bottom of the gully looking up it was obvious, for us anyway, that there was far too much spindrift cascading down. It would have to be saved for another day.

With that, the four of us climbed Tower Scoop a good short ice climb graded 3/4. Mike D and myself were climbing together and decided to carry on to the summit via Tower Gully and a somewhat large cornice. A 'white-out' on the summit added to our difficulty in finding Number 4 gully to descend to the hut.

The obvious decision for both our safety was to descend the easier ground of the walker's path and traverse back to the hut below Castle Ridge. It was inevitably a much longer trudge back to the tent, arriving bedraggled and soaked. 'Welcome to The Ben!' I heard voices say!

Dick and Martin were beginning to feel a little concerned and were glad to see us stumbling home in the gloom. As with all evenings after an eventful day out 'on the hill', tales of daring do were the talk over many brews until it was time to crash out in a warm sleeping bag.

The blizzard carried on all night and despite having to clear the tent of snow once or twice in the night, it was still half buried in the morning. At least it made for an easy decision as nothing could be done in the conditions. We packed a soaking wet tent and headed down for a very welcome brunch at Nevisport's.

Another short winter trip was far from wasted, so much learnt and so much fun. How I wondered, could so much fun, fuelled by so many new experiences, could be had at so little expense!

I crept into bed in the small hours of Sunday morning, woken after a blissful sleep to a welcome brew courtesy of Gary. Life it seemed, couldn't get much better.

It was always great to return to the familiar routine and enjoyment of everyone's activities; I felt it kept my feet firmly on the ground. Lynne was particularly overjoyed at this point, as she passed her swim coaching award.

Mum had been at the Sue Ryder Hospice nearly two months by the end of April, they were an exceptionally caring unit. We managed to visit two or three times a week, not knowing quite what to expect each time as it was a traumatic period for her. One visit could see her looking well and out of pain; the next could be a bad turn, enduring a lot of pain and terribly out of breath.

Over the first Bank holiday in May, I had planned to raise some sponsorship money for the Sue Ryder home by riding my bike from our home in Grove to Land's End in twenty-four hours. I certainly felt fit enough with all the cycling I had been doing to and from work. Friends, family and work colleagues from Oxford Instruments all contributed handsomely; added to which was the wonderful generosity of the company, which contributed with a cheque that matched the final sum.

I set off at 21.45 after work on May 2, having loaded as much as I could sensibly carry in the panniers and smeared as much Vaseline on my arse as was possible. I stopped for a quick 1-hour kip around 03.45, then on the bike again until 08.15 for a breakfast at Ilminster. Onward through Exeter around noon, followed by another short kip after Launceston. Head down against the prevailing breeze once more across Bodmin moor until 18.45, where I stopped for dinner, utterly famished.

Coincidently, the OMC had an outdoor climbing meet at Land's End and fortuitously one of the members, Brian C, passed me 15 miles east of Penzance. I was on a definite downer at the time, feeling the pain and having problems with the bike's gears. Brian and his passengers greeted me with horn blaring and whoops of encouragement, it was just the tonic I needed.

The damn bike played up on every incline, needing me to nurse it all the way into Land's End by 22.45 on May 3rd, an hour outside the planned time. Given the snags I had with the bike, it was good enough for me. I knew it was going to be good enough for all the kind sponsorship.

A couple of days was spent at Sennen Cove campsite, mostly recuperating, not having the energy to do much climbing. Brian gave me a lift to Penzance railway station, where I caught the train with the bike to Newton Abbott. A bus was needed from there to Exeter and it was thanks to a sympathetic driver that the bike came too. It would most certainly have been a gift to someone had he not allowed it on the bus.

From Exeter, I was met at Reading station by my brother Chris, who drove me home completely shagged. There was time and just enough energy for me to celebrate with the family a glass of champagne, courtesy of May, our friendly neighbour opposite.

I had not planned the sponsored trip to be so close to Mum's passing; but alas, by the following week she was in terrible pain that not even a higher dose of morphine could relieve. On Saturday, 11 May, Lynne, Gary, Nicky and myself drove over to see her and although it was obvious she was in agony, she still had a smile for the kids.

On Sunday, 12 May, I took a call from Chris to tell me Mum had asked to be sedated. I went over in the early evening, only to realise it wasn't going to be long. I zoomed back to Grove, picked up Lynne and was back at the Hospice by 21.30. At 22.15, Mum had passed away.

It was peace and pain free at last for her; four days before Gary's 9th birthday. She passed away aged sixty-two years young, not able to see her two grandchildren grow up beyond nine and six. However, it was a little comforting to know she had seen them both the day before.

I know she would have immense pride in how they have both made incredible and fulfilling lives for themselves. I'm sure she would have felt the same about her four other grandchildren, Cara and Rees (Pete and Siân) and Tom and Sam (Chris and Lez) who came along a few years later. Proud she most certainly would be to now see that Cara has a partner Siwan, and both represent The Wales women's national rugby union team. In addition, Tom is now married to Amy and Sam is married to Kelley.

Mum was a legend, a prodigy; she left a legacy, and maybe a gene or two, that will inspire her progeny for generations to come, not least for her two great-grandchildren, Chester (Nicky and Becki) and Anna (Tom and Amy) the latest additions to the family.

The following couple of weeks was difficult and confusing, having to maintain focus at work, being the same happy dad and husband, whilst helping my bros deal with Mum's cremation arrangements and the bitterness of her death.

A bank holiday weekend away to Symonds Yat on the river Wye helped begin the process of living with the loss. A mixture of cricket and rounders, walking over rickety wooden river bridges, cream teas followed by a pub in the evening all helped. We had a one night's stay and a great breakfast in a fifteenth century house, come B and B, before making our way home in the pouring rain.

The following weekend, Saturday, June 1 1985, Dick and I paid a quick visit to the Lakes, arriving at Stool End farm for 23.30 the evening before. We travelled over to Dovedale crag via Kirkstone Pass and climbed Dovedale Grooves at E1 5b, 5a, 5a, my first lead at the Extremely Severe grade. Great climbing was followed by a great pint at the Kirkstone Inn, before heading back and arriving home at 02.15 Sunday morning.

Weekend after weekend during the summer of 1985 was spent travelling somewhere or being involved in each other's activities one way or another. It was either up to Pete and Siân's on Anglesey or down to Mum's flat to help clear it out. To Easthamstead Crematorium, Wokingham to arrange Mum's funeral, or to sport presentations for the kids.

I was due to travel over to Los Angeles to help install and commission the equipment for Litton Industries that I had been working on for the last six months. The acceptance criteria had been met and signed off by the leading project engineer, but first there needed to be some important climbing to get under my belt before leaving.

A quick trip to Symonds Yat gave me my first lead success of an E2 5c on 'Wastelands'. That was followed a few days later with another short trip to North Wales to the famous crag of Dinas Cromlech, where I was overjoyed at climbing two famous Joe Brown routes. Dick managed to lead 'Cenotaph Corner' at E1 5c which I seconded, followed by my lead on 'Left Wall' at E2 5c.

I rapped down the route removing my lead gear, Dick was knackered after his great lead on Cenotaph, before heading back to Oxford with huge grins on our faces.

There was an equal feeling of success and satisfaction when I returned to work, as I had been given promotion to Production Manager of our Material Science Group.

I left Heathrow midday on Sunday bound for LAX International airport. It was going to be a very long three weeks away from Lynne and the kids. Little did I know at the time that climbing expeditions were going to make that a frequent event.

I had a free day following my arrival; the immediate priority being to find somewhere to boulder[23] to keep up the momentum in my climbing training. As luck would have it, I was told of a large boulder in an area known as Chatsworth Park, part of downtown LA.

I was not due to pick up a car until the following day, so as it was only a couple of miles out of town, the project engineer loaned me his bicycle. On both journeys to and from the boulder, I had not met another cyclist; in fact, I had the distinct feeling I was being looked at as some weirdo on two wheels. It appeared that cycling and walking any distance further than it took to get from a carpark to their multi-shop complexes seemed to most to be a complete waste of time.

Anyway, the boulder was an ideal feature for training and a getaway after work. There was plenty of chalk[24] on tiny crimps that assured me I was not the only silly bugger in LA.

Three weeks went very quickly for me at Litton. I had done as much as I could; it was then down to the Project engineers to get the thing running and signed off. I enjoyed the time in LA and the bouldering, however their lifestyle was not for me. I was extremely glad to get back to the UK, to little 'ol Wantage and to our rural way of life.

Summer and autumn passed very quickly too; a family holiday to Cornwall was a particularly great break with shorter trips to the lakes, the Peak District and Anglesey thrown in. There was also lots of climbing and training at local crags filling the gaps too.

One cold and snowy weekend in November, I took Gary to Cefn Gawr, the OMC club hut. It was damp and cold but he, unlike me, slept like a log. The following day we parked at the Pen-y-Pass car park, where we met up with Pete and Siân.

We all hiked up to the snowy start of Crib Goch via Bwlch y Moch and continued carefully over the sharp, snowed up ridge line with Gary on a short rope. From there, we decided to carry onto the summit of Snowdon via Crib y

---

[23] 'Bouldering' is a term given to a type of FREE CLIMBING in which short, difficult problems are climbed on large boulders or outcrops of rock. The climbing is generally executed at a safe height with reasonable landings, as the sequences can be extremely difficult on tiny holds (crimps) and falling off is common.

[24] Chalk as used in climbing, gymnastics and weightlifting is a compound made from magnesium carbonate. It is used on hands particularly fingers to improve friction and grip.

Ddysgl, where we found a spot out of the cold wind to pull out a flask of coffee and cheese sandwiches from the rucksacks. It was moments like these that mattered more to me than anything else.

We eventually descended the miners' track back to the car, my thoughts reflecting how impressed I was at the way Gary coped with the various situations. I sensed already that a seed had been sown.

Christmas 1985 was one of many spent at Pete and Siân's lovely old farmhouse on the Isle of Anglesey; it has pretty much turned into an annual tradition for the 'Hope gang' even today.

Pete was heavily into basketball and had rigged up a good court in their yard. Without fail, in whatever the weather, snow, rain or ice, we would be out there Christmas Eve or Christmas Day, mixing it competitively with as many as we could muster. It was great fun!

That in fact was quite tame to latter years when all the kids were growing up fast and motorised vehicles were raced round one of their large fields. A certain Citroen 2cv was shown no mercy as everyone tried to outdo each other, it only coming to end when its driveshaft and suspension were completely buggered. Happy days! Nowadays we still try to outdo each other with indoor games and quizzes, no less rowdy or competitive, still adolescents at heart!

It was at Pete's that Christmas, I realised my climbing training had slackened off. I searched high and low around the farmhouse, eventually finding a sturdy door lintel for 'pull ups' and a lengthy concrete partition to traverse. I was starting to take training more and more seriously to push my grades higher.

When we arrived back at Wantage, I was determined to plan my own climbing training wall at home, to have a facility immediately to hand and save unnecessary travel time. There was no such thing as individual and bespoke 'bolt on' climbing holds in those days.

I ended up making some wooden ones from bits of plywood and travelled over to the local railway line in search of flat pieces of rock or pebbles.

I bought a sheet of MDF (Medium-density fibreboard) and hung it at a 60deg angle from an RSJ (Rigid Steel Joist) in the garage. As many of the makeshift holds as possible, were drilled and bolted onto the board, giving rise to a fabulous asset for finger strength training.

To further my training at home and to make use of our end-terrace house at Grove, I also attached the same kind of holds to the outside wall. Araldite resin worked extremely well and with strategic placing of the holds on the wall, it gave an excellent traversing alternative to the garage board.

Now the fact that our end-terrace wall ran alongside a public footpath, did turn a few heads.

The public didn't really know what it was for at first. Until that is, they saw some weirdo with funny shoes on and chalk dust on his hands traversing the holds.

Kids would strike up some banter and try hanging from them. I would offer a few pounds to any of them if they could do a full traverse. Fortunately, they didn't, but it was great fun watching them and knowing they would desperately try giving it a bash when I wasn't there.

Great times and a definite step forward in raising my standard of climbing.

Chapter Seven
Alpine Initiation

The talk between the team (Dick, Martin, myself and anyone else we could cajole) was to make our presence felt in the Alps for the first time. However, some serious winter outings were needed in the UK before venturing out there and making a name for ourselves!

I have always looked forward to our British ephemeral winters as much as summers. The Lake District in 1986 was still a very reliable source for good winter climbing, with top class routes for the taking. Alas, global warming today is taking its grip on our planet in a more disastrous way than it was then, making winters as we once knew them shorter lived and less predictable, to the point where very soon it is likely we shall lose them for good.

January 1986 was out of the equation for me as I had another 'system' to install and commission for Oxford Instruments. The Litton project in LA had gone very well and many more companies were looking to develop similar technology. My forthcoming visit was to a company called Balzers based in Lichtenstein and would probably last nearly two weeks.

Early February was our team's first opportunity to get together and 'the Lakes' were looking white and iced up! Two top class winter routes were climbed by the three of us which more than made up for the travelling and shortness of a weekend trip. The first route was Inaccessible Gully on Dove crag, a grade IV/4[25], 2 pitch, 3-star climb.

---

[25] In simple terms, the grading of winter climbing is like the E grading system of rock climbing. In this case the first symbol is a Roman numeral (e.g. V), and represents the seriousness of a route with the second numerical symbol (eg. 5), representing the technical difficulty of the route.

The second route climbed the following day was on Black crag and aptly named Black Crag Icefalls, this was not a route frequently 'in condition' even back in those days, but we made the most of the rare opportunity, grateful of yet another fantastic grade IV/4, 2 pitch, 3-star route. One short weekend, two classic 3-star routes climbed, wonderful.

Two weekends later towards the end of a cold February, I had managed to sneak another few days off work to extend the weekend. We were on our way yet again, late on a Friday night to the Lake District, with plans to climb one route we had heard was in condition, then head on up to Scotland for further fun.

Dick and I met Martin and Mike W Saturday morning, and headed up to Honister Crag situated at an altitude of 350m overlooking the Buttermere valley. The crag which forms part of Fleetwith Pike's north face, contain a fine collection of pure icefalls if prolonged northerly or easterly biting winds have been blowing in.

Our choice of route was Honister Crag Gully, a 200m grade IV/4 line that splits the Honister face and soars straight up to the top of Fleetwith Pike. We split into two teams of two and enjoyed a very absorbing day, just managing to catch tea and cake at the local café in Borrowdale before heading back to Dicks place at Bowness-on-Windermere once again knackered.

Up reasonably early, the four of us headed for Fort William, arriving around 13.00. We were staying at the CIC hut for a few days, so essential shopping was needed, and although it was very tempting to take a few luxuries, the plod up the Allt a' Mhuilinn for three hours was very much in the back of our minds. We arrived knackered, but a brew and supper were prerequisites before sorting out gear for the morning then turning in to our bunks and away with the fairies.

Alarm woke us at 05.00 and already some keen folk were up and about. It goes without saying there is always kidology and bluff when it comes to discussing route choice with the enemy in hut life, no matter where or what country one is in.

A peek outside the hut confirmed it was a beautiful day and we would need to get a move on if we were to be the first at our preferred choice of route, 'Point Five Gully'. For those not familiar with winter climbing, it is always an aim to be first on a long route. Firstly, it allays the fear of debris, rocks or ice coming from above potentially ruining one's day. Secondly, it avoids any hold ups which can cause quite lengthy and serious situations, such as a benightments or accidents.

Point Five Gully is a classic grade V/5, 350m (8 pitches) long route and worthy of its 4 stars. It is possibly one, if not 'the', most famous ice gullies in the world, and as luck would have it, we were first at the bottom. We split into two pairs, Dick and myself, Martin and Mike W. The route looked awesome and I did feel some trepidation as it was my first serious grade V/5 route.

The climbing lived up to every bit of its reputation with great varied climbing and exceptional conditions of neve[26] and rime ice[27] throughout the route's length, so admired by our foreign visitors. We topped out onto the summit plateau to an amazing sky and exhilarating views.

Finding number four gully for our descent was more straight forward than the last time I was looking for it, and before long we were back at the CIC hut, chuffed to bits with another tick for the Sassenachs!

Up again at 05.00 the following day to make the most of the stable high-pressure weather. This time we were heading for 'Zero Gully', the sister route of Point Five and another 'must do' all time classic route. The route is graded V/4, technically easier than the Point, but nevertheless a serious challenge with poor belays.

It was the first grade V to be climbed on the Ben. We were first to the route again, except for one guy who was soloing and was already half way up the first pitch. As if that wasn't enough of a put off with the thought of him falling off above us, we came across blood and gore below the line that evidently belonged to falling bodies from a few days before.

We cracked on, dealt with the few technical difficulties, and apart from the lack of good belays making for a few worrying moments, enjoyed another magnificent outing to the summit plateau. The weather had closed in on the summit but visibility was good enough to find number 4 gully to descend to the hut. We were obviously very delighted to bag two amazing classic routes.

Not surprisingly, we were a little knackered the next day and not so keen to depart onto a third long route, although the star prize of 'Orion Direct' to

---

[26] 'Neve' (pronounced Nev-ay) is a wonderful climbing medium of snow that has gone through a metamorphosis of freeze and thaw that changes the character of the snow pack into a very firm/hard structure.

[27] 'Rime ice' is also a wonderful medium for winter climbing associated with the UK's closeness to its seas, its latitude and weather. Similar to hoar frost, rime is formed when supercooled droplets freeze and attach onto an exposed surface. All surfaces impacted need to be at 0degC or below causing the liquid to freeze instantly.

complete a trio of classic grade 5s would have been an amazing finale to the trip. The wind had got up and it was feeling bloody freezing. 'The Curtain' seemed more like the route of the day and a fitting end to our trip, another magnificent route and pure ice climb which is steep and no easy option at the grade of IV/5.

The wind ensured full concentration was needed, the ice was excellent if chopped about a little, but considering it is probably the most climbed route of its grade on the Ben, it was great. The ice cave belay atop the first pitch was novel, as was the contorted exiting onto the start of the second pitch.

All of us were 'done' by the time we got down to the car. It was time for a Nevisport meal and the long journey home. I made the most of my remaining day's leave, taking the kids to school, Lynne to work, washing a lot of smelly gear, and celebrating with yet another bottle of bubbly with Lynne in the evening as it was her birthday.

Two or three weeks had passed, and just as I was beginning to think that winter climbing was over, I received a phone call from Dick. He'd got hold of information that 'the Ben' was still in nick and worth one last visit. He suggested we make a long weekend of it with both families, stopping in the Lake District for a couple of days at their house at Bowness.

Both our families had met up a couple of times and got on well. Dick's wife and son, together with Lynne, Gary and Nicky travelled up in one car, whilst Dick and I travelled up a day later after work. Obviously, there was an ulterior motive behind the plan, which was for us to pop up to Scotland after the weekend.

We had a great couple of days all together in the Lake District, snow still laid quite deep on the high fells, which the kids loved. Tea and cake went down well, followed by a welcome dip in the indoor pool and spa at the newly opened Pillar club on the Langdale Estate.

By Sunday lunchtime, Dick and I headed for Scotland (I had managed to blag another couple of days leave) whilst his wife, Lynne and the kids headed back home. As luck would have it, the CIC hut had a couple of spare bunks and by 17.00 we were in Fort William, by 21.00 we were in the CIC with a brew on the go.

We were up at 08.00, quite late by climbing standards, especially as the weather was crystal clear and the Orion Face was looking alpine. Orion Direct is a 400m, grade V/5, 4-star route, and one of the finest winter climbs in Scotland, with its length and sustained climbing it takes on all the atmosphere of an alpine face. It looked in great condition and from what we could see, not a soul on it.

The face was open and extremely exposed. Between us we managed to navigate a line through the difficulties and find reasonable belays where it mattered most. We were back at the CIC at 20.30, twelve hours after leaving; my legs felt as though they were about to drop off, particularly as we had been on our 'front points' most of the climb. By 21.00 we were joined by Martin and Mike W, both eager to get on the face the following day.

Another 8.00 start saw Martin and Mike head for Orion, whilst Dick and I made for Vanishing Gully, yet another grade V/5, three-star ice route. We found just about enough energy to get that ticked and limp down to Fort William.

We relived the route again and again in minute detail the entire journey home. I suppose it's a process we all go through that helps a major achievement to sink in.

Orion Direct was first climbed in 1960 by two very talented Scottish mountaineers, Jimmy Marshall and Robin Smith. They had rudimentary climbing gear (nothing like the improvement in gear we had) and step cut their way up the face. It was an incredible achievement.

I had been completely absorbed, captivated and in a zone as never before. I felt confident that I had completed yet another apprenticeship successfully, and equipped myself with the skill and knowledge to take to the Alps!

As a youth I read Jack London's 'The Call of the Wild'; it struck a chord with me at the time. I also came to realise over those last few weeks of climbing, particularly with the bold, extreme end of climbing, that it bonds partnerships like nothing I had ever felt before.

The trust of putting one's life in a partner's handling of your ropes and vice-versa in dangerous, potentially dire situations, makes for a truly special relationship. Later, in the world's great mountains, I would come to realise how important that bond and synergy really is.

In my mind over the years, I have kind of drawn a simile between the challenges and situations that exist in mountaineering, to the challenges that I guess exist in hostile conflicts, and that exist in our emergency and rescue services. This is purely from the point of view of how it must bond individuals together, through a reliance and trust in each other when confronted with difficult, hazardous or potential death situations.

It was most poignant for me when we were about to embark on Zero Gully after stepping round the gore at the bottom of the climb, where clearly something had gone terribly wrong.

My generation are very lucky and should be eternally grateful that we have not been called upon to go to war. I can only imagine those poor souls (my grandfather, for one) who had to endure two horrendous world wars, like myself, did have that intense bond and trust in their comrades who were looking after each other's backs. Gary would also come to recognise this after successfully going through Sandhurst Academy and joining the Parachute Regiment.

Winter 1986 was all but done in the UK, although our first climbing trip to the high Alpine mountains in June was expected to have similar conditions. I managed to keep training going between our hectic home-life by installing my own climbing board in the garage. Fortunately, the previous owner was a keen car mechanic and had installed a useful RSJ (Rigid Steel Joist) inside the garage under the flat-roof.

I was able to hang one end of an eight by four sheet of MDF with two hinges to the beam, the other end touching the floor, giving an angle of around 60deg. I bolted on many holds made from bits of wood and drilled small bits of rock which made for a very convenient, albeit very strenuous, finger workout.

Training at the various locations that were now open to me was paying off. A few trips to Avon Gorge before the Alps, enabled me to keep my 'head game' positive with leads on great routes such as; Ladder of Desire E3 5c, Steppenwolf E3 5c, and Them E3 6a.

And so there we were, late June, Dick, Martin, Mike W and myself, heading down the Autobahn in Dick's BMW, having crossed the Channel around midnight. We were heading for the Grossglockner region of Austria. The mountain itself is the highest in Austria at 3,798m, and by all accounts is a magnificent sight from any point above the East bank of the Pasterze glacier.

As I recall, it was Dick who had a fascination for this mountain, and any route on its North face. The consensus from all of us after scanning through limited guide book information, was the Pallavicini Couloir, and that was only if we had everything going for us, of course.

We wasted no time travelling down towards the Heiligenblut district of Austria, stopping only for the occasional loo and coffee break. The cassette player banged out repeatedly to the sound of *when the going gets tough, the tough get going*, a hit song at the time by Billy Ocean; there was going to be no stopping us. Pulling into service stations the volume would be ramped up, and if we had Union Jacks, they would have been made obvious too.

Three out of the four of us needed to make the trip as cheap as possible, especially Mike W who was a poor university student. Three to one voted in favour of a bivvy wherever it was possible, instead of finding needless and expensive accommodation.

It didn't go down to well with Dick, who could afford otherwise, despite having tentatively discussed it prior to leaving the UK. The mood had changed a little due to the bivvy discussion. By the time we got to the Franz Josefshohe road terminus, overlooking the glacier and the Grossglockner, the mood had deepened even more.

The weather was bloody awful, rain coupled with extremely warm temperatures and low cloud, meant we were hardly able to see the mountain, let alone climb on it. The weather forecast from a local guide was not looking any better for the next few days either, it was time for brews and discussions to ensue. Needless to say we were all pretty pissed off.

It was fortunate that Dick had brought plenty of Hamlet cigars with him from the UK, for it was an addiction that kept him affable in adversity, not only for himself, but also for others around him so long as he had a good stock of them. I was to learn some months later, how much it changed his mood when his stash had expired. It prompted me thereafter to always keep a packet in the top of my sack!

We decided to head to the Northern Limestone Mountains of the Austrian Tyrol, particularly the 'Wilder Kaiser' or Kaisergebirge, Emperor Mountains, as they are known, in the hope that the weather was more stable there. Thunder, lightning and heavy rain accompanied us as we drove north. Our constant lookout for a deserted barn or anything else that offered shelter for an overnight bivvy was fading fast, as were the last glimmers of daylight.

Fortunately, we had moved away from the rain, and while on a quiet stretch of road we came across a freshly cut field of hay. It was too inviting to pass off and we were too knackered to look for anything more suitable. Sleeping bags were out in no time, hay was gathered as a mattress, and none of us could be bothered to make a brew. Rumbles of thunder could be heard in the far distance; I'm sure I wasn't alone in praying it was not going to turn into a night of cramp and discomfort in the Beamer.

I awoke to the wonderful sound of bird song after a blissful night's kip, quite happy to lay there soaking up the ambience before the compulsion of a brew dragged me out of my pit.

We were soon on the road again, heading for the great limestone cliffs in anticipation of climbing in a region that was often frequented by famous Italian alpinists like Riccardo Cassin, Vittorio Ratti and Walter Bonatti a few decades before us.

We drove high into the region as close as we could for one of the huts. Little time was wasted in sorting our climbing packs before hiking up in lovely sunshine to the hut. We sat drinking beer outside, still in the sun, but there was the ominous presence of darkening skies followed by the customary distant rumble of thunder.

We stayed the night, if only to secure a dry night and shake off the beers. Thunder boomed during most of it and I could hear rain absolutely belting down each time I was woken by the bombardment. I knew in my heart this first alpine trip was likely to end up in abandonment; it was going to have to go down as an experience. I was blaming Billy bloody Ocean for it all!

Again, we all knew it wasn't worth hanging around for the weather to improve; the latest forecast pinned to the wall by the hut guardian was confirming that. One of us bright sparks (not me) suggested we get out of the Dolomites completely, head to France to an area of limestone crags at Le Saussois along the river Yonne. It is an historical cliff, once used by Parisian climbers in the spring months before heading off to bigger alpine adventures.

The weather was dry at least, but I found the rock as slippery as buggery. The climbs were not bolted as such, best described as a mixture of British trad, pegs and staples. After a couple of routes sizing up the area, I was happy to take the grade up a notch or two.

I made a big mistake fumbling around placing gear whilst on steep, slippery ground. It was the last route I did in the area, then and ever since. Before I knew much about it, I was off, going what seemed a fair way, hitting the bulging wall below me, and it hurt…a lot!

Dick lowered me down to terra firma. I realised swiftly that I had busted at least a couple of ribs. It had to happen; the third disappointment of the trip and an unceremonious one it was at that.

The guys did what they could to help ease the pain. I have a photo of Mike W binding me up like a mummy, although I don't recall it, and a vivid memory of Martin giving me some medication from the team's medical kit. It certainly did the trick; I'm told I had a smile and a giggle for hours after.

I could not lay down to sleep as there was too much discomfort, but recall finding a position propped up in the back of the Beamer that got me dozing off. By now, it was obvious we were out of luck on this trip, we were beaten up, fed up and weathered out, needing to head home and regroup.

About 150km from *Le Saussois* and roughly in line with our travel home, lies the world-famous bouldering area of *Fontainebleau*.[28] Although our egos were properly dented, it seemed worthy of a visit, especially as none of us had been there before.

'Font', as it is known by Brits, has a variety of hard sandstone with a wide selection of graded climbs, most of which are hard even at the lower end of the scale. I remember thinking it highly likely our egos were going to get even further dented here too.

We slept in the forest, which was very peaceful and pleasant, although I didn't fully appreciate it at the time. The guys were keen to get some bouldering under their belt, even if it was rather a comedown from our original plans. As much as I wanted to join in, I could only wander around the area feeling sorry for myself and watch the guys at play.

Bouldering by its very nature generates a lot of falling off, and therefore requires reasonable landings. Fontainebleau has ideal soft landings mainly of sand and dirt. These days, bespoke bouldering mats are the norm and can even make rocky outcrop landings a possibility.

We stayed just the one day, although many enthusiasts stay for much longer, especially as bouldering has now become a recognised activity, no longer just a means of training for 'the greater game'. I crept into bed in the early hours, still strapped up and still in some pain. It didn't take Lynne long in the morning to realise what had happened. Bless her, in those days I got stacks of sympathy!

As with all my extended climbing trips, catching up with the kids and Lynne's activities have always been important to me. Reading through my diaries really does make me wonder how we managed to fit everything in. We

---

[28] Fontainebleau is a region south of Paris particularly famous for its amazing concentration of bouldering areas. French alpine climbers have practiced the art there since the 19th century. It is the biggest and most developed bouldering area in the world, situated in the *Foret Domaniale* (National Forest) *de Fontainebleau*.

had our first holiday abroad to the Algarve a few weeks after I got back, courtesy of Mum's legacy she had left to us brothers.

It was a magnificent week of sun, sand and warm seas for all. A novelty for us came from the women selling melons on the beach, one of the enjoyments we never quite get to experience on our regular Cornish holidays.

The back end of 1986 was all about work and climbing, particularly trying to get as many routes in as possible to keep the improvement going before winter. I was particularly happy with routes in the Lakes like, 'Manpower' on Goat Crag and 'Battering Ram' on Shepherds Crag.

At Avon Gorge with 'New Horizons', 'Arms Race' and 'Mirage', all of which were pushing me to my limits.

Just before Christmas, Lynne was very unlucky to have an ankle injury playing netball. Further complications set in after it was strapped up at our local cottage hospital.

Unable to put her foot down and becoming ever more painful, she visited our doctor who immediately ripped off the strapping and sent her packing to the John Radcliffe Hospital in Oxford. A blood clot had developed, and a course of Warfarin was required over 5 days before they would let her out.

She was extremely pissed off and very glad to get home; as were the kids, who were equally pissed off with my cooking.

Chapter Eight
Alps Revisited

It was always going to be difficult being a mountaineer living in Oxfordshire. However, I think I have proven, to myself anyway, that anything is possible if you have the desire and the will.

I needed to put everything on the table and be honest with myself as there was a lot going on in my mind.

I had a wonderful family, a good job that gave us a very balanced, contented way of life. I was besotted with climbing; it seduced me rather late in life, and although I was now well equipped with the skills, I was approaching forty years old.

The thought of turning professional and earning a living from it had seriously crossed my mind, but it would mean moving to the mountains or somewhere like the Peak District in the UK at least. It was also going to incur a lot of money and time to get professionally qualified.

The status quo won the debate and thankfully over the last thirty-five plus years I've not looked back. All the same, it has cost a serious amount of expenditure in travel alone. I am truly indebted to Lynne for putting up with my passion, for sacrifices made on our finances when that money could have been spent on our house, and not least for the endless encouragement she has given me.

The North Wessex Downs and Wantage are no substitute for the *Mountains or Chamonix*. The Downs, however, do offer some wonderful countryside for getting fit for 'the hills', whether that be cross country running, off road biking or hiking and camping. Added to which there are very few roads bisecting the downs, keeping cars out of sight and out of mind; tourism is minimal and cafes are plentiful.

With its central position in the bottom half of the country, Wantage gets more than its share of decent weather, and has some of the best limestone climbing in the country only an hour to an hour and a half away, cliffs such as Avon Gorge, Wintours Leap and Cheddar Gorge to name a few. Add another half hour to the journey and you are on the cliffs of the south coast, or alternatively the cliffs on the Somerset/Devon border, even the Gower Peninsula.

Some years Wantage gets fair dumps of snow, it did on one occasion in 2009 enable me to cross country ski from home to work at Dorcan, Swindon; a total distance of 20 miles along the ancient trackway known as the Ridgeway (Britain's oldest road), possibly the first to have done so.

It's a bloody marvellous part of the country. It has enabled me to keep up (nearly anyway) with Martin, a great mate and excellent Mountaineer. Martin was also a very good fell runner; one of his outstanding feats was to hold the *winter record* for the Bob Graham Round[29]. I also got into that hard game, but was always in Martin's wake.

After the Austrian misadventure, I had two further expeditions with Dick, one in 1988 to the Alps on the *North face of the Tour Ronde* and *Buoux* limestone, then further afield to Canada in 1990 for an ascent on *Mount Robson*. Robson was not successful for a few reasons, and I got rather frustrated.

Fortunately, Martin and I had a great Alpine two weeks in 1987 camping at Argentière, Chamonix. I felt I had more in common and more synergy in the mountains with Martin from an Alpinism point of view; it has remained that way to this day.

We packed my recently acquired Vauxhall Cavalier to the brim and drove to Chamonix, bivvying when and where it was needed. Our first Alpine route together was *The South Face of Le Pouce* (French route) graded TD+ and took us six hours of technical rock climbing. It was very sunny and very warm on the face, not the best place to run out of water.

We hit the summit in the dark and needed head torches to find our way. Desperate for water and somewhere to sleep, we stumbled across a cabin linked to 'The Index' upper cable car station. To our delight and whoops of joy the door was not locked.

---

[29] The Bob Graham Round is a fell running challenge in the English Lake District. It is named after Bob Graham, a Keswick man who in June 1932 broke the Lakeland Fell record by traversing 42 fells within a twenty-four hour period.

Expectations of water, a horizontal floor to sleep on soon vanished as we burst in and woke two British lasses who had been fast asleep and beaten us to it. After a brief exchange of pleasantries, we grabbed some much-needed water and proceeded to bivvy some distance away. I think we did nick a blanket or two at least!

We made use of the cable car the following morning back to the valley and spent the remainder of the day resting in camp. The next day was spent ascending the *Aiguille de Chardonnet* via the *North Spur* graded D/D; then descending via the *Forbes Arete* to give a splendid mountain days circuit. This gave us good acclimatisation for the next challenge *The Frendo Spur* on the *Aiguille de Midi*.

I saw this next challenge as the most serious yet. It is a long route, often enjoying a bivvy somewhere on route and although it only commands a grade of D+, it looks quite an intimidating line, particularly for a novice Alpinist. After a good day's rest, we caught the Midi cable car to the Plan de l'Aiguille (half way station), then approached the start of the route at 2582m via the Pelerins Glacier.

A mixture of moderate to difficult climbing mostly on rock in cracks and chimneys led to a horizontal shoulder. We had started later than planned and thought it wise to take basic bivvy gear with us; it was an opportunity not to be missed as we took full advantage of a small flat ledge with a commanding view over Chamonix. As my first real Alpine bivvy experience it was an absolute delight.

Tied in from my harness back to the rock face, I was looking forward to a good night's sleep, although with my feet very close to the abyss, I did wonder if I would wake up in a hot sweat.

In the morning after a brew and porridge, we tackled the crest of the snow/ice ridge. It was brittle, hard, steely ice, my first experience of it and so often encountered when climbing in the Alps. Getting axes and ice screws to bite was quite difficult, all the time balanced on crampon front points with calves screaming for a rest.

We eventually reached the upper rock rognon at 3700m that had some tricky climbing, made more difficult by me feeling knackered. Soon after that, I was very grateful to be on the final, straightforward snow slope to reach the horizontal ground of the Midi-Plan ridge.

It was getting rather late in the day as we coiled the ropes and headed for the summit. If we missed the last cable car down, it meant a night's bivvy in the ice tunnel, not ideal! Fortunately, the gods were on our side and it wasn't long before we were downing a beer or two in the famous Le Bar National on Rue du Dr Paccard, Chamonix.

We were both chuffed with what we had achieved and feeling more like Alpinists, *and* we still had a few days left. We savoured the successes we had achieved and dossed at the camp site all the following day, drinking vino and eating French bread with very smelly Camembert cheese.

The weather was still holding fine, and there was just enough energy in the tanks to take a hike up the Mer de Glace to the Envers hut, thoughtful of doing a couple of classic rock routes on the Envers des Aiguilles. The hut is in a fantastic location, I could have stayed there a lot longer.

Not too keen to rush out the door, we eventually headed for a classic line called *Children of the Moon,* a route put up by French Alpinist Michel Piola and graded TD+. It took us six hours round trip, but was a magnificent outing. I even have a photo of Martin leading a pitch with a slither of moon above him.

It wasn't without a little epic however, as on one of the rappels the rope jammed. The quickest option was to use a prusik or jumar[30] attached to my harness and ascend the jammed rope. I also protected myself by tying into my harness with the other end of the rope and re-clipping the bolts in case the jammed rope suddenly ripped out.

Martin belayed me up to where I released the jammed rope then lowered me down from an anchor I rigged. It all worked out fine, and was yet another experience learned climbing in the mountains.

A second route the next day called *Ambiance Eigerwand*, graded harder at ED, was yet again a magnificent outing; although we cut the route short, it was a great conclusion to the trip. The journey home seemed a lot shorter as we feasted off our achievements and more of the smelly Camembert. It took days to rid the car of the smell of cheese and nearly as long to remove tar from the lower half of the car, accumulated from the numerous road-works along the French motorways. I cared little, as it was a most magnificent trip.

The years of 1988, 1989 and 1990 were full of climbing and walking at various venues.

---

[30] 'Jumar' has now become a generic term in climbing to describe a means of ascending a rope. There are now a wide variety of ascending devices that have all but replaced the original method of ascending a rope known as 'Prusiking'. A sliding 'prusik knot' or friction hitch with a foot loop was an invaluable means of getting out of trouble.

One was to the Alps and Canada as mentioned earlier, others were typically to Avon, the Peak District, Lake District, Wintours leap, Cornwall, North Wales and Scotland. Climbs I was most pleased with during that period were:

Avon, *Krapps last tape, The Last Gasp, Ladder of Desire, Think Pink.*

Peak District, *Suspense, Time for Tea, Supra Direct, Desperation and Right Unconquerable.*

Lake District, *Jubilee Grooves, Prana, Guillotine, White Noise, Bitter Oasis.*

Wintours Leap, *The Jackal, Kaiser Wall, Never Say Die, Stairway To Heaven, King Kong, The Lurking Smear, Kangaroo Wall, Never Say Goodbye and Fly havoc.*

Wintours, in the Wye Valley near Chepstow, was a new climbing area to me. It formed an immediate attraction with its 300 feet of limestone cliffs and wonderful tranquillity.

We would combine family outings to most of those areas, with Lynne, Gary and Nicky going for walks with others while I climbed. On other occasions, we would all hike to the high Fell tops of the Lakes, to 'The Glyders' in Snowdonia and even to the summit of 'The Ben' (Nicky was barely 10 years old and coped amazingly).

During 1988 and 1989 I also signed up to the Mountain Leader Training Board as part of my early desire to perhaps make a living from the hills and mountains. I took the assessment programme for the Mountain Walking Leader Training Scheme and the training programme for the Scottish Mountain Leader Training Scheme. Even though I decided not to go in that direction, they were invaluable experiences, and I would recommend them to anyone interested in mountaineering.

1991 brought about another big decision-making time for me regarding work. I had been with Oxford Instruments for 10 years. I had tremendous respect for the company, its directors and many of the colleagues I worked with. Oxford had acquired a similar business to the Ion Beam deposition systems group, their location was based in Yatton, north Somerset, 11 miles south-west of Bristol.

A decision was made to relocate the Oxford technical and manufacturing team to their facility, as it had far more room for potential growth. The Oxford board of directors gave every team member very fair support and relocation packages, both financially and otherwise, to get the majority, if not all of us relocated to the new site.

For me personally, it was an extremely difficult decision. Gary was soon to take GCSE exams; Nicky was doing well in her new school; Lynne was in a good job around the corner from home. Above all, we were very attached to Wantage.

As Production Manager, I was fortunate to be offered a company car, giving me the opportunity to commute daily. I took full advantage of it, as it gave me breathing space to contemplate.

As Production Manager, I had my own set of standards, one of them was to be at my place of work on time, just as I would expect from my team. After four months or more of long days commuting 85 miles each way along the M4 and M5 motorways, I felt it was affecting home life and indeed climbing. I needed to make a quick decision.

Loyalty, respect and gratitude for Oxford Instruments were the most difficult aspects to turn away from, but in the end, it was necessary to leave. I'm in no doubt the company would have found a place for me back on the benches at Oxford; but I had made my decision.

One short climbing tale while working at Yatton was when Martin and I made a trip to Beinn Udlaidh near the Bridge of Orchy in Scotland for a quick ice climbing weekend. In fine winter conditions with perfect formations of ice, I led a vertical ice pitch called *Organ Pipe Wall*. Near the top, an awkward move on shite snow/ice was needed to finish the pitch and gain horizontal ground.

I planted my right axe in ice that I thought was sound, lifted my left axe to replant it, when unexpectedly the right popped out. I fell eight or ten feet onto the last ice screw I placed and fortunately it held, but with the force and pendulum of the swing I slapped my left boot against the ice and fractured my ankle (although I didn't know it at the time).

Martin lowered me down and we called it a day. I hobbled and crawled down to the car after about an hour and a half hour. Martin, of course, was giving me lots of encouragement from out in front, by shouting "come on, you old git, I'll race you to the car."

It was fortuitous that my company car I used to drive us north was an automatic; If I kept the left foot comfortable, I would be okay just operating with the right. There was no way I was going to spend time in Glasgow hospital! We eventually made it to the Lakes where I dropped Martin off then made it home without further incident. This time there was no hiding it from Lynne, as now the ankle was a fair size and very painful.

Next day at the Oxford Radcliffe Hospital it was confirmed I had a small fracture in the Talus region of the foot and plastered me up. I did turn in to work the following day, only to be told I was a daft bugger and to go home and rest up for a while.

Suffice to say, climbing was put on hold for a wee while.

Gary at Cleeve hill   *Nicky at Cleeve hill*

My first pieces of climbing gear

Me on 'Left Wall' – Dinas Cromlech (picture by Dick Patey)

Ben Nevis – Martin on 'The Curtain'

Ben Nevis – Ice cave belay on the 1st pitch

Ben Nevis – Me high up on 'Astral Highway'

Chamonix – Martin on the South Face of Le Pouche

Chamonix – Martin loving a Frendo Spur bivvy

Chamonix – The Frendo Spur ice arête

Me on Children of the Moon- Envers rock

Part 3: Early Expeditions

We are not Gods,
Just fragile human beings privileged to play,
for a few hours, a greater game.
To transcend the world of possessions, of material need and greed,
of fear and petty jealousies, of fraught relationships.
We have opted out, for this short time,
yet must return as surely as the sun will rise with a new day.
We are, however, forever changed!

*** Anon***

Chapter Nine
A Taste of Alaska

What an amazing part of the world, if you don't mind it being a little chilly at times that is.

The 49th state of America is huge and is the largest of all the US states, sitting up there in the extreme northwest of the country. It borders Canada, having the Yukon to the east and British Columbia to the south. Just across the Bering Strait to the west is Asia and Russia's Chukotka region.

I have only experienced a smidgen of that wonderful landscape, but to my mind it is most certainly a mountaineering paradise of extreme wilderness; yet has relative ease of access and is free of burdening bureaucracy.

As a comparison to the size of the British Isles, Alaska has a land mass of approximately 571,950 square miles with a population of less than 1 million. Compare that to Britain's land mass (including all our islands) of 121,684 square miles and a population of approximately 67 million and you begin to get the picture. The crown of Alaska is most certainly Denali[31] (Mt McKinley) standing at 20,320 feet.

By 1993, I had left Oxford Instruments two years previously, and was now working as an engineer for Biomet UK Ltd, an orthopaedic manufacturing company based in Dorcan, Swindon. I had taken a wage drop but there was an

---

[31] The name 'Denali' comes from the early inhabitants of the region and means 'The High One'. It remained that name until a prospector/mountaineer named William Dickey travelled in the area. He renamed it McKinley after William McKinley the Republican nominee for president in 1896. At 20,320 feet, Denali is the highest mountain in North America and because of its height and position just south of the Arctic Circle, it is arguably the coldest mountain on earth. Denali is one of the world's highest peaks rising from its relative neighbouring environments.

opportunity on the horizon as Production Manager. The Production Director, Norman Hibbins, was a friendly and very knowledgeable guy.

We got on well together. Having been there for 2 years, I felt it was not too cheeky to ask for a three-week holiday. I was desperate for an expedition.

Martin suggested a trip to Alaska, which fitted just grand with me. After lots of thought, research and planning, our primary objective was an attempt on the Kennedy/Lowe route on Mount Hunter (14,570ft) in the Denali range via the northwest face. Mt Hunter is also referred to by its native American name of 'Begguya' meaning Denali's child. We felt it a rather audacious route choice, as frequent attempted repeats of the route had been thwarted by poor snow conditions.

However, on the positive side, it is recognised for its quick, alpine-style ascent, relative safety, with one of the quickest accesses of any route in the range, ideal for our limited three-week trip. In addition, we were in an area where there were other opportunities should the attempt on Hunter go pear-shaped.

Twelve months of planning had come to fruition. It was May 1, and after our long flight to Anchorage via Seattle, we stepped into our £25 per night digs at the Chelsea Inn, Anchorage.

Martin was particularly glad to get there after his full body and baggage search at Seattle, suspected of being a drugs smuggler. I could do nothing but smirk, thinking all the while to myself that it would teach the bugger a lesson for boasting about all the exotic places he had on his passport, like Turkey, Nepal, Kenya and Kurdistan!

The next day, we picked up snow shoes and three weeks' supply of grub and were on our way to Talkeetna, courtesy of Denali Overland Transport Company. Talkeetna is about 110 miles north of Anchorage and about the same mileage south of Fairbanks. It is a unique town, still playing host to many prospectors as well as climbers and tourists when we were there.

For us it was our launch point onto our glacier base camp, around 7,500ft via Talkeetna Air Taxi. Although there was only Martin and myself, I think we must have used up the total payload of the Cessna's carrying capacity of three persons and hundred and fifty pounds of luggage. Paul, our pilot, did a great job of finding a hole in the clouds around 11,000ft to view our route on Hunter, before landing on the glacier adjacent to base camp.

We dug out a patch in the deep snow for our tents amongst the most spectacular scenery.

Mt Foraker, Mt Hunter and the Cassin ridge on Denali were but a touch away. Going for a pee every couple of hours with temperatures of -18degC (in the tent) was a pain in the arse. I was so very grateful for my pee bottle close to hand!

The following day, we wandered up to the base of Hunter and concurred with the guidebooks warning. Heavy snowfall during the winter and early spring months had left huge amounts of unconsolidated snow on the route, and looked particularly heavy on the upper triangle, it wasn't looking good!

The following day necessitated sitting out some bad weather and by the morning of the following day two to three inches of snow had fallen. The sky had cleared and it became very warm, we waited until 18.00 for cooler conditions before heading off and giving it a go.

Even with snow shoes it was heavy going in the deep snow towards the face. We stashed unnecessary gear at the base of the route and commenced our climbing. Initial conditions were ok, but worsened considerably by 02.00. We had been wading through a snow pack and were now waist deep on a 60deg slope. In serious threat of an avalanche, there was no other alternative than to beat a retreat.

Completely shagged and disappointed, we eventually rose from our pits early afternoon. Climbing teaches you not to be pissed off for too long, and sure enough after a few brews and plenty to eat, another plan was springing into our thoughts.

The West Rib on Denali would be an absorbing challenge, but did we have enough time and the right gear? We were quite sure our layering system and down gear would be adequate, but an extra 6,000ft in height could give problems with frostbitten feet. Our boots were designed for cold Alpine conditions rather than the high altitude conditions above 20,000ft. Undeterred, by 19.00 sacks were packed; we had 'borrowed' two sledges from base camp for extra gear and headed for the northeast fork of the Kahiltna glacier. We passed two Norwegian guys in retreat who had left earlier in the day than us. They offered us their stock of dried fish, which was very kind, but I must say, after sampling some, it was sent straight into the deepest crevasse.

We made camp on a flat spot at 8,500ft around 23.00 with a temperature of -22degC. Following a pretty sound sleep we were up at 10.00 for a brew and breakfast. We made progress to 10,500ft, where the weather was closing in fast, and pitched our tent in near whiteout conditions. It was a wild night and 28degC outside the tent.

Progress was made despite the weather to our camp at 11,000ft. At this point, we had decided that even the West Rib route was not going to be possible for us. We decided to make a move to the advance basecamp at 14,500ft used for the West Buttress route, stash some gear and food, then head back to our 11,000ft camp. The plan was successful and we made it back to camp absolutely knackered, just as the weather was turning stormy.

For three nights and two days we were storm bound, with nothing else to do except make brews, read a book and clear the tent of snow every two hours. twelve to fifteen inches of snow fell during that time and food was down to one Snickers bar and one apple each. A further decision was necessary; whether to retreat and lose our stash at advance base, or go for it. Whatever the decision, it would wait until the morning.

It was still snowing in the morning, but the wind had eased a little. We were not about to give in just yet. We left around midday as the wind had abated a little, until we approached the notorious 'windy corner' where winds had picked up again to 70–80mph. As we gained more height, it seemed we had got above the worst of the weather, and eventually made it back to 14,500ft camp at 19.30.

It was now day fourteen of the trip with little time to spare. The following day continued with stormy conditions and heavy snow. We were both feeling tired and beaten up by the weather, so it made sense to make use of the day drinking, eating lots and relaxing, in the hope of making it to 17,000ft on the West Buttress route tomorrow.

Day fifteen dawned bright and the wind had dropped. We made an early start for the col at 16,000ft; the ice was a better quality at this height and before long we were on the spectacular ridge, looking across arctic tundra to the north and amazing mountains to the south.

I thought our progress to this point was enough to get me acclimatised, but it was not long before feeling nauseated with the effects of altitude sickness. It was disappointing for Martin, who was going well, but I needed to get back along the ridge and back to camp.

I was expecting to feel shit in the morning but had slept okay and was actually feeling ok.

The weather had improved further, but we were running out of time with only five days remaining. Deciding on one last push, we traversed across the upper snow field to meet up with the West Rib route, which was steeper and more technical but quicker. We made use of the extended daylight at that latitude, and by 23.00 came to a useful bivvy spot at around 16,500ft, not far from a site known as 'Balcony camp' with at least one discarded tent that had been ripped to shreds.

It was an uncomfortable night with lots of wind and spindrift. A brew was on for 04.00 and we were on our way by 05.30. Both of us were suffering with cold feet, finding it difficult to keep warm.

Before leaving advance base camp, we had cut bits off our sleeping mats, shaped them to our boots and fitted them between boot and crampon in the hope it would to give a little additional insulation. Although we both had serious loss of feeling in our toes during the summit bid, I'm sure it prevented a more severe situation developing.

We climbed on mixed ground for 1,500ft, then a narrow snow/ice couloir for a further 1,000ft to reach the huge plateau at 19,500ft, known colloquially as the 'football pitch', where the West Buttress route also joined it. Within the hour, we were on the 20,320ft summit in perfect weather, later to be informed our ascents were the 4th and 5th that year.

We allowed ourselves a few moments to take pictures and celebrate before scurrying down to the plateau and descending the West Buttress route. It had been an extremely arduous round trip from the 14,500ft camp and back, further compounded the following day by the exhaustive return to our glacier base camp and exit point at 7,500ft, at times close to the edge of complete exhaustion.

A flight back to Talkeetna courtesy of Talkeetna Air Taxi that evening helped take the pressure off, as we needed to be back in Anchorage the next day. We were able to relax a little and soak up a beer or two in the West Rib bar, feeling ten feet tall.

All in all, a tremendous expedition, not as planned, but with a will to succeed, a companion to rely on, in mind blowing mountains, anything is possible.

I was sure we would be back!

During our ascent from the bivvy spot at 16,500 feet to the plateau of the 'football pitch', I experienced my one and only 'out of body experience'. A phenomenon still not completely understood, but perhaps caused by exhaustion, dehydration, or complete fear. Possibly a combination of all three!!

Chapter Ten
Running Wild

I had got into fell running partly because that's what you do if you are in the Lake District and it's pissing down, and partly because I had been running cross country or otherwise since I was eleven years old. It was in my blood.

At first it is torture and torment, but once you start to get 'fell fit' it becomes a great feeling, striding and gliding over the rocks and bogs of the fells and moors. It was certainly a key element in developing my fitness for mountaineering, as well as taking it seriously for the fell races I entered. I was even beginning to get Lynne, Gary and Nicky interested in a gentler sort of way.

I had officially entered the Ben Nevis fell race along with Martin a few months before the McKinley trip, and was to run it on September 4 1993. Not a great deal of training was done beforehand; but we were feeling fit, and looking to beat a time of two hours for the round trip.

I had run a couple of official races previously but on the day, this race felt rather special.

As a build up to the start, all competitors were paraded round the pitch of Fort William F.C behind a full band of pipes and drums. We were led out to the start line and given a brilliant reception. As in all cases when entering the same race, I ended up chasing Martin's heels with gritted teeth, hands on knees and arms pumping furiously for upward progress.

This was particularly the case beyond the half way point of the Lochan Meall an t-Suidhe up the steep flanks of the 'big bad Ben' via the zig-zags to the summit at 1,344m. When the summit 'trig point' had been touched, it was downhill pretty much all the way.

Now that sounds simple, but in fact it's the toughest, daftest fucking thing I've ever done in my life! Those skilled enough can remove their brain completely from their skull and launch themselves downhill at a phenomenal rate, and is a fantastic exhibition to watch. However, for mere mortals who leave half of it in and ticking over, it's fucking terrifying as you try to catch them up, all the time avoiding a fall that would result in certain admittance to Fort William General Hospital!

Martin recorded a great time a smidgen over our target in 2:00:59. I followed him in (as usual) with a time of 2:04:03. I was happy with that!

The winning time was 1:33:38. The men's record has stood since 1984, held by Kenny Stuart (1:25:34) and the women's record is held by Victoria Wilkinson (1:43:01) in 2018…amazing!

For me, 1994 came and went very quickly having started with a good winter icefall climbing trip to Chamonix and ending with a wet and not so positive summer rock climbing trip to Grindelwald and Leysin. Squeezed in between those trips were three fell races, all of which were first time entries.

The first was a tough 'Welsh 1000m Peaks' race, usually taking place on the first Saturday in June and covering 32km and around 8000ft of ascent. It was my longest race to date, and I crawled in 5hrs 43mins after setting off, barely able to walk to the car.

I recovered just in time to run in the 'Old County Tops' race paired up with Rob Blackburne (NZ), with Martin and Neil Walmsley from the Old Dungeon pairing up alongside us. This is a beast of a race covering 37 miles and around 10,000ft of ascent, but is a true classic. Rob and I were going well until high above Langdale where thick mist had set in.

We lost our way and lots of ground, eventually having to re-ascend a 1000ft or more to get back on track. Inevitably it meant being timed out at the 6th check point (Cockley Beck Bridge) after seven and a half hours running. The locals, Martin and Neil had a distinct advantage over Rob and I, knowing the ground like the back if their hand (our excuses anyway), they finished the race in a creditable time just over eleven hours.

My third and final race of the year was the 'Langdale Horseshoe', the shortest of the three that year, but still a hard challenge at 22km in length with 4757ft of ascent. I was happy with a time of 2hrs 47mins, and my body glad the fell running season had come to an end, for me anyway!

In no time at all 1995 was upon us, Lynne and I barely able to grasp that Nicky was going to be 16 years old and Gary 19. Gary had been unsure what direction to take after 6th form, he wasn't keen on going to university, and had decided to save up and see some of the world. On the 25 January, we hugged and waved him and a friend off from Heathrow, knowing it was going to be many months before seeing him again.

Fortunately, there were occasional telephone calls, nearly always reverse charged I may add, with one month's bill particularly sticking in my memory of over £700, and regular emails to reassure us that he was okay. What a difference video calling such as Skype, Facetime, or Zoom would have made in those days.

At the same time Gary left, Nicky was looking to find her way after she left school.

She realised that university was not for her and as parents do, we worked together on different ideas and options. Eventually with a growing interest of working on a farm, she enlisted at an Agricultural College and in parallel obtained part time work on a farm just outside Wantage. Nicky found the practical foundations at college interesting and rewarding, but didn't have the same feelings working at the farm.

There were a few issues that kept bubbling up, but inevitably the last straw for her was when tasked with artificially inseminating a thousand plus sheep. Poor thing; although she pondered for a short while, it didn't take her long to put an end to that career path. Fortunately, our philosophy of 'nothing ventured, nothing gained' has rubbed off, and with that she enrolled at Abingdon College on a business studies course.

Chapter Eleven
Defeat in South America

In 1995, I had managed to sneak another three-week holiday out of Biomet Ltd for an expedition, this time a long-haul flight to Peru, then to the HuayHuash region (pronounced way-wash) for an attempt on the West Face of Mt Jirishanca.

Our flight left Heathrow and landed at Lima on the 10 May having felt it was never going to end after transfers via Paris, Bogota and Quito. The usual team of dirt bags, Martin, Dave, Rob and myself, were extremely grateful to get into Hostel Roma, a positive oasis in comparison to the surrounding squalor outside.

After catching up on much needed sleep, we hit the high spots of central Lima in search of breakfast, a market to obtain expedition food then perhaps a coffee followed by a local beer, or was it the other way around! It was quite unexpected to see as many westernised fast-food establishments as we did, Pizza Hut, Burger King and McDonalds to name a few. I was sure these would get our full attention when we were back out of the mountains.

Our aim the following day was to get to the town of Chiquian courtesy of one of the notorious Transfysa buses. Our bus not only served our expedition, it was full to the brim of locals with their baggage and trunks. There were even a couple of goats on-board and caged chickens strapped above deck on the roof rack.

Very clearly, this had been a market day run for locals, and was hilarious to watch the disembarkation chaos at each village we stopped at. No sooner had the bus stopped than villagers were trying to get off with their wares as local kids were trying to get on and sell theirs to those that remained, chaos reigned supreme.

Eventually after many hours, many villages and much hilarity, we arrived at Chiquian, a much larger town than I expected at an elevation of 3553m and our launch point for the trek into base camp. It was also our last chance to gather any food supplies and to pick up a second-hand multi-ring stove if we could find one. Fortunately, the village had plenty of expeditionary cast offs, it was just a matter of searching round the various open stalls.

Our next priority was to acquire a reliable *arriero* (muleteer) and a few *burros* (mules) to help carry our rapidly expanding gear. Pelayo, with his cheerful smile fitted the bill well; he even offered to cook meals and remain at base camp for us when we were pushing on up the route.

Next day we were on our way quite early, after stacking loads on six mules bound for a village called Llamac. It was all going too well when without warning we were down to five mules. One of the stubborn buggers was having none of this malarkey and headed down a steep ravine, kicking and bucking for all he was worth.

We didn't know whether to laugh or cry as Pelayo chased after him, throwing sizeable rocks, shouting what we roughly interpret as something akin to what we were thinking! Fears of gear and food ending up in the river were allayed after we eventually retrieved and picked it all up. We never did see that burro again.

We arrived quite late at Llamac and pitched tents in what looked like a farmyard. We attracted a curious audience, mostly of lovely, happy smiling kids. They were even more inquisitive as we started cooking on our modern westernised equipment.

Another early start and longish day of seven hours had been enjoyed on a splendid trail that took us to a high point at 4000m and delivered us to our base camp in an idyllic area at the far end of laguna Jahuacocha. The sight in front of us was spectacular with the majestic peaks of Rondoy, Jirishanca and the imposing Yerupaja having looked particularly impressive.

It had concerned us that it was quite mild at 4000m and although it cooled down by night, there was little sign that ice was forming at our elevation. A day of rest and fishing for trout in the stream running beside our camp helped take my mind off the nausea and altitude sickness I was once again feeling. Poor Pelayo was suffering also, not with sickness, but with trying to get warm.

Between the four us, we had failed to consider if he needed a sleeping bag. In desperation, he evidently had to pull a tatty old mule blanket over himself along with anything else he could find that night. Not a good start to a working relationship on our behalf.

May 16 dawned cloudy. It was G's 19 birthday, and it had been four months since he left the UK. Although we were in the same hemisphere, I was missing the contact and chat that assured me he was still ok.

Our decision was to recce (reconnaissance) the area onto the glacier towards El Toro, with the intention of establishing camp 1 the following day. Dark clouds had formed and light rain had started; it wasn't looking good, so we returned to base.

The alarm sound at 06.00; there was no real need to rush about, but knew from yesterday's recce it was going to be a long day. I was still feeling shit, fortunately, so were the other guys.

I struggled to get Pelayo's porridge down, but a couple of brews helped, before we eventually left around 08.30 with heavy loads, it still raining. We worked our way up the glacier and through a very dangerous icefall, eventually dumping the gear at the 4725m contour, not as far as we had wanted camp 1.

The day's work had been done and by 18.30 as darkness closed in, we just made it back to base camp. Priority was to get a brew on and tuck into some of Lynne's fruit cake I had brought along, to grins all round. Inevitably, it wasn't long before rain started to hammer down once again.

Heavy rain prevented anything ambitious the next day; it was more about keeping busy and offsetting boredom. Rob, myself and Pelayo went fishing with hook and line, and to our surprise, ended up with two reasonable trout for lunch. A little further back from basecamp, a few Peruvian hill people were busy tending their crops of potatoes and sweetcorn in the rich soils at this elevation. They were marvellous people with huge beaming smiles and although we had a huge language barrier, we still managed to socialise a little.

Day ten dawned dry, and we needed to move up the mountain. We carried six days' supplies between us and made it to our previous dump on the glacier around 13.00. After a quick reshuffle of gear, we needed to head for a more favourable camp 1 position on the Yerupaja Chico/Jirishanca pass at 5,200m.

We made it to the 5000m contour, but not before surviving a huge avalanche going through the icefall, Martin being the luckiest at the back. I've never seen him run so fast! All of us were knackered and decided to set up camp where we were.

Next day, Martin and Rob bravely did a round trip back through the icefall to pick up the remainder of out gear; we then needed to get to the col that day, to stand a chance of succeeding with our objective. Heavy snow coupled with extremely warm temperatures had not helped at all, as very often we were wading through knee deep snow.

Gradients+Snow = Avalanches. Mountains have numerous defence mechanisms under their belt to ward off the climbing invader, including, crevasses, seracs, extremes of weather and avalanches to name just a few. There are many types of avalanches and many scientific reasons for their occurrence, which unfortunately, are too many to go into detail here.

By and large, it depends on the amount of snow fallen, the structure of the crystals as they fall through the atmosphere, the gradient of the slope and the 'stick-ability' to the surface they fall on.

Large accumulations of snow (50>80cms) can avalanche on slope angles as little as 25deg. Large slab avalanches can be up to a kilometre wide and over a metre deep at the crown (where it breaks). The destruction that a slide, weighing hundreds or thousands of tonnes, travelling over 100mph can do, doesn't bare thinking about.

It is something a climber wants to avoid at all costs, as the survival rate if caught in one is slim indeed.

*A publication entitled **'A Chance In a Million'** by Bob Barton and Blyth Wright is worth a read.*

Eventually we arrived at the col to find dangerous snow conditions and a huge crevassed slope. It prompted the decision to head back to our previous day's camp to tackle the complex slope the following day.

We were up early after a very chilly night to renew our attempt on getting to the col and beyond. Our energy levels were particularly tested at this altitude as we shared the burden of double trips to keep our supplies in touch with us. We reached the col in good time but progress through the heavily crevassed slope with uncertain snow bridges covering enormous gaping mouths was very concerning.

It took an age being careful to test the doubtful looking bridges. We were almost over the worst of it when suddenly Dave disappeared down a large slot. Fortunately, all four of us were roped together, enabling us to hold his fall, which prevented him disappearing too far down the crevasse. A little shaken but not stirred, he managed to climb out the short distance by himself.

Time was marching on and we decided to retreat to a horizontal spot on a rock-band and bivvy out for the night. It was late afternoon and the ominous signs of a storm was brewing. In no time at all, thunder and lightning were all around us. We crudely erected the flysheet of our bigger tent and crammed ourselves inside for what was to be a very wild and scary night.

The storm was indeed very close, if not directly overhead, with hail and snow falling heavily. It quickly prompted us to throw all our metal climbing gear out from the shelter, too fraught to think of anything else other than to get the fuck out of the situation as soon as it was possible.

After thirteen hours of self-pity under a cramped flysheet with barely any sleep, listening to the cracks of thunder and the smell of lightning induced ozone, it was a unanimous decision to bail out. We made two long abseils off the rock-band onto the glacier and made the long slog back to base camp.

It was extremely disappointing to be so close, yet so far, from our objective of Jirishanca's west face as we turned our backs on the mountain for the last time. Heavy hearts and mighty loads on our backs made the descent back to base torturous. Spirits were lifted somewhat when, to our delight, Pelayo had caught a few river trout which, with rice and potatoes, was woofed down in no time at all.

It was obviously disappointment for all of us as we came out of our comatose sleep. The reality of it all was that three weeks in those mountains is not enough, when the weather is not on one's side and the mountain gains the upper hand. We had attempted the climb 'Alpine style' and did most things correct, making decisions when necessary that kept us alive.

Some people talk of 'conquering' a mountain. In my view, there is no such thing, as 'to conquer' is 'to overcome and take control'. As mountaineers we achieve neither. A mountain will only let you stand on its summit if it chooses to allow it. Take it for granted and it will snuff you out in an instant.

We took a different route back to Chiquian through stunning gorges of pine, eucalyptus and mint, and after six hours arrived at the small village of Papillac. Very clearly the local people had seldom seen 'western gringos' through their streets. We were the talk of the village and the local kids couldn't stop looking and smiling at us. The village looked incredibly basic and its people impoverished, but everyone we met was wonderfully friendly and hospitable.

We arrived in Chiquian the following day and eventually bade farewell to Pelayo, thanking him for his kindness, patience, resilience and especially his cooking.

It didn't take long to be yearning for the mountains once again after arriving in Lima, except of course for the odd pizza, McDonalds and several beers. The pick-pockets of Lima had managed to steal Dave's altimeter watch from his wrist whilst walking through a crowded street, and Rob had been screwed with counterfeit notes when exchanging his dollars for the best price.

Lima was a typical city split between those that 'have' and those that 'have-not'. It was the first of many I was to experience through further years adventures. After every one, I have always been extremely grateful I had the luck to be born British.

It was, however, the most wonderful experience for me, and I'm sure I speak for the team.

Chapter Twelve
Mount Robson and Edith Cavell

Mount Robson at 3954m is a most impressive peak and after my failed attempt on the mountain in 1990, I was pleased Martin was available and keen to give it a try.

Due to its isolated position in the Canadian Rockies, it dominates the surrounding area and from any viewpoint, whether a climber or tourist visiting that part of Alberta, British Columbia, one cannot help being captivated by its majesty. It is not an easy mountain to tackle.

There are no easy routes up the mountain, each of them requiring quite a high degree of technical snow and ice climbing. Routes on the Emperor North Face require climbing to a very high standard.

In addition to the technical aspects, the weather on Robson must not be underestimated. It is very prone to sudden storms, snow and ice conditions can be very fickle and quite often the combination of both, deters climbers for a full year.

Our plan, if conditions and time allowed, was to climb a route on the North Face, or alternatively a line up the NE face, known as the Kain Face, a line that was taken by the first ascent in 1913, led by the Austrian guide Conrad Kain.

We took advantage of the time difference and made it to the very attractive town of Jasper, a former fur trading town, nestled in the grandeur of Jasper National Park. It was one very long day with our flight from Heathrow to Edmonton, followed by a Greyhound bus to Jasper.

By 01.00 the next morning, we were dossing in our sleeping bags beside a huge totem pole near the railway sidings.

Keen as ever to move on, we shopped for food then bused it to the Mount Robson Provincial Park headquarters to register our intent. I took advantage of the phone at the visitor centre to ring Lynne, the last time for a while, I had always tried to let her know we had arrived at our destination, especially not having mobile phones in those days.

After packing huge sacks, we made it to Kinney Lake only to realise the sacks were far too heavy for the hike to Berg Lake. The weight was split and with a more sensible load, made it to Emperor Falls camp with our first load through incredible scenery along the *'Valley of a thousand falls'*.

A reminder the following day as to how quickly the weather can change on Robson was waking up to torrential rain that lasted all day. We retrieved the second load left at Kinney and returned soaked to the skin, certainly enough for one day.

The next day dawned foggy but with height gain and a long day double hiking our loads. We arrived at Berg Lake camp with all our gear to a beautiful warm evening. We had travelled through scented woods of pine and aspen, with a huge variety of wild flowers.

The hike's crowning glory was the amazing view of Robson rearing up from the lake in front of us, the hike up to Berg Lake whilst staying at the various campgrounds or cabins is an adventure I would thoroughly recommended for any hiking enthusiast.

The previous days rain had been falling as heavy snow on the mountain, the North Face looked particularly 'plastered'. As we scoffed a bowl of soup followed by very tasty pancakes, numerous glances up the flanks of Robson told us the 'Kain face' was the more sensible option. A chat with the warden the following day confirmed it for us, as we learnt a few attempts on the mountain had been thwarted already and conditions on the Emperor Face looked far from ideal.

Although the day had started bright and cold, it was due to get worse the following day. It prompted us to make the most of the good weather and try for a camp on the Robson glacier adjacent to Extinguisher Tower. This we achieved without too much trouble through the crevassed ice-field.

Although one lapse of concentration on my part, ended up with a soaking wet boot, having broken through a shallow wet slot. I had forgotten the extent and pain of pushing my body through knee deep snow with a monster on my back!

We had put the alarm on for 05.00 and woke up to rain; there was obviously no need to rush.

Several brews later, it had begun to clear through and we were once again on the move. It was a particularly gruelling day through a heavily crevassed icefield, but we made it to 'The Dome' and our 2nd camp. I admit to another faux pas here, although it came with a bit of good fortune.

One crevasse was a little too wide to jump across with monsters on our backs. We had roped them one at a time across the slot, Martin's first, mine second. We were on our way once more, when I noticed I had lost my helmet, which I had presumed was now in the bowels of the crevasse.

We went back on the off chance, and lo and behold, found it had wedged 20ft down. Martin's bright idea of tying an ice axe on the end of a rope to carefully fish it out worked a treat; it wasn't long before we were on our way yet again. Anyway, we arrived at The Dome, set up camp in an amazing position at around 3070m with the weather prospects not looking too bad.

It was Sunday, August 3, and we had left the UK the week before. The alarm was set for 04.00; one peek out of the tent showed the weather had really 'clagged in', which sent me straight back into the sleeping bag. By 05.30 after a couple more peeks, the weather was showing signs of clearing which got us motivated for a brew at least.

Within the hour it was looking very positive, and by 07.30 we were on the Kain face. Ascent up the face went very well on excellent neve, and soon we were on the ridge. The weather had turned fickle once again, giving less than 20m visibility along the ridge.

I remember feeling that I would be very disappointed if we had to bail out at that point, but at the same time, extremely privileged to be there on the mountain. Suddenly, as if on cue with our emotions, the ridge was opening out before us.

The mountain was giving us a window of opportunity and we took it immediately. We negotiated our way through a magnificent gargoyle section of the ridge, but were becoming increasingly aware that the snow and ice was thawing fast. Finally, around 13.00 we were on the summit; completely shagged, very proud and very happy. Martin's tenacity and determined character played a significant part in getting us there.

Unfortunately, for one reason or another, there is never enough time to dwell on a summit for as long as one would like. We knew that descending the Kain face was not the place to be with elevating temperatures and with the snow/ice pack deteriorating rather rapidly. The first signs of small avalanche runnels were already noticeable as we arrived.

Judiciously, we tip toed down the face with crampon front points sinking further and further into the softening slope. High on adrenaline, we were grateful to reach our camp as small avalanche slides were appearing more frequently.

My notes remind me of a rather sleepless and restless night that was probably still due to adrenaline pumping round my body. At 04.00, I woke up to lightning flashes all around us. Martin, as usual, was oblivious to the fact until I nudged him back into our mountain world. We waited for daybreak to begin the uneasy descent down the crevassed ice-field.

Half way down the ice-field an obvious avalanche site was visible. Amongst the deep, compacted debris of ice blocks and snow, we came across a large amount of climbing gear detritus. Some of the gear had been uncovered, but there were large amounts still semi-buried.

I remember seeing a single mountaineering boot half buried, and immediately sensed a bad accident had most likely occurred. We hadn't seen it on our ascent up the ice-field, so at that point, were unsure if it had occurred to a team following us up or whether it was before we arrived on the mountain.

We eventually arrived back at Berg Lake in one piece and informed the warden of our sightings. A helicopter was sent up, and although we didn't hang around for the official news, the warden thought it most likely to be the gear belonging to a team who arrived just before we did that had been uncovered by the weather. Unfortunately, he also gave us the news that one person from that team had died in the avalanche.

News of a person's death in the mountains or wilderness is obviously very poignant, especially if it's someone you know, or the accident is close to when it could easily have been yourself.

However, mixed with that melancholy of thought, it generally returns to the adage 'when your number's up, perhaps it's better to be in a place you love, than be struck by a RTA or a terrorist's bullet'.

In any extreme sport, there is a risk of serious injury or even fatality which is accepted by those that play the game. That isn't to say it is taken likely, or there is any degree of blasé or arrogance. For me, it is the hope that the long apprenticeship and continual learning that I have accumulated, along with turning back if I felt the need, keeps me, if not always safe, a good distance from a fatal end.

In the twenty-first century, we have seen huge developments in 'high octane' extreme sports, balanced with prodigious talent and incredible technology that combines to make it possible.

'Risk' in these cases, moves to the 'high risk' category, and skill moves to the super skill level equivalent to an Olympic athlete.

I can only really speak for those extreme sports that indirectly surround me at my level, such as extreme high altitude mountaineering, hard mixed winter climbing and the incredible 'head game' of free soloing.

Another group of extreme sports to briefly mention here, as it worries me the most, is Gary's enjoyment of Sky Diving, Wing Suit flying and BASE jumping. 'BASE' is an acronym that stands for four categories of fixed objects to jump from: **building, antenna, span and earth.**

When BASE and wing suit flying combined a decade or so ago, the super ridiculous extreme sport of 'close proximity wing suit flying' developed. Wing suit flying only a few metres above a ridge line or similar terrain at around 60>70mph. I'm glad I know my limitations needed to feed my rat!!

I didn't care how late I laid in bed for the next morning, but as it happened, it wasn't that late.

I was not looking forward to the hike down the valley that was for sure! The aches and pains gradually eased with each brew and pancake we ate. We hit the park headquarters by the road head in one long day, just in time for as much coffee and cake we could eat. However, all the campsites were fully booked, leaving us little option to head back to Jasper and the convenient bivvy site we had found previously.

With around four days left of the trip before needing to head home, we hired a car and headed for the 'Miette Hot Springs', expecting to find a soothing natural hot spring. It turned out to be nothing more than a fancy swimming pool, so did an immediate U-turn and headed back to Jasper just as a spectacular storm kicked off.

The usual bivvy was out of the running, so we tossed for who had the car and who had the sheltered, cramped porch outside the local bank. I had the car, but I'm not sure I won the toss!

The following day, a wild walk to the 'Lost Boys' climbing crag gave us an opportunity for a quick rock route at 5.10d before heading to the Mount Edith

Cavell hostel. The plan was for a quick ascent of the East Ridge the next day. The weather was very poor again as we set off around 06.00.

It took around an hour and a half to the col and then soon after onto the ridge. Visibility was poor as we scrambled and climbed solo on mixed ground (mainly snow and ice ramps). Wind and snow had become very heavy, and although we guessed it was probably only a few hundred metres to the summit, we called it a day and battled our way back to the hostel.

A final day in Jasper gave chance to gather souvenirs for back home and to fully appreciate the fine alpine town that we had not really had chance to do. Jasper and the National Park offers adventures for climbers, skiers and outdoor enthusiasts alike, and welcomes over three million tourists a year.

Part 4: Short Stories/Long Journeys

Success is not final, failure is not fatal.
It is the courage to continue that counts

WC

Chapter Thirteen
Fun Together

1996 and 1997 were interesting years for all the family in many ways. Gary had returned from a world of adventure, having spent a lot of his time in New Zealand. He had commenced his trip not knowing what he might do thereafter, but returned home with a clear vision of getting into the Royal Military Academy Sandhurst (RMAS) and becoming an Army officer. He joined me on many local cross-country runs and climbing trips to get himself fitter.

As Gary was a non-graduate, he did not meet the initial entrance criteria. However, his sponsorship by the Parachute Regiment to RMAS obviously impressed, so was sent by the Army to MoD Worthy Down near Winchester to 'culturally broaden his horizons' on the Pre-RMAS (PRAMS) course. He threw himself at the challenge, did very well, and arrived at the gates of Sandhurst as Officer Cadet Lincoln-Hope.

Nicky was a little unsettled during those years, having decided university was not for her; it was taking a while to discover a job that interested her. I knew deep down there was a pull towards following her brother's footsteps with a journey round the globe, which I'm proud to say she did a couple of years later.

She passed her driving test, first time, which was one up on her brother, and prompted us to look for a cheap car that would give her the independence she needed. Of course, it had one condition, it required the necessary street cred.

Eventually, we settled on price rather than cred and arrived home one day with a Ford Fiesta. However, it didn't take long for the cred to evaporate, especially with a rather large crease in the rear bumper courtesy of her brother. An alternative car came on the scene. It was a neat, sporty Vauxhall Nova complete with a soft top.

All was fine, until I got a call from her one day to say she had an accident coming around a bend on a steep road leading down from the Berkshire Downs to Wantage. From a fair distance away, I was shocked to just make out on the distant hillside the familiar post box red car on its roof, it was off to one side of the road on a grass verge!

Unbelievably, Nicky came out of that unscathed; a few metres in front were trees, and to the nearside was a ditch and fencing. She was extremely lucky, as was her car; despite the car being muddied and bruised, we managed to get it repaired relatively cheaply.

It is an event of continual wind up for the rest of the family to play on to this day! Never though, have we got to the bottom of the real reason for the accident, other than her insistence it was a driver coming in the opposite direction over her side of the road, of course it was!

Lynne was still heavily into netball and showing no signs of giving up, even in her mid-forties. Needle matches often got quite dirty evidently, with her frequently finding the need to give as much as she received from women half her age. We were beginning to tackle more long distance and challenging hikes together, which over the following years, have been fantastic.

I was getting a good deal of climbing in, both on the rock and winter ice climbing. Rock climbing was mostly at Avon Gorge, Wintours Leap and the Lake District, although one weekend visit to Gogarth on Anglesey, North Wales, was to climb an amazing atmospheric route called 'A Dream of White Horses', a mid-grade route with huge amounts of exposure and excellent climbing. A climb that is not difficult to muse over from time to time.

Of course, winter climbing trips were quite plentiful during that period too, mainly in Scotland, the Lakes and the Alps.

I had also decided to join the born-again biker club. In the main, I saw it as a cheaper means of transport for my commute to work, rather than buy two cars. I had been running a second-hand Honda 125cc for over a year on L plates, much to the amusement of the shop floor employees I managed in my role as Production Manager, most of them had flash cars, as we paid them far too much!

Quite often I would get on the bike to go home, only to find some bright spark had written 'Pizza Express' or something similar on my very colourful red top-box at the rear of the bike, great humour which I must admit to missing!

Anyway, I hoped I got my revenge after passing my test later in the year. In those days, one could obtain a driving licence and go from riding a 125cc, single cylinder puppy, straight to a 1000cc, 4 cylinder beasty, which of course I did. I arrived at work one day on a beautiful blue and white Honda CBR 1000F; *that will show the bastards!* I thought.

My brothers and I have always kept close family ties with each other. Even each set of our kids, now in their twenties, thirties and forties are managing to keep that close bond between cousins and uncles.

Despite the age differences, there have been many fun gatherings, from the ski slopes of Aviemore and the Alps to walks in Snowdonia and Christmases on the beaches of Anglesey. It's very pleasing as a parent to know that they are making the effort too, because that's what it takes to keep strong family bonds.

One final adventure for me to mention during this period, was the opportunity Lynne and I had to purchase a small second home. I had started employment at Biomet Ltd at a very opportune time. Shares in the company were doing well and divvied out to all employees who had been there for the required period.

I also happened to be on a good salary as Production Manager. With our mortgage repayments on our house in Grove now quite small, we took the financial opportunity of a second home as being a good investment at that time, rather than move to a bigger house in the area. We had always talked of buying in the Lake District if we had the chance.

After several trips and viewings, we took possession of a flat in Collin Croft[32] in the town of Kendal, Cumbria. Kendal is a charming and historic town on the edge of the National Park and famous for its 'Yards', of which Collin Croft is one. It suited our outdoor lifestyle wonderfully, being around the Lakes, and remained so until 2010.

We both knew that going into the venture had a limited time frame, as finances were never going to make it affordable when we both retired. That moment approached in 2010; we did stutter for a while as to where we should spend our future years, but the pull of Wantage was far too strong. We sold up

---

[32] In the book 'The Yards of Kendal' by Trevor Hughes and Arthur Nicholls, their research shows the yards started life around the time of William, the Conqueror. "They were originally rented parcels of land or burgage plots, where cattle and sheep were kept. By the late eighteenth century, cottages and workshops were clustered into the cramped spaces with dozens of neighbours living cheek-by-jowl." Eventually, they were raised to the ground during slum clearances in the 1960s. Collin Croft was one of 17 yards converted into housing during 1985–1986.

on the Kendal house, never forgetting that wonderful period, always grateful for the opportunity and experience, our family and friends enjoyed there.

Chapter Fourteen
Along the John Muir Trail

As I mentioned previously, Lynne and I decided to broaden our adventures a little further while we were fit and able. It occurred in 1998, our twenty-fifth wedding anniversary and a year that was to have other memorable events.

The John Muir Trail[33] (JMT) in Yosemite National Park, California, was a big step for both of us hiking together. For starters, it was long, tough, and renowned for heavy spring snow in certain years. All very well for myself who was used to carrying heavy expedition packs for several days; it was a different ball game for Lynne.

The trail also necessitates carrying mostly everything needed for up to fourteen days on one's back, on a rugged, wild, high altitude trail. There were limited food restocking facilities, so at least five days food was included in the packs. Finally, there are very few escape routes.

We trained together with heavy packs, as we often did, on our local Berkshire Downs and White Horse Hill, clocking up the mileage. Having had previous experience of organising all climbing expeditions for ourselves (Martin and myself), I was able to have the enjoyment and interest of planning logistics for the Muir trail for Lynne and I.

Mid-July we were on our way out of Heathrow bound for San Francisco, having left Nicky in charge of the house for three weeks! It was always the intention not to loiter in the city at the beginning of the trip, preferring to head

---

[33] The John Muir Trail (JMT) cuts a journey through what many backpackers regard as the most famous trail with the finest mountain scenery in the USA. I's overall length of 211 miles from Happy Isles in Yosemite to Whitney Portal rises above 14,000ft. It has a delightful summer climate, but spring can often bring huge dumps of snowfall making the trail impassable.

straight out to the town of Merced, not far outside Yosemite National Park. A night's stay in a comfortable bed at the Ramada Hotel was all we were getting for the next fourteen days.

After a great breakfast, another indulgence unavailable for the next 2 weeks, we caught a bus into Yosemite village. I was grateful we had arranged the necessary trail permits back in the UK, as the place was heaving with tourists and hikers alike. We hurriedly booked a spot in the campground for the night, followed by sourcing food supplies, camping gas and of course a bear proof food canister. The canister was not cheap (approximately $75) in the village, but it certainly proved its worth on a few occasions.

We wasted no time the next morning after porridge for breakfast, a sharp come down from the morning before, and were soon on the JMT. The climate in the valley and at the start of the trail was extremely warm even in the morning. It was difficult to absorb the enormity of the place as we gained higher ground, particularly the spectacular granite monoliths of El Capitan and Half Dome.

The natural desire as a climber to feed the soul on that wonderful granite was overwhelming, but alas, it would have to wait. Our aim the first day was to make it to Sunrise camp, but the heat, heavy loads, and likelihood we were still acclimatising made us feel particularly knackered. We decided to pitch the tent a couple of miles short of Sunrise and make the most of relaxing away from the crowds.

We were up by 06.00 the next morning, and scoffed a bowl of porridge with honey and nuts before eagerly hitting the trail again. It was particularly noticeable with our height gain that the snow accumulations were getting larger and more frequent, albeit melting fast in the heat of the day. As we stopped for lunch, two guys approached from the direction we were heading and gave us 'heads up' that the trail ahead was blocked with huge dumps of snow.

The 'off trail' diversion took a considerable amount of energy and time, often in knee deep snow; it was clear we were not going to make our next camp 3 miles away at Tuolumne Meadows.

Cathedral Peak and pass lay before us. It was a magnificent view, too inviting not establish our second camp. We drank and ate well before emptying sacks and counterbalancing them over a tree branch behind us.

It was made clear to us by the Rangers before setting off, that black bears were frequently encountered on the trail. As we were spending a second night out of a designated camp site, sensible precautions should prevail, or so we thought!

Around midnight, the snuffling and grunting of bears could be clearly heard. The Mummy bears are so accustomed to human stupidity that they have learnt to send their little sons and daughters along the thin branches instead of themselves. From there, the little buggers hoist the sacks up and over the branch and merrily go to town.

Lynne was note taker on our trip. Suffice to say, "I have never been so shit scared in all my life" went for the both of us! Not knowing whether to make a loud noise or stay shtum, we decided on the latter and must have eventually nodded off to sleep. By first light, a recce of the debris revealed a bear canister that had obviously been padded around a little and rucksacks that were not badly damaged.

However, Lynne's little bag of cosmetics and toothpaste she had forgot to remove from her sack had either been eaten or applied. Two gas canisters had been removed from my sack and punctured, which must have left them extremely high or pissed off!

We were alive at least, and able to have a real giggle, although breakfast amounted to nothing more than a granola bar and water. It was a glorious morning as we packed the sacks and headed for Tuolumne Meadows through Cathedral Pass. The scenery was stunning, especially with Cathedral Peak glistening in the morning sun at nearly 11,000ft.

Cathedral Lake was clearly frozen and there looked to be further huge dumps of snow on the trail ahead. More diversions off the trail, often in knee deep snow, eventually saw us into The Meadows camp site late afternoon, greeted by a million and one mosquitoes. We took advantage of a café that was open and treated ourselves to burger, chips and salad, heaven!

Everyone we spoke to were extremely friendly, but gave stark warning of the frequency of bears seen around the site. One old boy however, got talking with Lynne and assured her that black bears would very seldom attack humans. Initially, it gave her more confidence, but helped little for what was about to follow.

Each tent pitch in the campground was supplied with a metal bear proof box. We obviously took advantage and emptied our pack contents into it, then placed the packs in the 'bell end' of our tent. It just so happened that the orientation we lay in the tent placed our heads closest to that end.

At around 01.00 and being a light sleeper, I heard that familiar snuffle! The bear must have got scent of my sack and in no time at all, snuck his bloody great paw under the tent flap and hooked it out. Lynne immediately woke up on hearing me shout, grabbed a metal pan and was banging for all she was worth, shouting "bear, fucking bear!" at the top of her voice.

I shot out the tent, forgetting I was only in underpants, as Lynne was still banging away. I was hoping he hadn't run off with my sack, as I saw his pretty large backside skulking into the night.

It was all over in a couple of minutes and I eventually found the sack not too far away. Other tent occupants had started to appear, but as I felt rather naked, I didn't feel like hanging around for a chat.

We slept well afterwards, eventually surfacing quite late. We shared chats and laughs of the event over breakfast with our immediate neighbours, it was surprising how relaxed everyone was after the event. We were growing used to the fact that bears were an annoyance more than too much of a worry, but complacency was certainly a mind-set not to get into.

Our next objective was Donohue Pass, at an elevation of over 11,000ft. I was beginning to fear too much snow, especially spring snow, had fallen over the year. It turned a journey that should have been reasonable pleasure into one of very hard graft.

A few miles out of Tuolumne, I realised a large storm was headed in our direction. We were in another particularly beautiful part of the trail, so having decided we did not want to get soaked through, elected to erect the tent and hunker down. As it happened, it was the right move, as a prolonged period of thunder, lightning and heavy rain stayed around us for several hours.

As darkness drew in, we both prayed for a bear free night and a good sleep. This was another unscheduled campsite without any bear protective boxes, only our own bear bin for food, which was left outside the tent and rucksacks buried amongst the rocks. Although restless at first, we both ended up having a sound sleep.

A clear beautiful morning greeted us, the kind of morning that makes one feel alive and special. I was indeed impressed and proud of how Lynne had coped with the last few days. Perhaps a lesser person would have struggled to carry on with the continual bear situation, let alone the toughness of the hiking under the far-from-summer conditions and the weight of our packs.

After a couple of brews and breakfast, we were once again on our way to Donohue pass. I feared the worse! Huge amounts of snow on a large boulder strewn, steep slope up to the pass greeted us. I could sense Lynne's apprehension before she said anything and decided to remove my pack, leaving it with her, whilst suggesting I went for a recce.

I was gone for around an hour; it was hard work making progress even for myself, in the snow pack and often bottomless gaps between boulders that had you sinking up to your waist. Before I got back to Lynne, I had already decided the JMT was not on for us that year. I knew she would feel disappointed and somewhat guilty, but what lay ahead was not going to be enjoyment for her, nor what we had planned.

There was of course some deliberation, but I was in no doubt it was not going to be enjoyment for her. We turned on our heels with a determination not to let it be the end of our hiking.

Our immediate plan though was to make it back to Tuolumne Meadows before the 'eating house' closed at 18.00. We promptly strode it out arriving back just in time for a good feast. We re-grouped the morning after, had a plan, and began a three-day hike with what we had come up with.

The first day took us on a trail North West out of Tuolumne to our first campsite at Glen Aulin. From there, the second day took us on a trail South West to the next camp at a frozen 'May Lake' situated around 10,000ft. Finally, the last day's long hike snaked us back to Yosemite village, via a punishing one hundred switchbacks.

The whole circuit was endowed with majestic peaks and spectacular waterfalls. But most important of all, our decision to retreat from the JMT left us with no regrets whatsoever.

At the campsite, Lynne was more than grateful of a lie-in and a long hot shower after nine days of hiking! However, there was one final bonus before needing to leave the valley.

We had just enough time left to hike up the relatively easy, albeit 6 hour, trail to the top of El Capitan, also known as El Cap, and probably the most recognised vertical granite monolith in the world. It is a jewel in the crown for hard core rock climbing, not only for those in the US but also the world over. I was elated just to be putting the tent up to camp on its summit, musing as I did about whether I would ever be good enough to climb on it!

We were the only team around, sitting there eating supper under a beautiful evening sky with the other great monolith of Half Dome in the distance. It was hard to drop off to sleep, not for the worry of bears, but because it was hard to let go of the billion stars under a massive dark sky, laid on top of a revered piece of natural wonder.

I guess we could have stayed there for days, but thoughts of the long trek back pulled us out of our slumber. One final spectacle for us to take away from the valley was the hike past the awesome 600ft plus Bridalveil Falls.

Next day, we headed back to San Fran via coach and Amtrak train, spoiling ourselves one more time in a Ramada Hotel. I did wonder at first if they would let us in, dressed as we both were like true dirt bags. A final two days on the beach at Santa Cruz wallowing in the sea and sun was a brilliant finale to celebrate twenty-five years of marriage. We were, of course, so looking forward to seeing the kids after three long weeks.

Chapter Fifteen
1998

Gary was finding life at Sandhurst his forte, whilst Nicky was doing well in a new career as a gym instructor.

I could have had a better start to the year! I had been experiencing a dull ache in my groin towards the back end of 1997 and had been putting it down to long periods in my climbing harness. By the end of January, along with Lynne's insistence, I decided to see my doctor. Doctor Teare, a wonderful GP for us, ever since the children were born, and Doctor Ambler, both suspected my symptoms were down to a little more than my harness.

I was referred quite quickly to the Urology department of Churchill Hospital, part of the Oxford Radcliffe Hospital. After two or three visits and one ultrasound scan, the histology showed a small tumour on my right testicle.

In March, after a small op, my Consultant Surgeon Mr Cranston was satisfied he had removed the tumour. However, he wanted a second opinion from a colleague in the Imperial Cancer Research Fund Unit, to see if any further treatment was appropriate for me. Around June, after two or three previous visits, another Consultant Surgeon, Doctor Ganesan, decided he wanted to be sure the tumour had been fully removed. The Biopsy report had shown that the tumour was a malignant Leydig Cell tumour, which was not common, and not a great deal had been learnt about it.

Anyway, "It has to come off for us to be sure," he said.

"What? I'm losing one of my balls?"

"Yes, but you'll be fine with one," he said.

That's all very well for you to say, mate, I remember thinking to myself, as I struggled to find anything else to take the conversation further.

The surgery was swift, in and out the same day, a bit like watching 'The Yorkshire Vet' on the television! There was a little ache that followed and a day off work, but that was about the crux of it.

As I was told not to drive, Lynne picked me up from the Hospital.

"I've had a meeting with Ivor Bolockov," I said.

"He sounds Russian, was he nice?" she said.

I pissed myself laughing, until the penny dropped for her, at which point she found it not amusing at all!

To close this little episode of my life, I cannot thank everyone enough for their swift action, their knowledge and expertise. We have come a long way in our understanding and treatment of various cancers, testicular being one of them. It was only three decades previously, when as a young lad, a neighbour of ours lost his life to testicular cancer, he was only in his thirties.

To every male out there, fondle yourself regularly and don't hesitate to get checked out.

March through to August 1998 was a busy period, it certainly helped take my mind off the testicular period. A long weekend at the beginning of March, skiing in Scotland, was followed by a few weekends accompanying Nicky with her new sport of women's rugby. She had gone along for training sessions with Reading Ladies RUFC.

Nicky was fit and strong through working at the gym which coupled with a good turn of speed and useful kicking ability, gained from her early days playing for Grove FC, she eventually made the 1st team squad. One crunch-match against Harlequins Ladies was very entertaining, with lots of skill displayed from both sides.

Harlequins eventually won 27-13, and the game certainly showed that women's rugby had bundles of talent that would eventually overcome old stigmas of the past. It is great to see that talent has manifested into the women's game we see today.

The girls had other talents that matched the fella's, off the pitch too. I can only bear witness to two of them; one being that they could drink like fish! Beer drinking competitions in the bar followed nearly every match, along with goodness knows what other alcohol concoctions. The record for a pint of beer down the hatch was seconds.

Another talent one of the girls had was sniffing a condom up one nostril and pulling it out through her mouth. I'm sure this was not such a novelty for a group of male or female rugby players, but it was sure a total novelty for me. In all the years of after match activities I had ever been involved with, I had never seen a condom go in and out like that!

Meanwhile, Gary (Lincoln-Hope; he changed his name by deed poll to take my mother's maiden name) was performing exceptionally well at Sandhurst. A 'Father's night' and 'Open Day' were treats for parents during each course intake, for they were a wonderful opportunity to view the RMCS inner sanctum, recognised as 'the national centre of excellence for leadership'.

Each commissioning course lasts for forty-four weeks and is divided into three terms of fourteen weeks, each with an interval between. Courses focus on military skills, fitness and decision making amongst others activities. The final term culminates in putting those skills learnt, into demanding exercises around the UK and overseas.

No doubt there were plenty of other unofficial skills learnt, probably best not mentioned here. One I am privy to however, was a cultural evening the group was sent on, to see *The Barber of Seville*. This received a sacking off in preference to another cultural experience at Stringfellows strip club.

At the end of each course intake, a Sovereign's parade ceremony takes place with various skills on display. This is followed by an award ceremony for a variety of achievements, the top honour being the 'Sword of Honour' awarded to the British Army Officer Cadet considered by the Commandant to be, overall, the best of the course. In September of 1998, it was a very proud moment for us to witness Gary receive that award.

It is concluded with the commissioning officer cadets marching off the parade square, up the steps of and through the entrance to Old College. It is usual for them to be followed up the steps by the Academy Adjutant riding a horse.

Gary passed out of RMCS as a Commissioned Officer in 2nd Battalion, Parachute Regiment. That was immediately followed by three months at Catterick Garrison, North Yorkshire, completing the infamous 'P' Company and Parachute course.

Time rarely stood still, as a Platoon Commanders battle course promptly followed and lasted for a further three months. Barely time to catch a breath, various tours of duty and Jungle Warfare Instructors courses, all followed in quick succession. Gary eventually left full time service in 2004 to embark on his own private business ventures, but continued a very active service in the UK reserves.

Somehow and somewhere I had managed to fit in a two week call up for jury service; a dozen or more visits to the oncology department at Churchill Hospital; Lynne's and my trip to Yosemite; and of course, a full-on job as Production Manager at Biomet Ltd. It was a very busy year but exceedingly rewarding.

10 November—Covid 19 Update:

It seemed inevitable that sooner rather than later, England would have to go into a 2nd lockdown. Cases were rising despite the introduction of the three tier system only two weeks previously.

As from the 5 November, England began a four week lockdown. It is not as severe as the 1st lockdown, as schools and nurseries will remain open for children's education and well-being. Industry will continue, but working from home wherever possible, should take priority. All non-essential shops will be closed for the duration.

The Government's growing fear is that, with the number of cases increasing rapidly and needing hospital treatment, particularly in Intensive Care Unit's (ICU's), could reach saturation point. Whereby NHS staff, hospitals and Nightingale hospitals will be unable to cope. That in turn, will lead to doctors having to make the unprecedented decision on selecting whose life to save. Not since the 2nd World War has this arisen in the UK.

To date, there are now 50,000+ deaths due to Covid 19 in the UK, the highest in Europe.

Chapter Sixteen
Rewards of a Bivvy or Wild Camp

The term bivvy is a derivative of the French word *bivouac*, meaning temporary shelter. They can be planned well in advance or as a sudden refuge to save one's life. Bivvies are also useful when a short overnight stay does not justify the expense of a B and B, campsite or other salubrious accommodation, especially if one is a member of the dirt-bag club!

The rewards of sleeping under stars and the Milky Way on a warm summer's night, or a pristine winter's night in the snow, tucked up in a cosy sleeping bag, out in the wild, are innumerable. Those occasions are very precious, though, especially in a UK winter; alternative 'sheltered accommodation' needs to be sought if the weather turns wild.

There is, of course, a danger the activity can develop into a perverse addiction, due to the fact so much fun can be had at so little cost! The following short paragraphs give a few memorable tales, exact details left out to protect the author:

Aviemore Railway Station

Much to our surprise, Aviemore was not over endowed with dry bivvy spots. On this occasion, early in our bivvying days, we had arrived for last orders at a pub just out of town with a Ceilidh[34] in full swing. An hour or two later after much banter with the locals, we trolled the streets looking to lay our heads. It must have been another hour or so, looking for somewhere out of the rain, that we were resigning ourselves to the car.

---

[34] A Ceilidh (Cayley) is a very popular Scottish or Irish social event with folk music, singing and dancing with lots of story-telling. It is commonly found in the Highlands of Scotland.

The railway station platforms were looking darker and more inviting by this time, so decided to have one last look. As luck would have it, a corner of the North bound platform was dark and quiet; even better, two flatbed trolleys were parked up, a luxury too good to dismiss. Sleeping bags were rolled out on a trolley apiece and we were soon away with the fairies.

Around 04.00, I vaguely remember half waking to the sound of a train pulling into the station. A little while later my trolley was on the move. *Am I dreaming, or is this for real?* were my thoughts.

I sat bolt upright with the hood of my sleeping bag tight round my head, just as the porter turned to see why the trolley was feeling so heavy. "Jesus fucking Christ!" he said, scared witless at the sight of me looking like a revived mummy.

It was the early mail train and he was about to load the daily newspapers onto my bed.

We had a good laugh and with that, I left Martin still fast asleep on his trolley, hoping he may get delivered to Inverness along with the papers, while I disappeared for the remainder of my kip in the car.

Lochnagar, Royal Deeside

After a lengthy journey up from Martin's in the Lakes one winter's day, the weather was less than pleasant as we arrived at Ballater. Our aim was to head down the valley of Glen Muick and park our car at Spittal of Glenmuick for a day's climbing on Lochnagar. It was around 01.00, and very few bivvy spots jumped out to welcome us, not surprising I guess, as the Queens Balmoral Estate was only a few miles away.

Anyway, we'd had enough of driving and eventually found a rather useful and well-built bus shelter. It was clean, dry and for the minimal hour's sleep we needed, it was ideal. We were both buried deep in our sleeping bags and sleep, well past our intended alarm.

Being a lighter sleeper than the Scrowston, I thought I heard voices, but struggled to determine at first if I was still dreaming. Through squinting eyes, I looked up to see a few school kids, obviously waiting for the school bus, giggling away at the dossers on the floor. Nudging Martin awake was hopeless, so I turned over hoping to fall back to sleep.

Ten minutes passed, the giggling was now a cacophony of noisy school kids getting soaked because two old gits were taking up their dry shelter. We had a good bit of banter with them, before they all got on their bus for school. We returned to peace and tranquillity and a very welcome brew.

Spittal Of Glenmuick

Following the night in the bus shelter, the weather was awfully grim and mild as we drove down the Glen and parked the car. Climbing didn't look on for the day, but we made the effort to walk into the Coirre and recce the cliffs for future adventures.

It was nearly dark by the time we got back to the car, thoughts of a brew, food and a bivvy were in that order of priority.

Unusually, we were the only ones in the carpark. I left Martin to get on with knocking up supper, while I nosed around for a likely dry spot to bivvy. There was little point in going back to the bus shelter, so it was either stay where we were, or try and find somewhere else in the dark, unlikely.

I had gone to the Gents toilet for a pee and ruled that out for a bivvy, being wet and very uninviting. Just on the off chance, I popped next door to the Ladies, it was pristine! It was more than spacious for the two of us. The floor was clean and dry, there were hand-driers delivering hot air, even hot water at the sinks, a three-star bivvy.

We bedded down half expecting to be disturbed at some point overnight, but left the car park in the morning having had a good night's kip and breakfast with no sign of anyone.

Argentiere Glacier, Chamonix

Our attempt on Les Courtes North Face, one of the most famous ice routes in the Alps, got off to a rather late start. By the time we snow-shoed up the Argentiere glacier and approached the hut, it was getting dark. Thoughts of a very busy, smelly hut and the need to be on the route before anyone else prompted us to look for a bivvy.

It was obviously going to be in the snow, but the forecast was for a clear, albeit cold night. 100m higher up the rocks from the hut was a snow-covered ramp, big enough for the two of us. Little effort was needed to dig out an open coffin each in the snow, and in no time at all, we were comfortable in our cosy cocoons, with a brew and supper on the go.

Climbing packs were sorted ready for a 03.00 alarm and a good route plan across the crevassed glacier to the foot of the face was memorised before settling down for an early night. It was extremely difficult to drop off to sleep, transfixed as I was, on the cloudless, starlit sky above. For me, big mountain faces at night, seem to grow taller and steeper, developing a mystical and spiritual reverence in the moonlight. It also identifies hidden characters in their faces, not noticeable during daylight.

I did eventually nod off, and we did hear the alarm at such an unearthly hour. We managed to be first on the face and succeed on one of the best mixed (ice and rock) North Face routes on the Argentiere wall.

Kingshouse, Glencoe

One other short tale to mention was a winter climbing trip to Scotland with Martin and his partner Carole, later to be his wife, who I had met for the first time.

As is always common with winter trips to Scotland, we arrived in the early hours. Having made it to Glencoe, the weather was dry and a pleasant night was on the cards. A quiet corner of the Kingshouse[35] carpark seemed a good place to bed down. We wasted no time in sorting bedding, lying like three slugs adjacent to the car for some sort of protection.

Morning came. I made brews for Martin and myself, clearly Carole was still fast asleep. We had a bowl of porridge and still Carole had not moved.

"Right, we'll be on our way then," he said.

"Surely we aren't leaving Carole like that on her own," I said, as it wasn't exactly the quietest corner of the carpark I had in mind.

"She'll be fine."

We drove off, leaving Carole rather exposed and pretty much in the centre of the carpark.

There she was, all alone, still lying in a sleeping bag, with her rucksack beside her, her sole possessions, as we drove off for a day's climbing. We eventually returned to the Kingshouse after gallivanting around the fell-side. I

---

[35] The Kings House Hotel is a famous historical inn at the eastern end of Glen Coe in the Scottish Highlands. It is situated close to Rannoch Moor and has a commanding view of Buachaille Etive Mor. It is a particularly famous spot for climbers to gather and share their tales. It got its name following occupation by the British Army during battles to control the area, in the aftermath of the Jacobite Rising of 1745.

was to say the least, still a little amused and a tad guilty as we met up again with Carole.

Carole was completely unfazed with it all, dealing with it as though it was standard practice. She had eventually spent the day skiing at the Glencoe ski centre, none the worse for the experience.

A Snow Shelter

No bivvy CV is complete without experiencing a snow hole or snow cave for shelter. The better ones to experience are when planned, rather than one needed in an emergency. Either way, once cocooned inside you are well protected from the elements.

Snow shelters can last for days, even weeks if enough work has gone into them. Some enthusiasts will take all the snow shovels, snow saws and tools necessary for a three-star decadent abode, but usually it's the standard climbing kit one has on them that needs to suffice.

A great overnight stay for me, was close to an area known as the 'Marquis' Well' just north of the Cairngorm summit. We probed an area to ensure the depth of snow was adequate, then got to work using the adze of the climbing axe to form a tunnel. Once long enough, we could start to work side-ways and upwards to enlarge the cave.

It took a long time with the tools we had, but it was an experience I truly savoured. There was nothing more gratifying than having a brew, cooking supper and sleeping in the solitude of our cosy white hovel.

The British countryside is our back garden and a veritable haven for learning.

It is there for all of us to gain both, physical and mental stimulation. Wild camping or an overnight bivvy are the mechanisms that help us be at one with the wilderness; **a synergy that is invaluable and should be on every school's adventure curriculum.**

An important addition to emphasise is that, any bivvy or wild camping trip, must undertake the fundamental principle and philosophy of leave no trace, AT ALL TIMES.

Good housekeeping and planning should be paramount. A good stout trowel will do the job in an emergency!

Chapter Seventeen
The Corsican Traverse

Corsica (Corse, in French) is a mountainous island with a length north to south of approximately 110 miles and a width of 50 miles. The island has been part of France for over two hundred years and is situated in the Mediterranean Sea, approximately 50 miles off the coast of Europe. The interior is mostly mountainous and particularly rugged in the northern half. Two of its highest summits (Monte Cinto 8,887ft and Monte Rotondo 8,611ft) are also found in the northern region.

The entire mountain regions are controlled by the 'Parc Naturel Regional de la Corse' (PNR).

Approximately a-quarter to one-fifth of the island is covered in forests of pine and deciduous trees, along with large areas of dense maquis. On the west coast, the mountains run down almost to the sea, where some of the best scenery and beaches in Europe can be found.

It was reading about the beaches and scenery that first attracted Lynne and myself to take Gary and Nicky to the island for a summer holiday. It was indeed a fabulous week of sea and sand for all of us. Nicky was content most of the time, lying on the beach drooling over the French Foreign Legion troops (a training base is located there) in their budgie smugglers, whilst showing off their physique!

While there, I read up on the official hiking route of the GR20 which traverses the islands inner landscape north to south. The GR (Grande Randonnée) network of hiking footpaths is very extensive throughout Europe, with the GR20 considered to be the most difficult of them all. The trail is 110 miles long and wholly mountainous, never dropping below 3,000ft, whilst reaching 7,245ft at its highest point.

A total of some 32,000ft of ascent and descent is hiked during its length. The crux of the GR20 is the traverse of the Cirque de la Solitude, a constant rocky scramble of considerable length. Several sections of fixed rope and metal cables are in place, without which, the traverse would be graded 'Moderate' on the British climbing scale. It seemed an ideal undertaking to follow on from our Yosemite trip two years previously. However, like Yosemite, it was not one to be taken lightly.

In June 2000, we arrived at Calvi airport after a magnificent scenic flight path descent over the mountains, some of the high peaks still harbouring lots of snow. The following day was spent in the usual way, gaining the odd map we could not obtain back in the UK, sorting food and other essentials. Our detailed handbook made it very clear that resupply of provisions along the trail was limited.

Provision for at least five days food was needed, especially if one wanted to avoid time consuming deviations off the trail. It also pointed out that water in the mountains, especially in the summer months could be hard to come by. Planning our overnight stays was important too, as wild camping in the PNR is forbidden. However, as we were particularly keen to camp rather than use the huts, we found there was no problem camping close to the huts for a nominal fee.

It is normal to expect the whole trail to take thirteen or fourteen days, with sightseeing and side journeys to the odd satellite peak. That didn't include time lost due to thunderstorms, quite often encountered in the summer. As time was limited to a two-week holiday in total for us, we hoped to get to the halfway stage at Vizzavone after ten days, enabling a short time to be spent elsewhere on the island, lazing on one of the beaches.

Our sacks were enormous as we set off on our second day from Calenzana, day 1 of the hike.

I was immensely impressed with Lynne's keenness to get going, given that there were 11 miles, seven to eight hours and approx 9,000 ft of total ascent and descent ahead of her with a huge pack. Perhaps it was due to the little porky I propositioned her with, downplaying the real scale of the thing. My penitence was to come out much sooner than I thought.

The following is an abridged tale of our journey:

Day 1—Calenzana to L'Ortu di u Piobbu

This leg followed a new route due to a huge forest fire destroying parts of the old route a couple of years before. It takes a lot steeper ground and negotiates several crag bands. This route, unlike the original route of day one, gives and takes no mercy. One gets an immediate taste of joys to come!

Day 2—L'Ortu di u Piobbu to Carrozzu (Spasimata)

Steep climbing continued through Col's d'Avartoli and de l'Inominata followed by steep descents to an impressive mountain setting where the Carrozzu hut is surrounded by high crags at around 4,000ft.

Day 3—Carrozzu to Ascu-Stagnu

A shorter day, albeit around six hours, provided plenty of exhilarating hiking and some easy scrambling interjected with a few difficulties. A rather dilapidated suspension bridge needed to be crossed before heading for a steep ridge, where metal cables helped progress over the rocks. A further summit ridge was followed for quite a distance before heading steeply down to the site of the d'Altore Refuge, burnt down in 1985. Here there were ideal campsites in preference to the new Hotel Ascu-Stagnu nearby.

Day 4—Ascu-Stagnu to Bergerie de Ballon

A thrilling day, although it was one Lynne was dreading. The infamous Cirque de la Solitude would naturally incur trepidation in hikers, not used to ground that requires a fair degree of competent scrambling with in-situ ropes and cables. As it happened, Lynne coped extremely well, especially as sacks were not getting lighter. We were both glad to get to the campsite where cheese, ham and plenty of water was available to purchase.

Day 5—Bergerie de Ballone to Castellu di Vergio

We were aware of falling a little behind schedule. Lynne was a different person having got the worrying Cirque behind her and was going strong! We leap-frogged the next planned campsite at Ciuttulu di i Mori, passing through magnificent scented woodland and wild wonderful scenery, clocking up around 12 miles and around eight hours hiking.

Day 6—Castellu di Vergio to Manganu

Another long day through woodland and steep mountain sides, always providing views of mountain peaks and steep forested valleys. Having climbed to a high point of Bocca Redda, our path dropped down to the beautiful Lac de Nino. A great spot to relax for a while and take a welcome dip.

Easy hiking led to a *bergerie* where we watched cheese being produced from the local's goats. Not far after that the Manganu hut appeared and at an altitude of over 5,000ft, it provided extensive views of the central mountains. For the first time in the night, we had been bothered by quite a large group of semi-wild pigs. Their snorting and mischievous knocking about of our tent was initially a little concerning, but eventually they must have realised we weren't about to offer them food and buggered off.

Day 7—Manganu to Pietra-Piana

Before setting off, Lynne had noticed one poor lad from a group of young German hikers in agony with blisters. He had made the classic error of buying a new pair of hiking boots just before the trip. Fortunately, our First Aid had the necessary kit which sorted him out and got him on his way. I did notice afterwards, that Lynne had given him plenty of spares, leaving our kit looking much the worse for wear!

We made tracks on steep, rugged ground up to the high point of the Breche de Capitello at over 7,000ft. Thereafter the route followed rocky ridges, at times needing care, as a slip in places, would have had serious results. The elevation we were at commanded fantastic panoramic views once again.

A good number of lakes set amongst the rocky terrain looked wonderfully inviting. The final ridge led to the Col de la Haute Route, the highest point of the GR at 7,237ft. From there a steep descent, with flagging knees, led us down to the Pietra-Piana hut. A large flat area for camping was ideal, as was the fencing surrounding it, to keep the noisy pigs out.

Day 8—Pietra-Piana to L'Onda

This was a shorter day, one that we might have combined with the previous days hike, had it not been for the fact that we were knackered. The route to L'Onda had long, sometimes steep descents through pine forests, the scent of which was exceptional. It followed two different streams on their meandering journey down the valley, which was in pleasant contrast from the rocky scrambling of previous days; such a pleasant hike that necessitated many stops and at least one paddle.

The hut eventually became visible in the distance and wasn't long before we were setting up our tent once again. The camping area adjacent to the hut was flat, grassy and clean, it was also enclosed like our previous site to deter the wild pigs. There was also a *bergerie* close by selling basic provisions and excellent cheese.

Day 9—L'Onda to Vizzavona to Calvi

Our end goal was just over half a day away; we both knew we had made the right decision to end our amazing journey at Vizzavona. But first we needed to ascend a steep, often rugged path, for around two hours up to the Crete de Muratello at just under 7,000ft. From there, a steep descent over rocky slabs and boulders took us down next to a stream and several waterfalls. Inviting as it was, we were keen to press on.

Finally, after crossing the large bridge at Cascade des Anglais and easy walking through scented woods, we arrived into the town of Vizzavona, altitude 2952ft.

It would have been very easy to have spent a full day in the wonderful mountain setting of the town; to have spent a comfortable night in a hotel and gorged ourselves on a savoury breakfast, something different to our accustomed bowl of porridge! However, we had arrived in time to buy tickets for a train that was to take us back to Calvi.

The thought of a day on the beach in the sun was too magnetic. After another amazing journey, this time on the scenic mountain railway, we arrived back in Calvi late afternoon.

It was one of the most amazing hike's Lynne and I have done. Although Vizzavona is regarded as the half way point of the GR20, we were delighted to have completed the best of the trail.

Mt McKinley – Mt McKinley from base camp

Mt McKinley – Storm-bound at 11,000ft

Mt Mckinley – Advance basecamp at 14,000ft

Mt McKinley – Bivvy on the West Rib (Nr Balcony camp)

Mt McKinley – Me on the upper section of the West Rib

Mt McKinley – Summit (4th party to summit that year)

Peru – After the avalanche

Peru – Dave rescuing the 1st Aid Kit

Mt Robson – From Berg Lake camp

Mt Robson – The Kain Face

Mt Robson – S.E ridge loaded heavily with snow

Starting the John Muir trail

JMT before the bears paid a visit

Camped on the summit of 'El Cap'

Nicky at Reading Ladies RFC

Gary receiving the RMCS Sword of Honour (picture by Tempest Photography©)

Camped on the GR20 near the Manganu hut

Lynne in the Cirque de la Solitude

Vizzavona railway station – our time was up

Part 5: Further Expeditions

Only those who risk going too far,
can possibly know how far they can go.

T S Elliot

4 December—Covid 19 Update

Just over four weeks and England is out of the 2nd lockdown. The 'R' rate has returned to below one. However, the objective on keeping the infection rate at that level, is still very much the Governments priority. To that end, a strengthened 3 tier policy is in place across the country. This will be reviewed every fortnight, but it is unlikely to differ until the relaxing of the rules for a five day period over the Christmas break.

Note! in less than a four week period, Covid 19 related deaths in the UK has risen to above 60,000.

On a positive note, the Pfizer-BioNTech vaccine has been approved by the MHRA, first in the world, and ready to start immunisations on high priority groups, as early as next week.

It has clearly been a struggle for millions of people one way or another.

Lynne and I have barely been able see Nicky and Chester for more than a few occasions over the ten month period. Gary and Izzy will be unable to sensibly come over for Christmas, so it will be well over a year before seeing them.

I'm getting pretty pissed off now with all the moaning and whingeing from certain elements of the population, of what they cannot do. I keep reminding myself of what our parents and grandparents went through eighty odd years ago at the start of another type of war.

My mother was sixteen years old at the start of World War Two and twenty-two years old at the end of it. Her education, along with millions of others, went out the window!

Along with that, 'fun' as a late teenager and young woman was fucked up too.

Chapter Eighteen
Mount Asgard, Baffin Island

Martin and I first caught a glimpse of the awesome Baffin Island landscape from around 30,000ft. It was on a flight from the UK, on our first mountaineering expedition to Alaska. For any mountaineer, the scenery of remote peaks jutting out of ice caps is jaw dropping, we knew sooner or later we would have to be down there.

Monday, 26 July 1999, we had both managed to wangle another 3-week holiday, it was getting harder for both of us to get that length of time in one go, without compromising our positions at work. Nevertheless, we were on a flight out of Gatwick bound for Boston, albeit one and a half hours behind schedule. After franticly trapesing our baggage around Boston airport, we eventually loaded it onto the connecting thirty seater plane on the tarmac, waiting to depart for Ottawa.

Ottawa was a nice airport, we found a convenient quiet, grassy spot outside the terminal to get our heads down until the next connection in the morning to Iqaluit, a small town on Baffin Island, situated at the north end of Frobisher Bay. It was great to eventually arrive at Iqaluit and Baffin Island, a dream come true.

Baffin Island is the largest island in the Arctic Archipelago. The Island was first discovered by Europeans in 1576 and used extensively in the whaling industry in the nineteenth and twentieth centuries.

However, archaeologists suggest a Pre-Dorset people arrived in the region on the east coast about three thousand five hundred years ago. Approximately thousand years ago the Thule people arrived over the Siberian land bridge. The Inuit people of today are direct descendants of the Thule culture.

The topography of the island is extremely varied, ranging from spectacular rugged mountain peaks over two billion years old and ice caps that are today's remnants of the last ice-age, one of an estimated twenty eight ice-ages. They share valley flats festooned with wild alpine flowers and arctic tundra adorned with the most colourful mosses and lichens.

Our final leg of the journey onto Baffin was to Pangnirtung[36] on the Cumberland Peninsula, situated between the Cumberland Sound to the west and the Davis Strait to the east. This was the launch point for our expedition.

We toured the high spots of Iqaluit with a welcome supper at a small local café serving sandwiches and best of all, large portions of French fries! By the time we got back to the airfield, it was made clear we were going to spend the night there. The village of 'Pang' lies adjacent to the fjord named after it, and consequently suffers from strong arctic cross winds. That evening they were very strong, so without further ado, we hunted for the best spot to doss.

For me, I rated this expedition as one of the best, one of which I could write reams on. But to try and keep the reader's interest, I've decided to precis events from my diary from here onwards.

Wednesday, 28 July—Lights went on at 06.00 in the airport lounge, we had a reasonable kip on the arctic floor. Winds had eased at 'Pang', and our flight was due to leave at 08.15, just enough time to walk to 'The Shack' for downtown breakfast.

It was not a given we would land at Pang airfield, weather there was still 'iffy' and we could easily have been turned back. Having piled everyone's gear on the plane, we all boarded, only to be told the plane was overbooked and two people needed to disembark. Fortunately, two tourists loved Iqaluit that much they were happy to stay there another night.

We arrived at a windy, bloody freezing Pangnirtung, immediately registering our intentions at the warden's office and stocking up on supplies. Next visit was to the local Inuit outfitter we had contacted back in the UK. He was to get us up the 22 miles of fjord by boat, to the landing stage adjacent to the majestic peak of Mount Overlord.

By 17.00, we landed and bade farewell to our skipper and adjusted to the sublime silence of our surroundings.

---

[36] Pangnirtung is an Inuit village situated in the Auyuittug National Park Reserve and is part of the Nunavut territory of Canada. It had a population of around fifteen hundred people by 2016. 'Pang' is central to any climbing or hiking in the Weasel Valley. Strict codes of conduct are compulsory and a permit is required. It is not uncommon to be in the company of polar bears in the Valley, particularly in winter.

Rather than hang around we made a move straight away, making the most of the Arctic's twenty four hour daylight and marvelled at the fantastic untamed wilderness that lay before us. It was inevitable we were going to double load gear in stages all the way up to base camp. By 21.00, we had ferried one load each up the Weasel valley to Windy Lake camp, suffice that it had been enough for one day.

Thursday, 29—Up early at 04.00, we had a quick brew before setting off down to Overlord with empty rucksacks to get the remaining gear. The packs were huge and seemed far too heavy, but eventually we made it back to Windy Lake by 16.00, knackered. Several brews and a large supper later, it was an early night to be ready for a repeat exercise the next day.

Friday, 30—Clear skies greeted us at 06.00. Two enormously full sacks weighing stupid amounts of kgs needed progressing to the next stage under the incredible bulk of Mount Thor. It had taken nearly four hours and after a quick doss and brew in the sun, there was no slouching in getting back to the Windy Lake tent.

Without the weight of the pack, I was able to appreciate the jaw dropping skyline of Mount Odin above the Weasel Valley a little more. I day dreamed as I went, wondering what the place would look like under a full winter blanket. The sky had turned a menacing grey as the stove went on once more. Pretty soon after, it started raining, the wind had picked up. It was time for another early night.

Saturday, 31—It was pissing down with rain and sleet as battle commenced to get a brew on, followed by half a bowl of muesli. Rucksacks were packed to the brim for the return journey to 'Thor'. It was then onwards with the load to Summit Lake camp.

Glacier stream melts had not troubled us up to this point. However, as we pushed through Thor camp and headed for Summit Lake, a wild river crossing was required. Not wanting to get gear sodden before the climbing stages, it left us with no alternative than to strip to our undies.

Adding boots and gear to the already ridiculous weight made the crossing tenuous to say the least. It also felt like icicles were forming where icicles should never, ever, be. At least, our sponsored Paramo gear was keeping our top half dry!

Eventually by 17.00, the tent had been erected, soup had warmed us up and curry with rice was about to be scoffed. The rain was still pissing down, but it could not dampen the spirits of the day.

There had been two profound moments of thought during that day of sack hauling. I knew Lynne and Nicky would be fine at home and thinking of me, but it didn't stop me worrying about them. Thoughts were also with G who, at the same time was in the jungles of Belize.

As I relaxed in the tent, it also gave me an opportunity to recall a specific memory of the day's progress, through the amazing, short life span of mosses and lichen underfoot. Martin and I were both sensitive to the exquisite colours and formations of the mosses, intentionally trying to avoid them, which of course, was impossible.

I frequently stopped to admire the patterns of lichen that had formed on the granite boulders, as if some Neolithic artist had painted them just ahead of us.

It was 21.00, still pissing down as I lay head on pillow. It had been a big day and I was completely knackered.

Sunday, 1 August—Still bloody raining, Barometer reading only 965mb. Skies were very grey, but needed to get the last haul up from Thor today. Left 07.30 and through the freezing river crossing by 08.30. Arrived Thor by 10.00, quick 'go-bar', then back to river crossing which was getting deeper by the hour.

Back at Summit Lake for 13.00, the wind had picked up and noticeably colder. It now felt it was coming off the Penny Ice Cap and necessitated extra warm layers for sitting around.

It was time to relax a little, take stock of the tremendous, pristine, but fragile wilderness and be so grateful of the privilege. Cloud was hunting the valleys from the surrounding peaks. "What's your thoughts on the next moves?" I said to Martin. "When should we head for advance base on the Kings Parade Glacier under Asgard."

Actually, they were rhetorical questions as I didn't give a toss!. All I want to know was what was for supper, I was beyond starving! "Macaroni and Veg Stroganoff followed by Apricots and custard," Martin said. It was great and in such a wonderful panoramic outdoor restaurant, but it was not nearly enough!

Monday, 2—Barometer reading was 970mb, it had been a howler of a night. Winds were very strong and rain had lashed down continuously. I had needed to pee desperately in the early hours, but was not about to venture outside.

The pee-bag let me down again with a tiny leak, my sleeping bag would need another good clean when we got back home. Fortunately, it missed Martin's bag by a smidgen and he was none the wiser.

The rain had eased a little, enabling us to negotiate the Caribou Glacier west of our camp, and then recce the moraine onto our entry point of the Kings Parade Glacier. We hoped it would lead to a favourable position for our final camp, under the North Peak of Asgard. The recce was useful, but for the remainder of the day, it was a case of soaking up the boredom, waiting for the rain to stop and eating while we had the chance.

Tuesday, 3—Today we met up with our first visitors, a small group of hikers making their way through the Weasel and Owl valleys across the Cumberland Peninsula to the east coast. We chatted for a while and discussed each other's plans. A great bunch of people, very interested to know how Martin and I got on. Judging by the food they left, I think they felt sorry for us.

It was midday before we knew it, still very overcast and raining. We decided to ferry gear to our final camp. It did turn out to be a great spot on a flat part of the glacier under North Peak as we had hoped, just a shame it had clagged right in unable to see much of the mountain.

By the time another day had concluded, the barometer had nudged up another 5mb to 980mb. Perhaps the weather was going to improve!

Wednesday, 4—Barometer reading 985mb. Another wet night (outside that is) but by 07.30, the sun was trying to show its face. Beans with bubble and squeak sorted us out, followed by grabbing everything out of the tent to dry. It was also an opportunity to have a good wash under a small meltwater waterfall, one or two degrees above freezing. The remainder of day was spent in chill mode, preparing ourselves for what we hoped was a turn for reasonable weather and start of the difficult stuff.

Thursday, 5—Barometer reading 990mb. The sky looked like a lot of wet blankets and it had been raining on and off all night. We had used more fuel than expected up to this point, so after breakfast I decided to make a quick, light weight run down to Thor to fetch some fuel for our depleting stock at base.

We had cached extra fuel at Thor for our journey back to 'Pang'. I left 'Thor' with the fuel around midday, the stream had grown even deeper and in full flow, which made the crossing gnarly. By the time I got back to base camp it was in blazing sunshine.

It was tempting to head straight off to our advance camp, but decided to sort a climbing rack[37], double check the rest of the equipment and discuss route plans in readiness for the next day.

Our primary choice was the East Pillar Route on North Peak, first climbed by Doug Scott's team in 1972. It is 1200m in length, graded VI, 5.10 and climbed by the team in a thirty eight hour continuous push.

As we got our heads down for the night, clouds were gathering once again. The barometer reading was up to 1000mb, fingers crossed it wasn't going to rain.

Friday, 6—Up for 05.45, quick breakfast and away by 07.00. We were at our glacier camp in good time with Asgard looking both awesome and intimidating. If we were slick, we estimated we had just about enough time to get up the route.

Heading down the Kings Parade Glacier, it wasn't too obvious where the route started. It was nearly thirty years since the Scott team had climbed it and likely the start had completely changed due to the glacier receding. After a lot of hesitation, a commitment was made.

The first couple of pitches went ok, but blanked out. A move to another crack system ended much the same way. Our plans were always to 'free climb' a route not using 'aid' to gain height, where we were now, was not going to be freed…by us anyway!

Our hauling technique was proving to be a heavy burden too. Failure on this route looked inevitable in the time we had left.

It was a big blow to our morale as we trudged up the steep icy slope back to camp. We discussed our backup plan over supper, which was for an ascent up the 'Original Route' first climbed in 1953 with a grade of VI, 5.8/5.9 A.1.

There was possibly enough time to succeed on the route, with the bonus of hopefully avoiding the use of 'Aid' on the A1 pitch.

Saturday, 7—Out of our pits for 04.00, gutted to see it was raining. No choice but to wait and see what happens. By 10.30, it was brightening up, a gut feel told us this was a window of opportunity. By 12.00, we had geared up, fed ourselves and were away.

A short walk off the glacier led us to a rock-band. We soloed several rope lengths until it got steeper, then roped up and alternated rock shoes with boots and crampons with frustrating regularity.

---

[37] A climbing rack is a term given to a mixture of mechanical devices that are placed into natural features of a rock route to protect a fall. They are either organised on the harness or on a bandolier over the shoulder.

We made it to the crux corner after six hours, the wet pitch usually aided at A1, Martin led through the pitch skilfully, cleanly and without aid to a ledge system. It was now 20.00.

For the next 600ft, we took alternate leads on perfect granite, climbing corners, slabs, chimneys and laybacks. There was no sun and the rock was wet in places, but it looked like we were going to bag it! We summited at midnight, just as the Arctic sun was caressing the horizon. The weather was closing in, we gave ourselves a few minutes to soak up the atmosphere then promptly got our arses off as swiftly as possible.

What had been wet or damp rock on our ascent was now verglas rock[38] on the descent.

Cold was getting in to our cores, rock shoes were wet, feet and hands were freezing, but our decision not to climb with bivvy gear meant the will to succeed was evermore mindful. Another fear factor to add to the mix was the daunting prospect of getting our abseil rope stuck and having to re-ascend it. Luckily, we got away with it.

Pitch after pitch of abseils, often through tricky ground, eventually saw us back at camp around 06.00 on Sunday, elated after eighteen hours of continuous climbing, but completely shagged. We had a quick couple of brews before bed for a few hours. I awoke around 09.00 to the sound of rain on the tent, our weather window could not have been any tighter!

It was easy just to doss, especially as it was peeing down, but the need to get going was priority. We were already into our fourteenth of nineteen days leave and it was to take three days to get back to Pangnirtung. Determined not double leg our packs out to Pang, we packed everything that had taken two carries to this point, into one monster.

There was nearly as much strapped to the outside as there was inside, the packs weighed around 80lbs. It was going to be hard graft for sure.

By 15.00, we were back at Summit Lake, feeling completely spent. It was as much as we could do, to fully hydrate and eat, before collapsing in to our pits.

Monday, 9>Wednesday, 11—I was still in bed listening to the rain after laying fourteen hours horizontal. Martin was in the process of making tea and breakfast, which naturally, I took full advantage of and had it in bed. "Must tell this to Carole," I wrote in my diary.

---

[38] Verglas is a French term for a thin coating of ice or frozen rain on an exposed surface.

Every bit of clothing seemed to stink, sleeping bag honked. I realised I needed a good wash, even though it was bloody freezing outside.

At least another 10 to 15lbs was added to the sacks, but we were still determined not to do two legs, at least it was mostly downhill. The large river crossing was still in full-spate, extreme care needed not to topple over with the monsters on our back. At least it wasn't necessary to strip off, I didn't give a toss what got soaked, including my boots. We got down further than Thor camp before putting the tent up on glacial flats and collapsing for the night.

The next objective was back to, or beyond Windy Lake. Several more stream crossings had sprung up with all the rain and glacier melt. They were an inconvenience but easy enough to tackle.

Yet again we were all in by the time the tent went up. Mozzies in their thousands were there to greet us which was a bugger, as the sun came out the scenery was amazing.

We made our final exhaustive haul to Overlord, by 13.00, feet and legs sodden due to more stream crossings. We cared not, it had been the best Mountaineering experience ever.

We radioed our outfitter for the pickup and before long it was back to Pang and a coffee.

I couldn't help but feel we deserved to be spoilt for one night and found a B and B with an Inuit family in town. A friendly, laid-back family who offered us Caribou stew. I had Martin's share, him being a veggie, it was fantastic.

We were fascinated by the diverse way of life in the family. On one hand the children were playing with all the electronic gizmos of western culture, whilst grandfather was sitting cross legged on the stone kitchen floor, tucking into raw seal meat he carved off the carcass.

Thursday, 12—After a very comfortable night, we were amazed at their kindness and hospitality. They also entrusted us to lock the house when we had finished breakfast as they were off hunting Caribou, Beluga and Seal for the day at their summer hut round the bay, amazing!

The rest of day gave us chance to have a good look around the Inuit culture and way of life. We also found out that, while away climbing, a Polar bear had been spotted on the outskirts of town and needed persuading to go elsewhere. Interestingly, the pack-ice could easily be seen off-shore in the Cumberland sound, the likely home of many more bears.

We arranged flights for the next day back to Iqaluit and Ottawa, and booked a night at Pang's campsite at the very edge of town, hoping the bear had well and truly buggered off.

Friday, 13>Sunday, 15—Our flight left Pang at 11.45 for Iqaluit, then eventually onward to Ottawa by late afternoon. After a night's kip in a corner of Ottawa airport, we devoured numerous coffees and fresh bagels, before boarding our plane back to Boston.

Saturday was spent in part, negotiating Boston airport, which always seemed chaotic. One favoured eating spot was the 'Salty Dog' on Boston seafront, serving excellent seafood, thoroughly recommended.

One only other point of note before concluding was our night's stay in Boston Airport. We had gone back through security to pick up our bags, stashed in left lockers. There seemed to be a particularly quiet spot to doss behind some stacked seats.

At around 06.00, I was nudged by a fretting security guard who couldn't believe we had evaded their scrutiny all night! I did try to be jovial, by suggesting there was a lot to learn about us Brits, but maybe it was a bit early in the morning to expect a smile back!

We walked a bit, drank coffee a bit, before arriving back home to the UK to our wonderful families. It had been an amazing adventure.

22 December—Covid 19 Update

Just when we thought it couldn't get worse! Along came a mutant that changed everything.

Our scientists (best in the world) discovered it and it has become particularly virulent in London and the South East. A new level of restriction has consequently been added to the Tiers, to try and stabilise the rising number of cases. Those areas are now in Tier 4, almost, but not quite equivalent to a lockdown.

The R value has gone up above 1 once more (1.2>1.5). There is serious and growing concern that other areas will follow shortly.

Our five day Christmas hiatus has been cancelled, only Christmas day is the new rule for three different households to gather and enjoy Christmas.

Europe has become extremely concerned, so much so, that the Port of Dover has been quarantined. France will not allow any form of transport (Lorries, cars, or trains) to enter France for forty-eight hours at least. It looks likely that all lorry drivers will have to undergo a Covid test and prove negative before sanctions are lifted. Up to three thousand lorries are 'stacked' on the M20 and Manton airfield in Kent. There are also numerous lorry parks in use, as is the inevitable illegal parking pissing many residents off.

Up to forty countries are now refusing entry to UK citizens by road, rail and air.

Latest at 23 December—Over 70,000 Covid 19 deaths have now been recorded in the UK.

France have agreed an end to the sanctions with our Government. All drivers must submit a negative test result before being allowed to enter France.

Other areas in the South of the UK, including Oxfordshire, will move into Tier 4 at midnight on Boxing day.

Chapter Nineteen
Cutting it Loose on the Moose's Tooth, Alaska

A yearning to go back to Alaska had been on both Martin's and my minds, following the successful expedition to Baffin Island. Nearly three years had passed since then, but it had not been without further fun and mini adventures:

Lynne and I had moved house to Mayfield Avenue, Grove, in 2000. We did it on our own over the course of a weekend, with the aid of a van from work and Lynne's mate, Maureen. A slightly larger detached house and thankfully, our last move. Where are the kids when you need them!

Martin and I had a trip to the Isle of Wight and climbed a fantastic adventurous route on a chalk ridge of 'The Needles' called Skeleton Ridge. A fuller report to follow later.

Two winter ice climbing trips were made to the French and Italian Alps.

A fiftieth birthday party had been arranged for me in 2001, between Lynne, Carole and Martin at 'The Old Dungeon Ghyll' hotel in Langdale. It happened to coincide with the outbreak of 'Foot and Mouth' disease that hit the UK. Farms and most upland areas of the country were out-of-bounds to walkers and climbers, it also affected trading severely for hotels like 'The Old'.

Martin had negotiated a deal with Neil Walmsley (landlord of the Old) on Lynne's behalf. It enabled friends and family to have the privilege of their own bar, with rooms for the night and Sunday morning breakfast thrown in, at a much-reduced rate.

It was a magnificent night, accompanied by Neil's Ceilidh that produced music for the night. The event also attracted three news reporters who had been travelling the area, reporting on the Foot and Mouth outbreak. They were quick to spot a good night when they spied one and indulged for the rest of the evening.

One of them was useful on the guitar and happily joined the Ceilidh. The gathering also made the local 'Westmorland Gazette' newspaper later in the week. Our three friendly guests reporting that, "much fun could still be had in the doom and gloom of Foot and Mouth."

There were some heavy hungover bodies by Sunday morning. However, Martin and I had been coy with our drinking, having already planned to sneak out the door before most were up, and head to Scotland for some winter climbing.

Lynne and Carole also cycled the coast to coast route from St Bees in Cumbria to Whitby in North Yorkshire, during the Foot and Mouth outbreak. They too, received wonderful hospitality wherever they stopped on-route.

1 May 2002: And So, to Alaska

A delay at Gatwick had more implications than we realised. It was compounded by absolute chaos and further delays at Houston immigration, resulting in a rescheduled flight to Seattle and Anchorage. Eventually, baggage and climbing gear was loaded straight through to Anchorage, whilst Martin and I transferred at Seattle without it.

At Anchorage, most of the baggage arrived safe and sound, but inevitably one piece was missing. I never cease to be amazed how often 'one piece' out of many goes astray. It was 02.00 and with twenty-eight hours of travelling behind us, it needed to wait until later in the morning for a fight to retrieve it.

Eventually, after a great breakfast downtown at 'Gwennies', followed by a couple of hours basecamp shopping, we retrieved the bag and boarded a shuttle bus to Talkeetna.

The atmosphere of an expedition is immediate when setting foot in a town like Talkeetna, a town in the heart of the Alaskan wilderness, surrounded by mountains. The smell of pristine air, the sheer ambience of the place, the scurrying of exited and ambitious climbers and the devoted work of the Air Taxi ground crews, brings it fully home.

A few new buildings had sprung up at Talkeetna Air Taxi (TAT) since 1993 as we arrived early evening. Their bunkhouse accommodation was certainly an improvement, it wasn't long before we got our heads down on a comfortable pillow.

It had been a lazy start the following morning, getting our gear aboard TAT. We were on the Ruth Glacier amidst more snow than I had seen in my life. I started slowly, helping Martin dig out the mandatory snow-pit for our tents, still feeling squeamish after filling a sick bag in the plane on route.

It is punishing work digging the pits, but has two distinct advantages. It keeps you warm in temperatures of around -15degC, and secondly it sure pays dividends in giving the tents a sound base over long periods in the snow.

Waiting for the sun to appear and hit the tent in the mornings played a key part of our drive and ambition. We still had big hearts and huge enthusiasm, but were no longer spring chickens trying to deliver the goods in a fridge or rather a freezer between -15degC>-25degC.

Our primary route in mind was the Southwest Ridge of Peak 11,300ft situated on the West Fork of the Ruth Gorge, first climbed in 1968 by Heinz Allemann and Niklaus Lotscher. American alpinist, Steve House raved about this route in an article, which had inspired Martin and myself to tackle it.

A recce to the foot of the route that day, took longer than planned, about three hours, due to the 3 to 4ft of snow that had fallen over the previous week. Snowshoes were our preferred choice and worked ok, although skis would have undoubtedly made it easier.

The following day was spent at base, dossing, drinking, eating and packing for an attempt the next day. The position of our base camp was very convenient for receiving weather updates from Paul and other pilots bringing tourists onto the glacier for short day visits. Our latest forecast was for low pressure coming in that very night, *surely it can't snow anymore* were my thoughts.

As the wind picked up slightly and snowflakes started to fall, I could not help but be transfixed by the most glorious single snow crystals, settling on my duvet jacket.

We were up with the sun, brew and breakfast had been scoffed, we were on our way with 60lb packs. I'm sure I remembered saying "I wouldn't do this again." It was sheer purgatory in thigh deep snow for the last third of the journey to the ridge. The spectacle of Mt Huntingdon's North Face was awesome as we passed it.

It was difficult to distinguish crevasse slots with the huge dump of snow and took a bit of navigating. It was then down to another digging session to get the bivvy tent into position. Finally, there was only one thing for it in those situations…

"Let's get a brew on, mate."

The weather was looking ominous again, frustratingly, whilst the ridge looked impressive, its flanks looked absolutely loaded.

Morning came, I needed to get a brew on, having been laid horizontal for fourteen hours. The weather had turned grim once again, putting another 2 to 3 inches of snow down. Visibility was extremely poor, crevasse slots that had been barely visible on our approach, had now disappeared.

Our prints from the day before had sunk and been covered, but were just visible. It was time to retreat back to base and seriously reconsider our options.

After tough going for four hours, barely making out our previous tracks, we arrived back at base camp.

Keeping occupied for thirty-six hours in our tent whilst waiting for the snow storm to give way, is always a test of physical and mental agility. Constant brews, eating and reading helped. Two American teams were the only other climbers at base.

John Sykes and his mate seemed friendly characters and helped break up the time with convivial conversations. Another small team were being guided by Jack Roberts, but due to different objectives and comings and goings, we seldom met up with Jack.

There was one occasion however, when we did, and it proved to be very fortuitous. Martin and I always try to have a 'plan B' for a trip, on that occasion it was the Ham and Eggs Couloir[39] on the south face of the Moose's Tooth in the Ruth Gorge. John and Jack, who knew the mountains and routes far better than we did, thought the couloir could be a good option, given the conditions. All we had to do was get there.

Martin and I have always climbed with the single push, light alpine style of climbing, which is pretty much the given style of climbing these days. It is a bold style and 'necky', but does give a greater chance of success in small weather windows. It also fits with our limited time off work, a continual frustration. The

---

[39] Ham and Eggs couloir is an ultra-classic of the Alaska Range. The route is graded moderate by Alaskan standards, V, 5.9, A1, 4, but gives a big Alpine feel. First climbed by Jon Krakauer, Thomas Davies and Nate Zinsser in 1975. Oddly it took another twenty years to have a 2nd ascent in the late 1990s. Views from the summit are truly awe-inspiring. It acquired its name so say, when the team had climbed continuously for twenty hours. Krakauer wrote in his diary, "if we had some ham, we could have some ham and eggs, if we had some eggs."

same light weight alpine style was undertaken on the first ascent, a very bold approach in 1975.

The approach was the first hurdle from our base on the west fork. The guide book describes it thus:

A long haul to the Ruth Gorge would take 3>4 hours. From there, an estimated 3>7 hours would be required to negotiate an icefall and upper glacier to get to the Root Canal glacier camp. The route itself would take anywhere between 8>16 hours of ascent, giving a total elevation gain from the Ruth gorge camp of 5,400ft.

Then of course, it is 4>8 hours of descent off the route, with probably the same lengths of time back to base as it took to get there.

These days, it is common to be dropped off on the Root Canal Glacier airstrip directly under the route. The airstrip was negotiated by our pilot, Paul Roderick, from TAT in the early 1990s, but renders the approach less of a commitment and test of one's Alaskan alpine skills.

Keen to get going, we ploughed through more falling snow and onto the Ruth Glacier. The icefall was obvious to locate, but plastered deep in snow. A maze of partially sunken crevasses identified the larger ones, but numerous smaller ones were hidden and gave us cause for concern.

The weather closed in further as we started up the icefall. A hidden gully was our objective half way up the icefall, we located it just as it was becoming perilously close to a white-out.

Our decision was unanimous, we stashed our gear and erected the bivvy tent for the night, then waited to see what occurred the next morning.

Another dump of snow had fallen overnight, making our tracks through the icefall below barely visible. We decided not to press on upwards under the conditions. Instead, it seemed to make more sense to leave our gear at the icefall, using the time to go back to base for a restock of food and fuel in anticipation of a prolonged siege.

It was a fretful, time-consuming period, finding a safe way off the icefall down to the glacier; with snow falling heavier, it was obvious time was going against us. Constant decision making, led us to choose 'the devil we knew' particularly while our tracks could be seen. We also didn't want to be caught out between a tent at base and a bivvy tent on the icefall. Sense prevailed, it was back up the icefall to the bivvy site while we could.

As we hunkered down, there were the roar of avalanches everywhere. Strangely we hadn't got depressed or pissed off with little technical climbing thus far. I think the focus of correct decision making, absorbing the experience and above all, survival, took our minds off that.

I had been very grateful of the snow goggles Nicky had loaned me just before leaving. They helped tremendously identifying our passage through vague footprints and covered slots in the icefall.

A cold night (-25degC) had Martin and I sharing my Thermarest somehow. His decision not to bring his from base camp and rely on just a foam mat was brave, but useless in those temperatures. I found myself waking constantly, more off it than on, probably subconsciously avoiding his snoring and farting, in fairness, we were both beginning to stink by then anyhow.

A bloody cold dawn brought clearing skies. But with it came frustration, as we still needed to return to basecamp for resupplies and Martin's thermarest.

Even though we had lighter sacks, it still took nearly four hours plodding through deep snow to get back to base. Endless brews and fully fuelled with some quality Army rations, courtesy of Gary, we hit the sack knackered.

Morning dawned bright and clear, teasing us again no doubt!

We woke to the sound of an early aircraft depositing visitors onto the glacier and became the centre of attention. It must have been a strange sight for them to see just the top of our tent and our heads in our dugout home. By late afternoon, we set off once more back to our bivvy site and arrived around 21.00.

Too cold and knackered to do anything than get into our pits. A lot of effort had gone into the trip so far, and it was beginning to tell.

Another morning dawned clear but bitter, with a strong northerly wind. We were away quickly, heading upwards again at last, pleasantly surprised to be soloing several pitch lengths up the gully on fantastic neve. Steeper, less secure ground involved roping up, until eventually breaking out on top of the icefall.

A further hour's plod got us to the upper glacier camp. It was an awesome place to pitch a tent, under our intended line splitting the south face, to a col below the summit of the Moose's Tooth.

Two other teams were at base camp, Russian and US. We spoke briefly with the US team who were planning to climb the same route. Their intention was to lead off the following morning, as was ours.

Courtesy often gets lost climbing in mountains, but being British, we made it clear we would give them a good head-start before we set off.

It took little time to pack a light sack before getting our heads down. We had done it so often, it could probably be repeated with eyes closed, bivvy bag, down jacket, nutrition bars and water, no sleeping bag keep as light as possible for an expected round trip of 15>20 hours.

We were up for 05.00; the weather was on our side but there was no movement in the Yanks quarters. They must have heard us getting a brew on, as the next thing we heard was all manner of clamour.

We were true to our word, as frustrating as it was, but let them get a good start on us.

I led the interesting first couple of pitches on rock that went at about Severe (UK rock grade) with big boots and crampons. Martin led through on the next pitch of good steep ice and cruised the subsequent couple of pitches. By now, we were had caught up with the Yanks, it was time for gentlemanly conduct to politely end!

Martin led pitch seven, a steep, 90deg ice wall, in very good condition, an absolute joy to climb, at last feeling we were 'feeding that infamous rat'. I was quietly thinking my rat had been fed on one or two occasions already. I led through and found the same quality climbing on pitch nine.

We were climbing well on alternate leads, occasionally making use of old in-situ pegs and tat at belay stances, but avoided the use of 'aid' throughout.

Pitches eleven through to seventeen through a long narrow couloir often produced excellent, tricky climbing on thin, vertical sections of ice and mixed ground.

My calves were by now screaming for a break, the previous day's efforts were catching up with me. I seem to constantly remind my buddy I'm not as young as him, but it always has little influence.

A short rest helped a little and it seemed there was only a few pitches to the top of the route.

The ground levelled off with a couple to go, before long we had made it to the col, an absolute brilliant line with an amazing panoramic view. Surrounding peaks of Denali, Huntingdon and Mount Barrill, together with extensive views of peaks along the Ruth Gorge, blew my mind.

We rapped the twenty odd pitches back to base, always under nervous tension, hopeful the ropes would pull through each time, always with a mutter to each other "it's never over 'til the fat lady sings." Perhaps it was the praying rather than the muttering, that enabled us to get away with it and be back at our camp by 21.00.

It had taken fourteen hours round trip and we were chuffed with ourselves, especially being old gits the wrong side of fifty (well, me anyway). The two Russians, who we hadn't seen before we left, were also mightily impressed. They had watched our progress and success throughout and commented on the speed of our round trip.

It was a restless night, due in part to my body aching everywhere, but also part hunger and dehydration, part exhaustion, but mostly due to the bugger next to me, snoring his block off.

We were obviously not in any hurry to get up, but wisdom jerked us into getting back down the icefall while the weather held. More rappels and down-climbing the hidden gully led onto the icefall.

Grateful our tracks were still reasonably distinguishable, we staggered onto the Ruth glacier once more. It was enough for another day, so without further ado, the tent went up, a brew and supper went on. We were exuberant bunnies.

The following morning was windy but less cold; remaining dregs of our porridge were scoffed, then we were away with the monster packs for the last time. A few paces outside our tent I came across two dead Snow Buntings laying in the snow. I guessed they were part of a flock driven up the glacier by the strong wind, it then must have got all too much for them, poor things!

Arriving at our base tent, we were chuffed to see that Jack and his clients had welcomed us back with some makeshift bunting. They had flown out of the gorge but left numerous modified marker wands[40] around our camp. 'God save the Queen', 'well done boys', 'ham and eggs for dinner tonight', etc, etc, were flapping in the wind. A brilliant touch, which made us feel even more exhilarated with our achievement.

May 16 2002, it was G's birthday and my thoughts were with him, I wished him a great day, although I had no idea which part of Africa he was serving in.

Eventually, Paul from TAT was able to fly us off the glacier camp and back to Talkeetna. He did us proud by flying close to our route, enabling us to capture a great shot of the route from the air.

---

[40] Marker wands are tall thin sticks with florescent flags on the top, for identifying a safe means of passage when weather has closed in and visibility poor. Typically, they would be strategically placed in the snow at specific distances becoming a God-send, when whiteouts have blended the horizon with the ground.

Back in Talkeetna it seemed very quiet, particularly as conditions were improving and stable high pressure was building. We took full advantage of the 'West Rib' bar, keeping well-oiled with many of their namesake beers. Food in the 'Road House' especially their breakfasts, were to die for, and we took full advantage.

Inevitably it was time to head home to adorable and understanding families after three weeks of a fabulous expedition in a truly magic part of the world.

Tribute to Jack Roberts (29 May 1952—15 January 2012)

Martin and I knew Jack for a very short time, but he instantly came across as a genuine friendly guy. A truly nice person interested in other people's interests and achievements, reflected in his welcoming reception for us at base camp.

He was obviously a very capable Alpinist, Mountaineer and climbing Guide. It was extremely sad to read of his death in 2012.

20 January 2021—Covid 19 Update

Tier 4 restrictions were not enough to prevent an escalation in the spread of the new UK strain of virus. A 3rd lockdown came into force in England on the 5 January 2021 and unlikely to be relaxed until at least mid-February.

The new strain is >50% more transmissible than the original, consequently the number of cases and deaths have risen dramatically.

To date;

Current registered cases in the UK are 3.5 million, over 39,000 of which are in hospital.

Current number of Covid related deaths has exceeded 93,000 (1,800+ of which were recorded in the latest twenty-for hour period).

Two vaccines have been clinically approved for use in the UK so far, Pfizer-BioNTech and Oxford-AstraZeneca with over 4.6 million people vaccinated.

A third vaccine has also been approved, Moderna, but this is still in production and unavailable.

Lynne received her first jab on Friday, 15 January as a key worker at Grove Pharmacy.

Chapter Twenty
The Old Man of Hoy

It's a little tongue in cheek to include this chapter under the title of 'expeditions', but it sure felt I'd been on one each time I got back home. I had visited the Old Man twice, once in 2005 with Martin and again in 2011 with Chris Brockbank and Maureen O'Connor. Chris is a good climber and friend I met at a climbing wall after my retirement from Biomet.

He worked as a Project leader for a Rehabilitation centre and our trip was a sponsored climb to raise a bit of cash for the Rehab. Maureen (Moby) was a work colleague, good friend and climber who came along on that occasion as team photographer.

Hoy is the second largest island in the Orkneys and boasts perhaps the highest sea cliff in the British Isles at 1135ft (346m). St John's Head. Viewed from the ferry or south from the cliffs near the Old Man, it is a truly awesome site. A few lines have been climbed on the face, all in the 'Extreme' grade.

The 'Original Route' back in 1969 was climbed by Ed. Ward-Drummond and four climbing partners after several days siege. In 1970, Drummond climbed another route with his partner O. Hill, an even more outrageous line, and named it 'Longhope Route' in memory of the local lifeboat that was lost at sea, along with all eight crew members.

The Old Man of Hoy sea stack is equally as impressive. It towers 443ft (135m) as an immense column of Orcadian Sandstone rising out of the sea, whilst firmly fixed to a plinth of granite. It was formerly an arch attached to the mainland until everything except the stack collapsed into the North Atlantic. It is a climbers 'super tick', made famous in 1966 by the BBC's first live outside broadcast featuring many well-known British climbers.

Leaving the south of England with a thousand miles round trip ahead of you, two sea crossings and the potential of a 6 mile hike before even seeing the stack, does makes you think twice.

In 2005 (another eventful year), I headed north and met up with Martin in the lakes. Barely stopping to draw breath, we continued the journey, eventually stopping north of Aviemore in the Highlands for the night and customary bivvy. In 2011, our bivvy site was on the sands of Dornoch beach, sited on the mouth of the Dornoch Firth, a fine doss, especially as it was preceded by the local fish and chips.

From Aviemore, Martin and I continued north on the A9 coast road to the historical town of Thurso, the northernmost town on the British mainland in the county of Caithness. A touch further was the port of Scrabster and our ferry across Stromness on the Isle of Hoy, however, that was going to have to wait for the first ferry the following morning.

After getting our heads down, we headed in the morning to get tickets and sort out our gear. The waiting room was pretty much strewn with our climbing and camping gear, as we chose what to leave behind us in the car. Soon enough, we were boarding the ferry and heading out to the Pentland Firth.

I was particularly dreading the crossing with my feeble stomach, having read many tales of the Firth's boisterous seas. Conflicting currents run between the North Atlantic and the North Sea, making the relatively short hop to mainland Orkney reasonably treacherous at times.

I was lucky on both occasions as the sea was kind to me. We sailed close to the west of Hoy first passing Rora head, then 'The Old Man' and the intimidating St John's Head, a third of it shrouded in brooding cloud.

Stromness is the second most populated town on the mainland, after Kirkwall to the east, the principal town of the isles. Little time was spent in the town on our inbound journey as we were keen to get across to Hoy. A small fishing vessel doubled up as a ferry and before very long we were crossing the western fringes of Scapa Flow to the island.

Landing at the tiny jetty with only a couple of others passengers brought home the isolation of place for me; it had been a tremendous experience even to that point. Without further ado, we set off like laden donkeys with big sacks and carrier bags of food in each hand.

In 2011, we had the sense to organise one of the few taxis on the island to meet us at the jetty, but Martin and I always liked to do it the hard way!

Fortunately, we were in luck when a kind local offered us a lift to our destination, the Bothy at Rackwick bay on the rugged west side of the island.

The Bothy is basic but roomy for Scottish bothy standards and has a hearth for a fire, benches and a large table to sit at. Best of all, it's free. It was a great place to stay for a few nights on both occasions.

We met a local volunteer warden during both stays, and I would like to take this opportunity to thank him for the fantastic job of keeping the place habitable, particularly when it could be so easily abused.

To anyone staying there: please make sure you leave it clean and leave no trace.

As for Rackwick bay, it's a wonderful location and must have one of the most picturesque boulder beaches in the world. Sandstone boulders of all sizes and colours, have been deposited on the beach over the millennia. Each one has been weathered and wave washed, rounded by the tides, enhancing colourful symmetrical rings hidden beneath their surfaces, as if exposing annals of their life.

We quickly made ourselves at home in the bothy, eager to take a recce of the stack while the weather was not on our side for climbing. A diagonal track leads up leftwards from the beach, then onwards up the hill for around forty-five minutes. The first sight of the Old Man was seeing his flat top protruding beyond the summit of the hill.

Without perspective, it was yet to inspire. It's not until progress is made from that point, where every step forward exposes a little more of his height, that the picture begins to unfold.

Finally, when stood at the edge of the cliff, you're sure to be guaranteed one of the most awesome spectacles in the UK. It's hard to describe it as anything other than 'fucking gobsmacking'.

Once over the initial excitement, my heart started to sink slowly into the pit of my stomach at the thought of climbing the bloody thing. I think Martin was feeling the same, well I hoped he was, maybe he was just being coy! I remember Chris B having a similar reaction to me in 2011!

We took a good look at our intended line, being the Original route on the east face (graded HVS/E1) which conveniently faces the landward side of the stack. We were pleased to see an in-situ abseil rope in place between the 1st and 2nd pitch, but not so pleased to see an abundance of fulmars lining the route. These seabirds are famous for their defence of chicks and nests, by puking with unnerving accuracy at any dirt bag climber heading near them.

With a little anxiety, we returned to the bothy, to form a plan and hope the weather would play ball. A few old logs had been left by the hearth, the temptation to light a fire was too great, especially as supper and a glass of wine was almost ready to accompany it.

A quick glance at the local weather forecast was indicating a short window of improvement for the following afternoon. We sat beside the burning logs, fingers crossed, before tucking into a well-deserved bowl of soup, with the roar of the waves crashing on those age-old boulders. Could life get any better?

Morning came with little sign of improving weather, it was spitting with rain and clag shrouded the top of the hill. I spent a good hour or more on the beach taking picture after picture of the magnificent boulders. Suddenly, right on cue, it got brighter. Loitering suddenly turned to scurrying back to the bothy, wasting little time as we grabbed already packed sacks and made for the hill.

Luck was on our side, the weather was improving all the time as we headed up the hill, then down the cliff to the foot of the stack via a vague track. As a further bonus, it looked as though we had the place to ourselves.

A touch of nerves to start with was allayed by confidence in our ability once on the move. Martin led the easy first pitch of about 65ft up the initial shattered pillar, to a comfortable stance. It was pleasing to see (as previously mentioned) the in-situ abseil rope in place from the top of pitch 2 down to the stance we were on.

This is needed to ensure a safe line of retreat to the stance, instead of dangling helplessly on the end of a rope in free-space unable to swing into the face or back across to the stance. However, I wasn't totally convinced of our safe return, as the sheath of the Kernmantle rope was stripped completely off in places, revealing the guts of the bare nylon core exposed…*and not entirely intact.*

The 2nd pitch starts with a slanting, downward traverse leading to the base of a hand crack and the start of the crux pitch. Not one for loving hand jams (or experiencing many), I overcame the first small crack and overhang onto a small ledge. From there, a wider crack, too wide to hand jam but not wide enough to bury myself in, was tougher.

Fortunately, with the advent of 'cams' for protection, the climbing was less serious than it must have been on the first ascent. I do admit to clipping an old wooden wedge (original ascent), though only for protection, buried deep in the crack under the large roof. The exposure up the crack and round the roof at that point was full-on. With the combination of challenges that are thrown at you as you battle up the 100ft pitch, it ranks as one of the finest pitches I've done.

In 2011, I suggested to Chris he should lead the awesome 2nd pitch, as I had already led it in 2005. Standing on the stance of the first pitch, I became aware that time had moved on a wee bit and things had gone very quiet on the 2-way radios, (a bonus in communications over the first trip with Martin).

His words will live in my memory forever, as in reply to my asking, "how's it going, mate?" it was simply: "I'm fucking shitting myself." I had to admit to more than a chuckle, as I knew exactly where he was, it was further immortalised because Chris rarely swore!

I knew he was more than capable, but it really went to show the nature of the pitch. Imposing, awkward moves with full exposure, accentuated by the crashing of waves below and made even worse by the nature of the soft sandstone that gives ball-bearing like texture for both feet and hands.

The following 210ft or more gave easier, but nevertheless interesting climbing on ledges, corners and chimneys, until leading to the base of the sensational, vertical and final 65ft corner crack. It was delightful climbing on excellent rough sandstone, with bridging and big jugs for holds, a truly fitting finale that led to the small, soft grassy summit on the UK's most inaccessible summit.

I swear I felt the stack sway, but it was probably me and a wobbly head. Although, in a full-on Scottish storm it surely must!? One thing is for sure…it's not going to be standing for much longer, particularly in our changing climate, so get on up there while you can!

Rapping (rappelling) multi-pitch routes always leaves me with the unnerving feeling of ropes getting jammed, no matter how careful we are. The potential on the Old Man is quite high, but we got away with it…twice!

The battered and slashed in-situ rope held up okay however, it did prompt me to take a spare rope back in 2011, in case the one in place then needed changing.

The Pentland Firth gave my wimpy stomach something to think about on our return to the mainland in 2011. That soon got forgotten on the long journey home, as we reminded ourselves of the route and the adventure continuously back to Oxfordshire.

It was also a privilege to help Chris with his sponsorship for Gloucester House.

A truly marvellous adventure and super addition to any climbers CV. On both occasions, we climbed the Original line, but there are four other quality routes higher in grades that are waiting for those who have the skill to test themselves.

Meanwhile, life was not all about expeditions, that's for sure. I mentioned earlier that 2005 was another eventful year, in fact, 2004–2006 was certainly a busy time for us all.

Nicky was finding her feet with Triathlons, ultimately dedicated to some serious training and producing some very good times. She was to compete in a dozen or more tri's during the period, ranging from Helvellyn in Cumbria to London, Blenheim, Milton Keynes and Eton to name a few. We were supporting whenever we could.

Gary was involved with the military, but also looked towards building his own security business, both taking him abroad for one reason or another. On one occasion, when he had more than five minutes in the UK, we both manage to fit in a few days on the Isle of Arran.

It was a great opportunity to catch up and spend a couple of nights under the stars whilst traversing the A'Chir Ridge. A 3 star route comparable in interest to the Skye Ridge, only slightly subordinate due to its shorter length.

Lynne and I also had a grand few nights under the stars whilst completing the Lairig Ghru mountain pass circuit in the Cairngorms.

For me, it was probably the busiest period for rock and ice climbing that I can remember. Visits to Avon Gorge, Pembroke, Lower Sharpnose, Peak District, Lake District, Baggy Point as well as frequent visits to Wintours Leap, helped raise my game. I was particularly pleased to climb some memorable routes at the E3 grade at most of the venues, even more pleased to get a couple of E4's under my belt.

As for winter, visits to the Cirque du Gavarnie on the French, Spanish border in the Pyrenees, followed by the Lofoton Isles of Norway (more detail later) and La Grave in France certainly helped to improve my winter climbing.

A memorable short visit to 'The Ben' and the CIC hut, enabled Martin and I to tick the classic ice line of Astral Highway on the Orion Face. A brilliant climb graded VI 5.

Chapter Twenty-One
Jebel Toubkal and Moroccan High Atlas

It seemed very weird that we had packed our rucksacks and left behind ice axes and crampons. Strange not to have included a climbing rack of any description, stranger still, we were going somewhere warm, indeed hot, instead of somewhere to freeze our nuts off!

I think it was me (not totally sure) that had suggested to Martin we should take our other halves, Carole and Lynne, for a good trek in the mountains.

Carole and Lynne had already enjoyed trekking in the Dolomites and the Picos De Europa, and they were keen to go elsewhere outside of Europe.

Morocco, Marrakesh and the High Atlas Mountains came out top of the short list to visit.

It was in 2006, at the back end of July that we hatched a plan to spend two weeks visiting Central Morocco, taking in Marrakesh, the Toubkal circuit via Lac d'ifni and, if enough time was left, a visit to the coast at Essaouira.

It was a bit touch-and-go when the time came as to whether we should go or not. Lynne had an important operation in hospital less than a month before we were due to fly. The surgeon advised her to take it easy for a couple of months, he would certainly have given her a bollocking if he knew our plans and the weight of the rucksack she was going to carry. But not one for listening to me or doctors, our plans remained unchanged.

Our flight out of Heathrow landed at Marrakesh via Casablanca, with enough time to find a reasonably priced hotel and try a recommended restaurant overlooking the souks of the renowned Medina. The hum of the square was every bit as we had read about, as were the endless stalls of spices, fruit, figs, dates, jewellery, carpets and just about anything you could name.

Marrakesh has a far greater African feel than Casablanca or Rabat to the north. The air (outside of the medina) is fresher and being Morocco's fourth largest, thriving city, it attracts traders from as far away as the Sahara and the High Atlas.

Like all cities, it has its share unemployment and therefore its share of beggars and informal, rogue guides (known as faux guides) trying to make a bob or two.

The following morning was spent gathering supplies and trying to find gas canisters that fitted our camping stoves we took with us from the UK. After a long, hopeless search for the gas canisters with the correct fitting, we ended up buying matching stoves and canisters, so we could get on our way.

The sacks were monsters, and fair play to the girls, especially Lynne, they were taking more than a fair share.

We had done some homework on what bus would take us to Imlil, a village at the start of the trek at an elevation of 1740m. As we waited at the bus stop, a guy in a large pickup offered us a lift (like they do) to our destination for 200 dirhams (around £13 sterling). After a little haggle, we got him to agree 150 dirhams, and we were on our way, pleased, that the journey would have taken a lot longer by bus.

We needed no excuses for a quick coffee at a local bar, before heading off on foot to the hamlet of Aroumd. Although the hamlet was south of Imlil and thirty minutes in the wrong direction, it happened to have the only campsite in the area. It was in poor shape, leaving little option than to set the tents up in a small, dusty parking area. Close by, a cheerful Berber ran a café doing very little trade, he was more than happy to knock us up a large omelette and veg lasagne for us to share and tuck into.

The next morning, we headed for the trail proper, climbing gently on a rocky north east trail through the village of Tamatert. From there, the path headed east and climbed steeply to the col Tizi n'Tamatert. It was early in the day but already very hot, it went through my mind that shorts and a thin T shirt was a far cry from the gear I would normally be wearing on our adventures.

A battered old wooden and tin shack, known as *Bivvy The*, was selling soft drinks and mint tea; we had already sweated enough and weren't at all ashamed to stop for one. Soon it was onwards, on straight forward but rather rocky ground surrounded by arid landscapes. It was typical of the trail, views only broken from time to time by adjacent valleys, lush terraces and neat Berber houses, on our journey towards the small village of Ouaneskra.

From Ouaneskra, it was around 2.5km to our final stop for the day at Tacheddirt (2300m). Rather than use any of the Gites or CAF Refuges on the circuit, we had planned to use our tents throughout. There was a reasonable site to set up camp just south of Tacheddirt, close to a stream (Irhzer n'Likemt) a reliably good water source.

Even though villagers used the water, we chose to sterilise all water we drank with either Chlorine tablets or our two Katadyn water filtration systems brought with us from the UK.

After a good rest and breakfast, we were keen to move on. According to our notes from the guide book, the next leg was around five hours with 1200m of ascent and 900m of descent. The going was slow and tough as we gained height to Tizi Likemt at 3550m, especially as we gained the last few hundred metres on the mother of all scree slopes.

It had taken a good few hours to the col, with a couple of hours still to go. A rocky descent led through irrigated pastures into the settlements of Azib Likemt at 2650m. This small basic hamlet is occupied during the summer months by Berber people to grow crops and feed cattle, the fertile valley gave a pleasant change from the arid landscape higher up.

We set up camp just to the south of the settlement, once again close to another river called the Assif Tifni.

The next leg of the journey was to the relatively large village of Amsouzert, a journey of between seven to nine hours and 15kms. The well-worn trail took us from the campsite up the mountainside to an amazing gorge formed by Assif n'Tinzer (river). The trail routed itself close to the river for several kilometres passing lush pastures and impressive cliffs, until climbing steeply to the col of Tizi n'Ouarai (3120m). It was bloody hot all the way.

I believe it was at this point I started to feel the effects of the heat. I should have known better, I was drinking lots of water but little else, certainly not replacing the body's essential electrolytes that were being diluted by the plain water and by calories being consumed.

I was aware of the grand vista laid before us but paid little attention to it, more annoyed by the way I felt.

The trail meandered down to the small settlement of Tagadirt. I could have called it a day there with the way I felt. Eventually, we made it to the outskirts of Amsouzert (1740m), it was as much as I could do to rid myself of the rucksack and collapse on the ground of a small courtyard, propped up by a wall.

I craved cans of Coca-Cola or anything fizzy…strange, as I usually hate the stuff. I was so annoyed with myself; I craved fluid and food but couldn't eat a damn thing.

We set up tent close by, I didn't care where, just wanted to crawl inside and lay down. Eventually, Martin and the girls got some soup and sweetened brews on the go. Slowly I came around, but it took a considerable time.

I had never experienced the effects of dehydration and heat exhaustion anything like that before, or to this day, even with all the long distance running and mountaineering over the years. It was certainly a lesson learnt the hard way.

It had been a restless night and I was still feeling somewhat fragile as morning arrived. The guys had looked after me and because of that, I was able to enjoy with them an amble into the village.

In just about every adventure I have done, there has been opportunities to learn something new or reasons to be humble. The Berber people we met were no exception, even though they are only just able to eke out a living to supply little more than their basic daily needs. As we in affluent UK, had just moved into the 21st century, I couldn't help feel these guys were a century or more behind us.

Carole, a teaching assistant in Cumbria, got chatting to an old boy who had a connection to the school in Amsouzert. It was essentially one classroom, with basic equipment. Amongst other things, it obviously had a leaky roof, as half the floor was covered in water.

He didn't mention the water or any other 'nice to haves', just delighted in showing us round and what the children learnt and got up to. The distinct impression I got as we walked through the village, was one of cheerfulness and togetherness, no matter what adversity came their way.

We eventually made a gentle move off on the next leg to Azib lmi n'Ouassif. It was an elevation gain of some 1100m, a distance of 10.5km and was going to take at least six hours.

Firstly, it was an interesting trail to Lac d'Ifni, mostly a 4WD track to start, then a steep rocky trail to the north east side of the Lake. It had taken a good two and a half to three hours as we dropped down to the Lac, before being able to enjoy a break, with a soak of the feet to cool off. It would have been very easy to have enjoyed the break a lot longer, but we needed to move on.

The next part of the trail was a slog across the flat, hot, dry part of Lac d'ifni for around 1km. Then a steep ascent through a rocky gorge, wilting once again in the heat of the afternoon sun. We made it to our next camp area, just above an area known as Azib lmi n'Ouassif. Amongst the large boulders in the gorge, there were many flat, albeit rocky, camp spots. It was just as well there were a good few spots, as we were surprised by the number of other tents already erected (all the same, so assumed a guided party), particularly as we had seen very few other hikers up until then.

The area was at a cross roads of steep gorges, it was likely other groups had come in from different directions, or possibly trekking our circuit the other way. Hastily and not being too fussy, we stuck up our tents, as it was obvious more hikers *and their mules* were coming our way.

As night closed in it was noticeably colder, duvet jackets were on early. It turned out to be a great place to camp, lots of ambience, the sound of small waterfalls and an almost full moon that crept into the gorge.

Next morning, we were away in good time, heading steeply up the rugged, rocky track to a Col and high point of Tizi n'Ouanoums (3600m). It was a strenuous climb and took us around one and a half hours. A chill wind had taken the edge off a hot trek up, but that was soon lost as we headed down the other side on loose, rocky ground. The Toubkal refuge came into view as we left the steep ground behind us, and not long after that we were taking a well-earned breather, slumped against the walls of the refuge.

There was no temptation to stay in the busy refuge at all, instead we set up camp downstream to enjoy a much quieter evening. The plan was to have an early night in readiness for an early start to Toubkal's summit the following day.

The Lac d'Ifni trail with its high passes gave excellent opportunity to acclimatise in readiness for an ascent of Toubkal.

Having left our camp early as planned, we all found the hike up to the summit straightforward and without any altitude symptoms. We passed some hikers who were suffering the effects and almost all were coming up directly up from Imlil, staying one night in the hut, hoping to summit the next day.

Only one patch of old snow was noticeable on our way down off the mountain. However, darkening skies were coming in from the south. It was looking ominous as we hastily packed away our tent and kit in the hope of reaching Imlil by late afternoon.

Just as in any mountainous area, the weather can take a sudden change and change it certainly did. Thunder and lightning had already reached the skies above Toubkal as we scurried hurriedly down the rough path. We entered the

Berber village of Sidi Chamharouch just as the heavens opened, firstly with rain, then hail the size of marbles.

In true Berber style, they made us welcome and ushered us into one of the huts. Within minutes, we were drinking sweet tea, watching hail and water carve torrents through the village muddy street.

The darkening stormy sky made night seem imminent, with hail still pounding the village, we were not going anywhere in a hurry. One friendly Berber insisted we stay the night in his stall of carpets and souvenirs. It wasn't long before he created a space and in no time at all, our sleeping bags and mats were out and we were tucked up for the night.

It was a very comfortable night. We had an early brew, offered a few dirham to our friends for their hospitality, and bade farewell.

We were back at Imlil within a couple of hours, looking for a well-deserved coffee. Then back to Marrakesh where Lynne and I hunted down a reasonably priced hotel for the night, not far from the walls of the Medina. Carole and Martin had sourced alternative accommodation, but we met up again in the evening for a meal and a good long walk around the amazing souks.

With a couple of days left, we all hopped aboard a local bus and mixed it with brightly clad locals along with chickens, goats, fruit and veg bound for the coastal town of Essaouira.

A beach, a beach, my kingdom for a beach! More to the point, a dip in the ocean. It was so bloody nice, I had been thinking about it since our return to Imlil.

Essaouira is the most popular coastal town of Morroco and is known as the 'windy city'. It has a long sandy beach and a relaxed atmosphere, making it the favoured attraction to tourists and locals alike. For many, the reliable wind, also makes it a popular destination for windsurfers.

The old city of the Medina has a historical mix of Portuguese, French and Berber architecture. Within the walls are cafes, artisan stalls and workshops, neatly set up around tranquil squares and narrow lanes.

Lynne and I had left it rather late to find a comfortable room for the night, forgetting it was the height of the tourist season. Within a short walk from the Medina however, we found a hotel with one remaining room. All four of us met up in the evening for a good recce of the 'Old city' and the historical harbour. It was also an opportunity to take full advantage of our hotel's relaxing atmosphere and its licence to sell limited alcohol.

The following day, it was back to Marrakesh and the UK, to end what was yet another tough, but most memorable adventure…oh, and as I so often forgot, BACK TO WORK!

16 February—Covid 19 Update

We are now half way through February and still under lockdown. A review of the current rules will take place on the 22nd by Boris Johnson and his team.

Since the last report on the 20 January, the situation for the NHS and lives of many people took a terrible turn for the worse. Although many people would hurry to bring politics into it, it was due mainly to the significant increase in the transmission rate of the new variant.

The UK has now recorded the following:

The number of new **UK daily Covid cases** *reached a record, 38,905.*

The **daily UK Covid death toll** *reached a record, 1,820.*

Total cases have reached, 4.05M.

Total deaths have reached, 118K+.

The South African variant has been detected in the UK, necessitating specific testing areas being targeted to control the spread.

The UK has published a 'red list' of some 30+ countries that are not allowed entry. Air passengers who have come from, or who have passed through any one of the red listed countries in the previous ten days are not allowed into the UK, unless they are UK citizens or have residence rights. They must then quarantine in a government approved hotel for ten days without exception, and at their own cost.

Two self-tests for Covid 19 must also be carried out during that period. Failure to do so, risks a £10k fine or a possible ten year jail term if deliberate avoidance has been proven. As for passengers flying in from non-red listed countries, UK citizens or otherwise, they must quarantine for 10 days at their residential address specified.

Who would want to put themselves through all this, knowing in addition that we are in a 'lockdown', with nowhere to go for at least another four weeks, beats the crap out of me!

On a positive note, the country has reached its mid-Feb target of 15.5M vaccinations. The ambitious target was to vaccinate everyone over the age of seventy by 14 February.

Chapter Twenty-Two
Christmas in Patagonia

"Bugger," Martin and I said in unison, as we sat bolt upright from our slumber in the tiny cave. Water was pouring down the angled roof, soaking our sleeping bags. Our boots and rucksacks that we had left out to dry were also sodden.

We had been pleased with our progress the day before, in getting to a high point on the slabs beneath our objective, the Central Tower of Paine. The weather had taken a further turn for the worse, with wind speeds picking up from around 30mph to something more like 50mph. The rain was turning horizontal. "Welcome to Patagonia" was what I was going to hear from a variety of sources for the next eight weeks.

It wasn't until I took early retirement from full time employment in 2010 that I could contemplate the dream I had been harbouring for a couple of decades. I had always been inspired and captivated in my youth by famous explorers such as Sir Francis Drake, Ferdinand Magellan, Captain Fitzroy and Charles Darwin on their explorative voyages to Patagonia on HMS Beagle.

The dreaming was further enhanced when I took up mountaineering and came across pictures of the Towers of Paine and The Fitzroy range. Natural wonders like those would have to be visited before old age got its grip on my body!

Fortunately, that interest was shared by three of my friends, and over a two year period of cycling, kayaking and climbing trips, we hatched a plan that formed the origins of a South American adventure. It was a plan that would span two months or more away.

I've always been eternally grateful for Lynne's encouragement and understanding in my climbing activities and of course the costs that are incurred. This trip would add another dimension to that, as it was to be the longest expedition away by far. It would mean being away for Christmas and New Year for the first time in forty years.

The adventure was divided into five phases:

Phase 1—The eastern seaboard of Argentina.

Approximately twelve days of travel by public transport down the eastern seaboard of Argentina. Starting in Buenos Aires and finishing in Puerto Natales. Visits included Puerto Madryn, The Valdes Peninsula, Sarmiento and the Petrified Forest Park.

Phase 2—Suffering the Paine.

Sixteen days to try and climb the Central Tower of Paine in the Torres del Paine National Park.

Phase 3—To trek the Full circuit of the Paine National Park.

Phase 4—Kayaking and travels 'in the spirit of HMS Beagle'.

16 days to kayak the Paine massif watersheds of the *Grey and Serrano* river systems. Then travel by boat through the Magellan Strait and Beagle Channel to visit Navarino Island, Tierra del Fuego and Ushuaia.

Phase 5—The Carretera Austral (route 7).

Twenty days to travel 1000kms along the Austral highway from Punta Arenas to Puerto Montt.

Our team of like-minded radicals consisted of:

Martin—who unlike me, was still in full time employment in the Lake District, but was able to secure three weeks off work to join me to attempt a line on the Central Tower. The Towers are renowned for hostile weather, many teams have waited months at base camp for the weather to be favourable. Our total of sixteen days was always going to be a touch and go challenge.

Maureen (aka Moby)—a work colleague, close friend and capable climber, she was keen to join the team. She would be keen to join in as much of the trekking, kayaking and adventuring as possible.

Michael, brother of Moby who lives in New Zealand is an avid cyclist and kayaker.

The Plan:

Michael, Moby and myself would team up together in phase 1, to explore the natural wildlife along the east coast and the Petrified Forest inland at Sarmiento.

It was likely that Moby and Michael together would try and complete phase 3, while Martin and myself waited out the weather for phase 2.

Irrespective of our success or failure on the Towers for phase 2, Martin would have to return home, leaving the three of us to complete phases 4 and 5.

I have written an in-depth account of the trip, entitled **Chilled Out in Patagonia** *(some 50+ pages), so the following account is only a precis.*

Patagonia and most of Sub Antarctica, Tierra del Fuego and Cape Horn (49deg to 56deg South) have delicate ecosystems, not colonised by modern man. Many areas are completely uninhabited and make up one of the few temperate forest zones left on the planet. They remain virgin due predominately, to their wildness, remoteness and savage weather and are identified as one of the world's 37 most pristine wilderness areas.

However, where it can be touched, one cannot help being overwhelmed by the raw splendour of those lands, mountains, rivers, seas and oceans. They must be seen for oneself to fully appreciate the full beauty and rawness of their existence.

The story unfolds towards the end of November 2013, which in Patagonia, is the beginning of the Austral summer.[41] As it happened, it was an exceptionally stormy period even for Patagonian standards and although we didn't realise it at the time, the UK was experiencing a similar pattern of weather.

Moby and I arrived in Buenos Aires and were due to meet up with Michael. Unfortunately, he was going to be delayed a few days and would catch up with us later.

Long range overnight buses have secured the primary means of transport over Argentina's rail network (which is now almost non-existent) with the *Andesmar Bus Company* proving to be the best of the bunch.

We caught the overnight bus to Puerto Madryn from a chaotic Buenos Aires bus terminal, together with extremely heavy sacks and haul bag. I had stupidly volunteered to take all the climbing gear with us all the way to Puerto Natales.

---

[41] 'Austral' is the term used in science to describe the southern hemisphere, in this case the summer.

The bus companies generally supply a basic breakfast, lunch and supper inclusive in the fare, whilst the locals bring their own giant flasks of coffee or traditional *Mate*[42].

After a twenty hour journey, we arrived at the outdoor orientated town of Puerto Madryn, then hired a vehicle and moved onto the Valdes Peninsula nature reserve. The peninsula is famous for its marine animals such as, whales, particularly the Southern Right whale, sea lions and elephant seals. Tall cliffs and sea platforms of limestone contained an abundance of fossils.

Two days on the peninsula and a night's bivvy gave us ample time to witness it all. We were certainly not disappointed.

We learnt to book tickets for an onward journey well in advance, as some towns the bus called into had passengers quickly filling seats. A couple of ex-mining towns were not worth the overnight stay, but Sarmiento was a small village with a neat campsite. It is famous for its Petrified Forest Natural Monument[43], 30kms to the south and was certainly an amazing environment to walk round.

The journey down the eastern seaboard went well. The only hitch for a couple of days was when the Chilean border guards went on strike over pay. It meant the journey to Puerto Natales did not go entirely to plan, as it required a diversion via Punta Arenas. It wasn't all bad, as it was a very pleasant city to investigate, one we knew we must return to.

A mind and body that has endured Patagonia will never return to the way it was.

December 1 (day thirteen), We had met up with Michael and the three of us were looking forward to a rest day. We were in Puerto Natales waiting for Martin to join the team, I was certainly looking forward to the climbing.

He eventually joined us albeit a day or more overdue, thanks to another bout of lost luggage, with him having to spend two nights waiting for it at the airport.

---

[42] Mate (pronounced mah-tay) is the National drink of Argentina that boasts multiple health benefits. It is a ritual rather than merely a drink and is usually shared amongst friends and family. The leaf is chopped and mashed in a gourd (the drinking vessel) and formed into a paste, hot water is then added. Drinkers sip the liquid through a silver straw.

[43] Sarmiento Petrified Forest Natural Monument is a forest of fossilized wood of primitive conifers and palm trees from around 66 million years ago (the Cenozoic period).

Much to our surprise, it was bloody chilly in Natales, even though it was the beginning of summer. A light dusting of snow had fallen to a few hundred metres, ominous signs were in my thoughts!

Preparations began immediately. We met up with our agent, *Andares Patagonia,* to collect our climbing permit, only to realise a full day was going to be wasted obtaining another permit we hadn't realised we needed. This permit allowed entry to the National Park and could only be gained in person from CONAF (Chile National Parks Authority) headquarters, a six hour round trip…if we had a bloody car!

It would have been a lot longer by bus, leaving us no other option than to hire a car.

A further day gathering provisions and packing the customary enormous sacks, was followed by a two and a half hour bus journey to our start point at Hostel Las Torres. Unfortunately, Martin and I were now down to just fourteen days for the climbing.

We had arrived at Las Torres camp site late afternoon, prompting tents to go up straight away. Better to make a brew and have supper, with plans for an early start the following morning.

Our objective over the following two days, with the help of Michael and Moby, was to get to *Japones camp,* known unofficially as the 'climber's camp', the highest camp site up the Ascencio valley at an elevation of 700m and 12kms from our campsite.

There were a lot of trekking parties on the trail, it was fortunate we had not booked beds at either of the two huts we passed on the trail to Japones, as they both seemed rammed.

It was the inevitable double load carrying game again, even with Michael and Moby's help. Eventually though, we made it to Japones, the only team at the site (trekking parties are not granted permits for Japones camp). Tents went up quickly, prompted by the weather feeling ominously cold and very windy.

Supper was soon on the go in the rather draughty cabin known colloquially as 'the shelter'. The shelter paints a misleading image of its structure and ability to keep out wind and rain.

Heaven knows what it must have been like before a local climber volunteered to spend two months over the winter trying to improve it. Armed with only a saw, axe, plastic sheeting, string and surrounding drift wood, he patched it up to allow a basic area for cooking and cowering from the weather. It turned out to be a trial of endurance simply eating and trying to keep dry and warm, whilst maintaining jocose attitudes and brave faces.

The night had been extremely windy with huge gusts screaming at the mountains and ripping at the trees around us, the temperature registered 8degC. The shelter required a few basic repairs before we needed to venture up the trail and locate a way onto the western slabs below the Towers.

The trail took us through woods of Lenga and Ash trees, many of which had been uprooted by the ferocious winds. Soon we were negotiating boulder fields and snow drifts. Within an hour of leaving camp, I felt I had been gifted instant entry into a different world. A wonderland of huge monoliths forming a circle around us, most of which had unclimbed faces.

Fresh snow plastered the mountains and low cloud shrouded the summits, it looked more like a winter's day on 'the Ben' than summer in Patagonia. It was at that point my thoughts of success were being sowed with seeds of doubt. Getting up onto the wall, let alone gaining a summit was looking decidedly bloody slim. However, if I was honest, it mattered little, I felt privileged just to be there.

We ventured far enough to view the access slabs, then retreated to basecamp. In doing so, we stumbled upon a natural bivvy cave, formed by a huge boulder propped up by another. It had been used by many teams over the years, made obvious by the addition of numerous plugged up holes and small rock walls.

Back at base, it was clear Martin and myself were going to spend time on the attempt. It prompted us all to agree that Michael and Moby should leave and focus on their challenge of trekking the Paine circuit.

And so it was over a period of ten days, Martin and I made our attempt on the Central Tower.

The cave became our second home and shelter out of the incessant weather fronts of rain and snow that swept through. Retreating to basecamp, then advancing to the cave repeatedly between the fronts became a regular pattern. Temperatures never rose above +5degC and dipped to 0degC on occasions. The river Ascencio ran adjacent to basecamp, a blessing as our primary water source, but head-numbingly frigid for a wash.

In the main, the cave was a welcome hovel out of the violent, hurricane force weather, but hopeless when it rained heavily. The angled roof had a seam of quartzite running across it at half height. That was the point where water running down the angle would terminate and drop onto us, soaking everything below it.

There was little option other than to shuffle down to the end of the cave in a half sit, half crouch position and wait for daybreak.

We did manage to get at least some absorbing climbing in, getting to a high point on the slabs. Estimating it to be within 5 or 6 pitches from the col between the North and Central Towers, the lower granite slabs were either covered in snow or running with water. Crampons and a single axe helped us gain ground steadily.

We climbed solo on those delicate slabs, both confident in our ability. One steeper pitch required roping up as placements for the axe and front points became thinner. The top of that pitch was our high point and where we were to finally retreat from.

When realisation struck that time had run out for us, we made one final ascent up the slabs and successfully retrieved our mangled gear from the ensuing maelstrom.

Martin and I had given everything, we knew we couldn't have done more. Would I go back? I would, given we had learnt so much. It would have to be on the strength of a good weather window from Puerto Natales though, especially now, at the ripe old age of seventy.

It was time for Martin to head back to the UK. We cleared Japones camp, but left two packs to return for. Halfway down the trail, we met up with Michael and Moby who had successfully completed the circuit. Bless them, they had not wasted anytime in coming back up to Japones to help us. Martin was getting short on time and so it was agreed he should scamper down the trail on his own, while we removed all the gear.

We bade farewell and looked forward to catching up sometime in the future.

The three of us woke to a beautiful morning back at Hostel las Torres. I was still in a somewhat sombre mood, having failed on the Towers. That was soon put to bed when I received a beautiful text from Nicky:

Hi, Dad, good to hear you are safe. What would life be like, if we had no courage to attempt anything we dared to dream?

I was soon out of my sullen mood. I realised once more that success is not the essential factor in life. Surviving failure is also a significant part, particularly in the face of adversity, in challenges of the unknown, or living life on the edge.

Not only that…we still had the other half of our adventure to look forward to. Phase 4 was now the focus.

The kayaking was going to be a challenge that was sure, but visiting Tierra del Fuego, Navarino Island and Ushuaia was more like a holiday. We had two days to recover from Torres del Paine before the kayaking. It seemed a good opportunity to revisit Punta Arenas and whilst there, book ferry tickets for the journey through the Magellan Straits and the infamous Beagle Channel.

I hadn't been able to have a conversation with Lynne for a good number of days, it was essential to find an Internet café as Christmas was only a few days away. Fortunately, there were a couple to choose from and we had a great catch up.

It was going to be tough, but a comfort to know she would be spending Christmas 2013 and the New Year with Nicky. Gary on the other hand, was now living in Kenya, running his security business and developing a second one, Skydive Diani.

We found Punta Arenas a majestic city, full of parks, outdoor markets and grand colonial buildings. Just as special, we discovered Café Tapiz, they had coffee and cake to die for, and of course, we more than made up for the previous fortnight's deficiency.

And so, to the kayaking.

The Grey and Serrano watersheds came straight off their respective glaciers. The Grey merged into the Serrano to become one wild river, meandering its way westwards towards the Fjords of the Pacific Ocean. None of us had the knowledge or experience to undertake the journey alone.

Antares Patagonia supplied our guide 'Arek', a great guy who was an intrepid kayaker with some amazing long-distance expeditions under his belt. We were to spend four days and three nights wild camping to get to our exit point.

Undaunted by another wet day, we were up early and tucked into a hearty breakfast at Casa Lucy's, our B and B. We met up with Arek and travelled back into the Paine National Park to Anatares Patagonia's kayak centre, based on the shores of Grey Lake. We geared up and sorted ourselves out, before loading kayaks to the brim, both inside and on top of the hulls.

It wasn't long before the excitement started. Our first objective was to head directly off shore to explore a large sculptured iceberg that had carved off the Grey glacier. The wind was winning the fight just to free ourselves from the beach, lots of laughter ensued but not a good start to our intrepid adventure.

Eventually we gave up the fight to the iceberg, turned 180deg to the south and headed down stream.

The scenery, tranquillity and raw nature of the Paine wilderness was most profound from the viewpoint we had from the kayaks.

The river posed no real technical problems, although it was abundantly clear that such a mass of water with complex, conflicting currents, needed to be expertly read and navigated with caution. In addition, the current carried us at amazing speeds, sometimes up to 20km/hr. Vigilance was paramount as huge broken tree branches were often just visible above the water line, occasionally and dangerously in the centre of the river.

We kayaked for around four to six hours each day, only stopping to have a pee break or make camp. On every occasion, it was in the wilderness of untouched beech trees, dripping with 'old man's beards' (a parasitic lichen that thrives in damp, pristine conditions). It mattered little about the rain as we explored patches of the sub-Antarctic tundra, while Arek spoiled us with his great suppers. Kayaks would take a while to unpack and repack each morning, but the whole process was part and parcel of the amazing experience.

Strict fire regulations and precautions are necessary in the park, especially as a huge fire in 2012 destroyed hundreds of acres.

All too soon we were on our last leg of the journey that took us 22km down river to a Rangers post below Cerro Balmaceda. At that point, the Serrano watershed we had travelled enters the fjord Estero Ultima Esperanza on its way westwards to the Pacific Ocean.

We pulled into our last camp below the spectacular Lago Serrano and snout of the Serrano glacier. We had made it to the fjord, our destination before being picked up by boat in the morning, **Christmas Day!**

Two final, unexpected treats came before leaving that morning.

Firstly, Michael suggested a walk to explore the snout of the glacier via the shore of the Lago, while Arek produced supper. It was an amazing sight, it almost felt the wall of ice was within touching distance. Furthermore, we managed to grab bits of ice from the shore to take back to camp and enjoy our version of Pisco Sour[44].

---

[44] Pisco Sour is a cocktail of South American cuisine. It has a liquor base and the 'sour' is citrus juice usually of lemon or lime. Ice can be added to taste.

The combination of the drink and Arek's meal, which started with a delicacy of tree fungi (hongo dihuene), made it feel we were truly at one with the wilderness.

Secondly, we decided to portage the kayaks up to the Lago in the morning, then see how near we dare get to the snout of the glacier. It was +1degC, Arek thought we were bonkers, but couldn't leave his protégés to have all the fun.

Morning came barely above freezing, hail and snow was almost horizontal. Mike and I were in the double kayak, Arek joined us in his single. We weaved our way through small bergs to within sniffing distance of the glaciers face. We paddled our way back and forth along the stretch of the ice wall, revelling in the sight of the massive wall of ice, a magical couple of hours and a truly awesome Christmas present.

The four days kayaking was a wonderful wilderness experience, it had certainly 'fed the rat'.

Time had moved on quickly, and realised we needed to get a move on too. It was a quick change out of wetsuits, followed by a hasty pack away of our camping gear in preparation to be picked up by boat. In no time at all, kayaks were tied to the top of the captain's cabin (a sight to behold that would never happen in the UK) before landing up the Fjord at a local Estancia (ranch) for Christmas dinner.

We joined other tourists from the boat for a splendid lamb BBQ (asados) in true Patagonia style, courtesy of the ranch owners, going back for second and thirds until we were completely stuffed.

Within a few hours, we had returned to Puerto Natales and returned the kayaking gear to Antares Patagonia, very grateful for their professional advice and help on both our climbing and kayaking trips.

Twenty-four hours on, we had repacked for the next leg of the adventure and were on-board our ferry, the 'Austral Broom' at Punta Arenas, bound for the Straits of Magellan[45] and eventually our destination, Navarino Island, a journey of around thirty hours.

---

[45] The Magellan Straits were explored and fully navigated by Ferdinand Magellan in the sixteenth century, during his circumnavigation of the globe in 1520. The Straits are named in his honour. It separates mainland South America from Tierra del Fuego and is an important natural sea passage between the Atlantic and Pacific Oceans. The wild waters of the passage are well respected even to this day.

Our ferry left the wide body of the Straits after a couple of hours, at the point it heads North West to the Pacific. We headed south, taking smaller channels and fjords until reaching the famous Beagle Channel.

The channel is at the extreme southern tip of South America and is partly in Argentina and partly in Chile. It separates Tierra del Fuego from several islands, one of which is Navarino Island. The channel is named after HMS Beagle, which became famous along with two explorers on board, who sailed the waters in 1831.

Captain Robert Fitzroy was the young commander of the ship and was to complete a survey of Patagonia and Tierra del Fuego. Whilst a certain Charles Darwin, a naturalist, was to study a huge range of species that subsequently led him to produce his work of scientific literatures called *The Origin of Species* and the *Theory of Evolution by Natural Selection*. Both of which are considered the basis of evolution and biology as we understand it today.

We entered the Beagle channel at its North West fringe, having been on board for around twelve hours. As with Patagonian buses, our travel by ferry also included basic meals in the price of the ticket. Daylight was upon us as the Captain announced breakfast.

We guessed it was the familiar cheese and ham sandwich with a small cake to follow, inevitably it was the same for lunch and supper. No matter, I was constantly hungry, and grateful for small mercies.

Dramatic scenery was unfolding to our port side as I ventured on deck. Mist and light snow added to the ambience as the Cordillera Darwin came into view, along with glimpses of Mt Darwin (2488m).

As we headed east, glacier snouts of Alemania, Francis, Romanche and Hollanda respectively dropped into the channel from the mass of the Darwin Icefield high above. The panorama was truly one of nature's wonderful works of art, and all the while surrounded by pristine ecosystems of temperate rain forest, kelp forests and intricate sea floor habitats.

It suggested to me that any mountaineer would be in the same state of euphoria as I was, given the masterpiece unfolding before me, my thoughts constantly drifting away with the need to be there.

It was difficult to drag myself off deck and away from the scenery, even as darkness set in. We had been sailing for twenty-four hours and I needed to get my head down for a few hours.

Eventually around midnight, and after thirty hours sailing, the ferry docked at Puerto Williams, the capital town of Navarino Island. Travellers could remain on board to continue sleeping until the nod from the Captain to disembark came at 07.00.

A couple of days were spent exploring the island, thriving in the remoteness of the place, careful to avoid the outrageous beauty of sphagnum mosses underfoot. We visited Puerto Toro on the eastern side of the island, once a bustling port in the late nineteenth century. It is one of the remotest southerly settlements in the world before reaching Antarctica.

As the crow flies, it is approximately 50kms to Cape Horn National Park, and not much further to Antarctica.

All too soon, it was time to catch a small ferry across the Beagle channel to the town of Ushuaia. A town I obviously hadn't researched properly as my pre-trip idea in was one of a sprawling, retro sixties frontier town. It was in fact, a much larger, modern town, full of B and B's and hotels doing good business.

Ushuaia was a hub for Antarctic cruise ship passengers coming and going to the continent. When those ships docked, the streets filled with tourists not too dissimilar to a weekend in any town on the south coast of the UK.

We spent New Year's Eve and day in the town, and made the most of wandering the freshly snow covered local hills.

By January 2, heavy snow had fallen, down to 200m, even though it was summer. It made for an interesting journey back to Punta Arenas over various high passes. We had left Ushuaia at 08.00 and arrived at Punta Arenas at 01.00 the next morning.

One thing for sure when travelling in remote parts of the world is to expect anything. Strong tides can hold up ferry crossings for hours, as can Chilean customs seeking out Argentinian tourists trying to smuggle 'god knows' how much meat across the border.

One woman had a suitcase full of beef, probably to feed her hungry family, or possibly to sell at a market. Anyway, there was no way the sniffer dog was going to miss that lot!

The last leg of the adventure was *The Carretera Austral or Highway Route 7*

Formerly named Augusto Pinochet Carretera Highway, it ranks as one of the world's ultimate road trips. It runs north to south, close to the Pacific rim of Chile and is 1240km long.

Mostly unpaved, the highway runs alongside ancient forests, glaciers, pioneer farmsteads and turquoise rivers. It was completed in 1996 under the rule of President Augusto Pinochet and took twenty years to complete. Its purpose was little to do with pragmatism, more to do with the symbolism of tying disparate regions of the country together.

Most of the adventure is simply navigating the miles of gargantuan ruts, potholes and landslides. Sections of the highway require ferry crossings that are now totally inadequate for the increasing volume of traffic.

It does, however, make for a 'must do adventure'.

The three of us were going well, pulling together in times of need. The following three weeks were going to need much of the same.

At Punta Arenas we hired a Nissan 4x4, pretty much an essential tool for the journey as it turned out, if travelling the full length of the Carretera it is most wise to use a 4x4. However, we did come across some hard-core cases of people cycling the route.

From Punta Arenas, our journey would take us approximately a 1000km north to Puerto Montt. From there, Michael would head further north to Santiago and then home to New Zealand, while Moby and I headed northwest back to Buenos Aires and the UK.

We planned our itinerary for the journey back in the UK, and pretty much kept to it for the three weeks. There were some unexpected bonuses during the trip that secured it for me as being one of life's great adventurous travels.

Many side trips that I could easily elaborate on would be too much for here, so I will mention them briefly, for anyone interested.

We were keen to start heading north, if only for some sun and warmth for a change. At Cerro Castillo, a Chilean border crossing into Argentina (one of a few borders that occurred on the Carretera), we sailed through unusually swiftly, or so we thought. After 5 miles of what appeared to be *no man's land*, we came across the Argentinian border control.

As is quite often when things are going well, there's often a kick in the nuts. We had failed to notice that our friendly Chilean border guard had stamped all our passports with Entrada (entrance) rather than Salida (exit). The smugness on the face of the Argentinian guard who had picked up on it, was a sight to behold.

He revelled in the fact, along with his mates that they had got one over on their 'superior comrades' at the other border (something that doesn't happen very often we were told). We laughed along with them, but was a pain in the ass, to travel all the way back to get it re-stamped, correctly, and waste over an hour.

One issue that needs careful thought, is where to re-fuel. We perhaps take that for granted in the UK and Europe. There can be huge distances between fuel stops on the Carretera. Even then, there's high probability that the one you're aiming for has sold out, or you're at the end of a very, very long queue.

Moreno Glacier—Place to Visit #1

The local authority has made the most of passing tourists, by making excellent access to the snout of the glacier. I've seen many glaciers in my life but the Moreno is extra special. As with many glaciers these days, it was very active with huge chunks calving off quite frequently.

One huge mass of turquoise ice calved off while we were there, creating a massive bow wave, all caught on camera.

We moved on and camped overnight, relishing breakfast in the sun for a change.

El Chalten and the Fitzroy Range—Place to Visit #2

One doesn't have to be a climber to be gobsmacked at the sight of this wonderful natural spectacle, located at the southern end of the Patagonian Ice Field. Travelling inland had become warm and dry, but quickly changed to a chilled wind and rain as we entered town. The micro climates in the southern Patagonian Mountains can extremely fickle. A comfortable B and B had overridden the initial idea of putting the tents up for the night, particularly as the weather had turned foul.

The weather in the morning had improved as quickly as it had worsened the day before. We chose a day hike up to Glacier Piedras Blancas via Laguna Capri, which happened to be a common base camp for an ascent of Mount Poincenot.

It was a shame not to spend longer in the area, but after filling the fuel tank, we headed north once again. We headed east inland for a while, then a long drive north, through wide open plains aiming for Rodolfo Roballos and the Chilean border.

Fuel consumption was particularly poor on the gravel roads, we were lucky to make it to the next fuel stop, unfortunately ending up at the back of a queue. Through our pigeon Spanish, we established a delivery was not due for three hours or more.

When the fuel finally arrived after a very long wait, it wasn't the ESSO tanker or similar I was expecting. No of course it wasn't, why would it be, in the middle of frigging nowhere? Instead, a 4x4 Jeep pulling a 500 gallon drum on wheels with a hand pump turned up. Nevertheless, we had a good laugh and were eventually on our way.

It was around midnight as we approached the border in the middle of nowhere, the sky as black as soot, and not a soul in sight. High ridges were outlined against the dark sky as was the millions of stars. We then noticed a sign that said border closes at 20.00.

Suddenly, two border guards approached holding torches in one hand, and the other very firmly gripping the obvious weapon attached to their hip. For a moment the situation was quite tense, but once they realised our intentions were honourable, they were very hospitable.

So friendly in fact, that they would not see us putting tents up at such an unearthly hour, instead offering us an old room with a stove and sink, which we gratefully accepted. They even asked us politely, if we could be away for 08.00, just in case they got into trouble.

Caleta Tortel—Place to Visit #3

A few camera shots for nostalgia of our grateful abode, saw us away by 07.30 and heading north for Cochrane and Caleta Tortel, 185km away. Two and a half hours got us to Cochrane for a coffee break and stretch of the legs.

It was raining 'cats and dogs' as we approached Caleta Tortel, via a small road off the main Carretera highway from Cochrane.

The weather was kind of expected for a coastal village perched high above the mouth of the Baker River, the largest river in Chile! It is surrounded by huge forested hills, fjords and channels close to Golfo De Penas and the Pacific Ocean.

The village was founded in 1955 to exploit the Cypress forests for wood (Guayteca Cypress) that abound in the area. For most of its history, the only access was by air or sea.

There are no streets or roads, instead the village is completely constructed around the Cypress trees. Its timber is used for walkways, houses, and stilts on which they are built, enabling them to cling to hillsides around the inlet. The road that leads from the village to the Carretera Highway at Cochrane was only built in 2003.

The sun did come out in the morning, making a stay in one of the basic B and Bs, (or a plusher one if you're lucky), worth the detour off the main drag.

Lago Tranquilo (Lago General Carrera)—Place to Visit #4

Onwards once again, not stopping at Cochrane, we were now aiming for Puerto Guadal, on the shores of Lago Tranquilo. That was how the Lago was named on my map, but I believe it's known as Lago General Carrera now.

As the former name implies, it is a very peaceful, very calm and idyllic location, hopefully it still is after nearly ten years. The perfect spot to take a break in the sun, from the dusty and somewhat noisy gravel section of the latter part of the highway.

It was well worth seeking out the 'Emilia Ester campsite' well marked on the map, but not so easily found outside the village. Eventually, a small sign and short track led to a little house, next to the campsite. We roused a friendly old boy who couldn't understand a word we were saying, but knew what we wanted and made us welcome.

The lush grass and camp areas above the shore of the lake, as well as the surrounding mountain views, were magnificent. However, first impressions of the adjacent communal log cabin for cooking, washing and showering were not so pleasant. It seemed a rather dirty, forgotten place, obviously used at some point due to the rotting meat in the fridge, dirty crockery in the sink and general dross laying around. We set too and it didn't take long to make it clean and habitable.

I was more than happy to soak up the sun and peace, whilst Michael and Moby chose to drive the four hour round trip to Chilli Chico, an area famous for cherries. I also wanted to catch up with Lynne as I hadn't spoken to her for many days.

Our journey continued towards Bahia Murta, wondering as we drove what was going to turn up next. We had travelled through many valleys, one stood out with high glaciers, tumbling waterfalls and splendid flora. Mont San Valentino (3910m) on the northern tip of the Patagonian Icefield stood out majestically against the clear sky to the west.

A sign caught our eye as we neared the village of Bahia Murta, it was hosting a rodeo and drawing in the crowds. We pitched our tents on the local common, sharing it with a couple of horses, a few goats, chickens and the occasional feral dog.

The Rodeo was a lively, keenly contested affair amongst the local Gouchos, it was well attended and everyone very friendly. Best of all, the local beer was on sale and needed sampling. All in all, it kept us well entertained for the whole evening.

Cerro Castillo Camp—Place to Visit #5

Days had flown by, it was now day fifty-four of our trip. We left Bahia Murta and headed for a pre-planned hike up to Cerro Castillo camp.

It was a three day round trip that wound its way 13km up the mountain side, to an ideal camping spot amongst a sheltered wood, below the high peak of Cerro Palo (2191m).

In 1976, a New Zealand expeditionary climbing team visited the area and had chosen the area for base camp.

The area was known to be seldom visited, and our two days of hiking in the area to interesting points on the map bore witness to that. It was yet another wild, unspoilt environment worth the effort. One interesting moment came when particularly strong winds picked up, forcing all of us on all fours and threatening to rip us off the hillside.

It is worth a mention here that, throughout the whole of our travels in Patagonia, we were all mindful of the need to be environmentally aware in our surroundings, and sensitive of the places visited. Body washing and washing of utensils was never done directly in rivers or streams. It was always done away from them. Use of bio degradable soap along with packing everything out was a no brainer, something that came natural to all of us anyway.

Back on the road, the next port of call was a 100kms journey to Coyhaique, the small capital city of the Aysen region of Chile, founded by settlers around 1929. It nestles amongst the mountains on the western seaboard, and although it has an oceanic climate, it is somewhat protected from heavy rainfall.

Although only 100kms along the Carretera, the journey went particularly slowly due to the rugged road conditions. It was certainly one of the stretches that made us grateful for the 4x4 vehicle. We stayed the night in Coyhaique, but finding our B and B very scruffy and the town nothing special, we were eager to move on the following morning.

Ventisquero Colgante Glacier—Place to Visit #6

The road out of Coyhaique to Park National Quelat became very interesting, very soon we were in much wilder countryside. The gravel roads were rougher and steeper, with increasing numbers of hairpin bends, the 4x4 was certainly proving its worth. Great ferns towered over us along the edges of the forested tracks, and an abundance of Gunnera manicata (known as Brazilian Rhubarb).

By mid-afternoon, a campsite run by the local CONAF (National Forest Corporation) authority looked too inviting to pass over. The site was very cheap, had great spacious camping spots, clean toilets and drinking water. After sorting ourselves out, we took a hiking trail high above a river valley, leading us towards the Ventisquero Colgante Glacier.

It took us through enormous Gunnera plants, exotic flora and huge trees of the Redwood genus, very easy to imagine we were in an Orwellian movie. As we approached the viewpoint, the untouched raw beauty of the place was climaxed by the roar and thunder of a gigantic waterfall, dropping a thousand vertical feet from the distant glacier high above, to the river below.

Hot Springs of Los Termas—Place to Visit #7

Approximately 20kms along the road from the CONAF campsite, we passed a sign advertising the privately owned 'Hot Springs of Los Termas'. In the morning sun, it was far too inviting, situated as it was, in an idyllic position on the eastern shore of the Ventisquero Fjord. Three plunge pools at slightly differing temperatures up to 40degC, followed by a dip in the fjord at around 6degC, was everything the body needed after days on the Carretera.

For the equivalent of £20pp, it felt a bargain, and we surely made the most of it, particularly as we had the place to ourselves.

Northwards on the road once again, we camped the night at Lago Risopatron. Apart from trying our hand at fishing, the only recall to memory was the hundreds of huge biting horse flies.

Speeding on, our next spot to visit was the village of Futaleufu. As we headed there, it was interesting to see a gradual change taking place in the Carretera. From dusty, potholed surfaces, there seemed to be an impressive scale of road works and transformation to a Tarmac surface.

We guessed there was a general plan to extend it along its entire length. Who knows, it may well have been converted by now. Great for the local communities, I guess, but less fun for the likes of us selfish visitors!

Rafting the Futaleufu—Place to Visit #8

Futaleufu struck us immediately as a nice clean town, not unlike a small European Alpine town. We stayed a couple of days, mainly because Michael had done his homework about the infamous rafting to be had on the Futaleufu River. It is one of the premier white-water destinations in the world, with several rapids up to grade 5.

Its glacial snow melt waters carve their way through volcanic mountains and drop as much as 5500ft below the surrounding peaks. It seemed an adrenalin rush not to be missed.

The name Futaleufu is an indigenous Mapuche word, meaning *Grand waters'* and locals quite often refer to the valley as *un paisaje pintado por dios*, a landscape painted by God.

We had obtained a good deal from Christian and Carli, our rafting guides from *Patagonia Elements*. The following day was brilliant, it was a real buzz for me, having never rafted before. It was a terrific experience, negotiating grade 3, 4, and 5 sections, never worrying (didn't have time to think about that), always exhilarating and without doubt, leaving me in awe and appreciative of the immense power of the water.

After several kilometres and a couple of near 'throw outs', we headed to a pre-determined exit point. 'Back paddle, back paddle' a phrase to live in my memory for a very long time.

I could go into a lot more detail, but must leave it simply as, **a definite endorphin release!**

Chaiten Volcano and Alerce Forest—Place to Visit #9

A last destination worthy of a mention is the town of Chaiten. It is located at the northern end of the Carretera Austral.

In 2008, the nearby volcano of the same name erupted unexpectedly for the first time in over seven thousand years, forcing the entire population to evacuate the area. The town also suffered severely from earthquake aftershocks, as well as from ash feet deep from the eruption.

By the afternoon of the following day, an ash plume had spread across Chile and Argentina to the Atlantic Ocean in the east.

It was proposed to rebuild the town elsewhere away from the area, but that was ultimately disbanded in preference to rebuilding the town on the existing site.

We parked the car and took a vague trail up to the caldera rim at more than 3,600ft above sea level. The scene was both amazing and sobering as we hiked through a region of thick ash and devastated forest. The three of us stood on the caldera rim viewing the central plug, and as we did, small plumes of smouldering sulphur could be clearly seen and certainly smelt.

Another CONAF campsite just outside Chaiten was our pit stop for the night.

It was inevitable the campsite and region were getting busier as we approached the end of the remotest part of the highway. However, a walk through an amazing forested area of *Alerce trees (Fitzroya cupressoides)*[46] had pygmy owls watching our every move out of the corner of their eyes.

These were the 9 most interesting places to visit, as side tracks off the Carretera, should anyone be interested. There were probably many more we missed.

We were now on our last days together of an amazing adventure. It took a full day and three ferry crossings to arrive at our destination of Puerto Montt at around midnight.

It was there the following day, that Moby and I bade farewell to Michael. He continued his journey north to Santiago, where he deposited the 4x4 (as pre-arranged) at an *Alamo* car hire centre, before catching a flight back to NZ.

We on the other hand, caught a bus to Bariloche[47], where our favourite bus company, *Andesmar,* took us the long journey back to Buenos Aires and a flight back to Heathrow.

It was a fantastic adventure, made more so with the friends I travelled with. The couple of 'downers', particularly failing on the Central Tower of Paine, paled into insignificance when reflecting upon the huge experiences and wonderful knowledge I gained.

A simple case of believing dreams can be achieved if we have the courage to do it, NH.

---

[46] Alerce or Fitzroya cupressoides tree is a genus in the cypress family. It is a single living species of tall, long-lived conifer, native to the mountains of southern Chile and Argentina. An important member of their temperate rain forests.

[47] San Carlos de Bariloche (more commonly called Bariloche is a town in Argentina's Patagonia region. It borders a large glacial lake surrounded by the Andes. It is known for its Swiss Alpine architecture and chocolate. It is a popular base for skiing and hiking. Often compared to an Alpine Chamonix.

Fauna worth a mention:

Armadillo, Austral Parakeet, Austral Flamingo, Black faced Ibis, Black necked swan, Carancho, Condor, Elephant seals, Fox (Patagonian), Fur seals, Guanaco, Huemal (rare deer), Orcas, Scorpion, Skunk, Torrent ducks, Whales (Southern Right) Woodpecker (Magellenic).

Chapter Twenty-Three
Korichuma, Bolivian Success

The Quimsa Cruz

A new route on Korichuma in a seldom visited region of the Bolivian Andes. Korichuma South East Buttress, (500m, TD)
   Martin Scrowston and Mike Hope 12>13 June 2019.

I wrote the above article in full, for The Climbers Club Journal 2019–2020, as did Martin for The Fell and Rock Club. Both are available to read, so I won't go into the full details here, just a selected few paragraphs.

I was being seduced once again by the thought of climbing in the high mountains. The attraction of basic living, harsh conditions and a degree of self-denial, coupled with pristine environments and exploratory new routing is something one either loves or loathes.

Martin, my climbing partner for nearly forty years, had been on to me for 'an adventure' into the bigger ranges for a couple years; the excuses I had come up with were wearing a little thin.

We have climbed together in many parts of the world and the passion is certainly still there, but fitness, poor acclimatisation and being not far off seventy played a big part on my mind.

However, it would be a fitting 'swan-song' for my high-altitude mountaineering days.

Our objective was a small range of the Bolivian Andes, south-east of Lake Titicaca and La Paz, called the Cordillera Quimsa Cruz. At about 40km in length it is the continuation of the Cordillera Real, with the massif of Illimani, 6438m, close by.

The highest summit in the range is Jachacunocollo at about 5800m. There is however, still confusion about summit spot heights, peak names and new route details due to lack of both accurate mapping and an organised climbing information centre. More popular for its early twentieth century mining rather than mountaineering, it nevertheless has seen a few parties interested in its peaks.

Our chosen basecamp was beside Laguna Choco Khota, with the main peak of interest being Quri Ch'uma also named Immaculado, but now more commonly referred to as Korichuma, 5312m. From the limited information available, we felt this peak had the best opportunities for new routing.

Flying into La Paz airport at 4100m and staying in the city not much lower at 3640m affects nearly everyone. I knew it would certainly affect me.

After a few days in the city acclimatising, we eventually headed out for base camp in our 4x4 driven by 'Freddy' courtesy of our outfitters 'The Adventure Climbing and Trekking Company of South America', headed up by Fabricio. The 4x4 vehicle was essential for the 6hrs it would take to base camp on the very narrow, steep mountain tracks.

We could see our mountain in the distance down the valley, but had no way of driving the vehicle across the numerous wide and deep trenches, purposely dug out by feuding miners and locals over mining rights.

Expeditions generally require overcoming hurdles in some form or other. This was no exception. If it wasn't for a local Llama farmer called Cerilio and his rather dilapidated off-road motorbike, the outcome of our trip could have been very different *(more on that in the full article)*.

Korichuma lay in front of us looking spectacular. We were already plotting possible lines in our minds as we completed base camp duties.

June 10, I was awake and up by 07.00, not able to lie horizontal any longer. I wasn't surprised at how tired I felt, having still not really acclimatised. I certainly didn't feel like dashing up to any summit that day.

In the end, we decided to acclimatise further by ascending slowly, each with a light sack, to locate the best passage onto the snout of the glacier, to find a reasonable spot for a bivvy and to get a closer look at possible lines. Although the miners' tracks had a negative impact on the otherwise pristine landscape, they certainly made it easier to access the lower slopes of the mountain.

June 12 and we were ready to give it a crack.

It was a day of leisurely packing and dossing in preparation for the hike up to our bivvy site. Flat spots were not in abundance but we eventually settled on a couple that nestled in tyre tracks carved by large mining vehicles. It was then certainly time for a brew.

Now it's not often we both make schoolboy errors at the same time!

I had changed jackets at the last minute, and forgot to transfer my lighter. Martin however, did have his, but it failed dismally to produce a spark.

While I went on the hunt hoping to find one in an abandoned miners hut nearby, Martin explored a couple of rusting mining vehicles around our bivvy site.

He was in luck, an old abandoned generator had seen better days, but the battery was still in situ. He had the brainwave of reversing the polarity of the leads. By merely touching the second lead on the terminal, it gave a huge spark, nearly costing him his eyebrows, but enabled him to light a stove. We were lucky to recover from our faux-pas and fortunate to have a couple of brews and a freeze dried meal before getting heads our down.

June 13, a full moon overhead made the mountain a beautiful sight.

An essential brew and a quick breakfast were excitedly downed by 06.00 as we geared up for the climb. From our advanced position, it was clear the lines we thought might be possible were now clearly not in condition. Our revised line would take us onto the ridge east of Korichuma summit.

Approach to the foot of the route was pretty much crevasse free, but a slog in the much less firm snow than we were expecting. Martin took the first lead on a slope angle of about 60 to 70deg. We alternated the first few pitches on improving névé, whilst using adequate protection from the odd ice screw to rock protection off to our left.

I was feeling the pace and the altitude. Martin combined the last two pitches that got us onto the ridge after a gnarly bit of mixed climbing towards the top. Our intention was to take the rock ridge to the west, but the line looked super serious. Huge monoliths of teetering granite were not what we had expected from our lower viewpoint.

There were two options open to us. The first was an obvious bale out down the way we had come, which neither of us wanted. The second was a rappel down a seriously loose gully on the North side. We belayed off a solitary Rock 7 and rappelled a full 50m down the very poor gully. This was followed by a traverse of some 750m on a diagonal line across a granite boulder field, to a much broader channel, that was key to getting us back on the ridge.

The broad channel involved scrambling through mixed but much safer terrain. We were both quite knackered in getting onto the ridge, me more so. We were now only 300m from the summit and after a breather, we continued along the straight forward ridge line to celebrate achieving our new route.

It was late afternoon as we chose our line down the south-west face with care. One or two 'slots' needed avoiding but, it went smoothly despite the long, calf-screaming descent. Within two hours, we were off the glacier, heading for our bivvy spot. Martin was keen to carry on down to basecamp, I was just keen to collapse into my sleeping bag at the bivvy, then meet up in the morning.

After a couple of days recovering, it was time to decide what to do next; there was a degree of disparity between us. I sensed Martin was keener than I to hang it out and perhaps take on a further challenge. However, from what I saw, I struggled to be inspired enough to rekindle the energy and enthusiasm needed. On top of that, the weather was on the change.

We brought our extraction from basecamp forward by three days, and were grateful once again to Cerilio and his motorbike for getting us out of the valley. The mountains were soon in near white out as Freddy arrived for the ride back to La Paz.

A big thanks to Fabricio Escobar of for his hospitality and outfitting service, 'The Adventure Climbing and Trekking Company of South America'.

We were left with a few days to explore more of the area and more of La Paz, its tremendous colourful side of life, rather than its poverty and pollution.

One such sojourn was a trip to Lake Titicaca and short stays on the islands of Isla del sol and Isla de la luna, both of which have many trails across them with links to the first Incas.

Judging by the number of people (particularly younger generation) attracted to the islands, it certainly appeared to me they were on a typical student 'bucket list'.

We hiked and bivvied our way on several trails but the islands themselves left no real lasting impression on me. It certainly reminded me yet again, how fortunate and lucky we are to have the myriad of wonderful and historical islands in the UK.

One such memory however will linger with me for a while.

Having decided time was up on the islands, we headed back to the town of Copacabana for our return bus journey to La Paz the following day. In usual tradition, we were on the lookout for a quiet bivvy spot to see the night out.

After what seemed like hours of walking up and down the long beach, we gave up and found the nearest thing to a flat spot. Very clearly every mother and brother had descended on the place with music and barbecues raging into the early hours, it must have been a bank holiday for them I think.

A few feral dogs had caught my eye, probably thinking us two gringos were easy steal for some grub, but I think Martin was unaware or paid little attention. Anyway, it was now well past midnight and pitch black as we laid out the thermarests and sleeping bags. I for one was looking to rest a very weary soul. Within minutes, a couple of the not to diminutive dogs wandered up and got rather close as if to see if they could snuggle up.

Scrowston was a way with the fairies as usual once he laid his head on the pillow or rucksacks in our case. I, on the other hand, was beginning to feel a trifle uneasy.

Very soon half a dozen of the buggers gathered round us, one at the back of me only a little distance away, made me feel particularly twitchy.

Growling and some in-fighting started as if they were trying to prove what alpha male was to be in charge of the two weirdos laid in their cocoons.

With little movement coming from the body next to me, Martin that is, not the dog, I was beginning to shit myself. I grabbed a head torch, threw a few stones and 'eff offs' at them, but knew it was never going to be sleepy time for me where we were.

Eventually, I managed to rouse Martin from his coma and filled him in on the events of the previous hour or so. I was not going to leave him to the dogs, but at the same time expressed the need to move somewhere else, sharpish!

It was probably something like 03.00, as we trudged down the beach with sleeping bags and rucksacks slung over our shoulders looking for another spot to die for a while. There were bloody dogs everywhere, obviously making the most of the free left-overs from all the nights partying.

We ended up in the local market square bandstand as it seemed the quietest spot around. That was until around 05.30, when locals started gathering and assembling their wares around us for what was obviously going to be market day in a short while. It was not the best end to an expedition, but we soon laughed about it.

We arrived back in La Paz, sank a few beers, shopped for souvenirs to take back home and wallowed in coffee and cake. Exhaustion had evaporated, for me anyway, I was at last able to recollect with pride what we had achieved.

Mt Asgard – Base camp view of Mt Breidablik

Mt Asgard – On the Caribou glacier towards North Peak

Mt Asgard – Descending the Kings Parade glacier

Mt Asgard – Steep granite on the South Face of North Peak

Mt Asgard – Crossing one of the many melt waters

Mt Asgard – Summit of North Peak at midnight

Mt Asgard – Spent at Overlord – waiting for pickup

Mooses Tooth – Ham & Eggs couloir (right of centre)

Mooses Tooth – Bivvy camp below peak 11,300m

Mooses Tooth – Avalanches in the Ruth Gorge

Mooses Tooth – Upper glacier icefall

Mooses Tooth – First pitches of the couloir

Mooses Tooth – Martin on 1st crux pitch

Mooses Tooth – Back at the Root Canal glacier camp

Old Man of Hoy – East face (HVS/E1)

Old Man of Hoy – The fabulous rocks of Rackwick Bay

Old Man of Hoy – On the crux 2nd pitch (picture by Moby O'Connor)

Nicky going well in the Blenheim Triathlon

Gary on his 16th birthday

Patagonia – The Towers of Paine

Patagonia – Base camp home for 16 days

Patagonia – Home for too long

Patagonia – Kayaking up to the snout of the Serrano glacier

Bolivia – Korichuma (East Buttress – 1st ascent)

Bolivia – Cerilio's help to basecamp

Bolivia – Summit of Korichuma

Part 6: Alpine Adventures

Ability is what you're capable of doing.
Motivation determines what you do.
Attitude determines how well you do it.

Louis Holtz

Chapter Twenty-Four
Winter Icefalls, Canada and Europe

It only took one brief glimpse at a picture of the frozen *Weeping Wall* in Jasper National Park, Canada, to make it an essential addition to our winter climbing tick list.

So it was in March 2003, Nick, Chris, Martin and I were on our way to Calgary, for a date with the frozen 'vertical football pitch', as the massive wall of ice is colloquially known.

First, we were to pick up some wheels at the airport, and meet up with Mel and Ian, two friends of Chris', who were going to put us up for the night in Calgary. Both were very pleasant and friendly people as we talked into the small hours. The following day they pointed us in the direction of Canmore, our base for the next few days.

Canmore sits in the Rocky Mountain's west of Calgary at an elevation of around 4,500ft, slightly higher than the summit of Ben Nevis in the UK.

We headed to an area known as the *Junk Yards* for a quick couple of ice routes and our first taste of Canadian winter climbing.

We got a good deal at the Bow Valley Lodge that enabled the four us to get properly sorted, make use of the kitchen and relax.

The following morning was an inevitable lazy start, before heading for *Grotto Canyon* and another few interesting routes.

We were beginning to get a feel of the place, but with the need to accrue a few more routes under our belt, we chose another well-known climbing area, Lake Louise in Banff National Park, and the mighty Louise icefalls, an hour's drive from Canmore.

Approach time to the ice falls was approximately 40mins round the lake from the famous Lake Louise Chateau, a miniature replica of which had been sculptured in ice on the grounds adjacent to the lake. It was an amazing piece of artwork.

As the air temperature was around -28degC, we were assured the lake was well and truly frozen to walk across. It certainly added a little more spice to the walk in, as well as a little more anxiety and caution!

My thermometer at the base of the route read -26degC; the low temperature made the snow very crisp and squeaky. The clear blue sky made for a truly alpine ambience, and ice that had metamorphosed into a surface akin to glass.

The first 'thwack' of my ice axe bounced off.

"Mmmm, it's obvious a little more subtlety is required to climb this little route, boys," I said.

We soon got the measure of the conditions and thoroughly enjoyed the three pitches of climbing at a grade of WI 4/5, the steeper top pitch, particularly so.

It was inevitable we all suffered with the 'hot aches'[48] given the temperature. But the pain was worth it for the joy of climbing the 110m of beautiful blue ice, and further justification for coffee and cake back in Banff.

The following few days had snowed on and off, but we did manage to get a few more routes in at different crags. 'Professor Falls' and 'Haffner Creek' were two of the best.

A days skiing was slotted in, but hardly the proverbial 'rest day'. Particularly with temperatures of -25degC, added wind-chill and my inability to stay upright for very long. It did cross my mind however, that Nicky and Gary would have loved the wonderful snow conditions for skiing.

Ian (Chris' mate) had arranged a ski-mountaineering weekend, bless him, I knew I was sure to be at the back of the field. Ian and a couple of his mates met the four of us at Bow Lake. We skied across the lake, did a little avalanche beacon/search practice, then toured through a forested trail up to a Canadian Alpine hut for the night.

Two feet of snow fell overnight, and of course, most of the lad's eyes lit up, eager 'to get at it'.

I knew instantly I was doomed, but tried to remain cheerful in adversity (a phrase that has stuck since an old school report).

---

[48] 'Hot Aches' is the very painful effect when warmed blood starts recirculating back into very cold fingers. Intense cold constricts the surface blood vessels, and hence slows blood flow. If the condition continues for longer periods, frostbite will start to take hold.

As expected, the experts romped away, and hard as I tried to keep up, the inevitable nose dives would result. Getting back upright in two feet of powder snow with a monkey on my back was bad enough. But then somehow having to reset oneself on skis was indeed a joke.

Much swearing occurred during my inept descent, mainly due to pride, but we all had a good laugh back at the cars, and as I looked back with hindsight, I loved every minute of it.

Finally, we journeyed to Icefields Parkway via highway 93 and booked into the Ramparts Creek hostel, looking forward to visiting *The Weeping Wall* the next day. The hostel was a wonderful place with pine dormitories, good cooking facilities, wood burning stove and outdoor sauna.

Soon enough we were stood under the 'vertical football pitch'. It had been nearly a year since first noticing the amazing wall of ice in that picture. Everything about the place was an ice climbing paradise.

Eventually, Martin and I put nerves to one side, and climbed a brilliant four pitch line of WI 4/5 super ice. Three long abseils later, two of which were off Abalakov threads[49], we returned to our sacks at the base of the route as thick snow started to fall.

To end a fine day, Nick had knocked us up a fine *Kedgeree* for supper, complimented with plenty of wine.

To add another twist to the trip, the following morning we were told by the park warden that our road south back to Canmore was closed. Extensive snow high up was in danger of avalanching. Not only that, the road north was about to be closed too…for at least two days!

Avalanche blasting was about to take place. He was prepared to escort us out to the north to the David Thompson highway junction, but it was to happen immediately.

Faced with little other option, we hastily packed the car and prepared for a rather longer journey back to Canmore. Our journey to the Weeping Wall from Canmore was around 75kms. Our diversion for the return to Canmore was around 420kms, via Rocky Mountain House and Cochrane.

It was a bugger of a journey, but at least we had got one route under our belt on the mighty weeping wall, when it could so easily not have happened at all.

---

[49] Abalakov thread, is an ice protection technique for belaying or abseiling. It is named after its innovator, a Soviet climber named Vitaly Abalakov. It is a skill that needs practising before trusting its security.

Our final day of climbing was in Johnson Canyon near Banff. A beautiful spot with an interesting walk in. Thunderous water under one of the icefalls made for extra ambience. Although water at the back of the icefall was running fast, there was still strength in the ice to make it climbable.

To end a fabulous two weeks, our final evening back at our Canmore lodge was spent in the outdoor hot tub with plenty of beers and an amazing vista of the Rockies.

Another marvellous and adventurous trip, full of unexpected friendliness and hard-fought fun.

Winter Icefalls (Europe)

Winter icefall climbing in Europe has the advantages of being particularly reliable, relatively cheap to plan, and easily accessible, and because of that, those regions over the last few decades have become very popular.

Primarily, a frozen waterfall is a magical transient thing, a different world for climbers to enjoy. It is the synergy of colour, shape, verticality and their ephemeral nature that give them the attraction to seek out and climb.

To know that a small rivulet or cascade of water in the summer can become a vertical candle or solid wall of ice in the winter makes it a form of alpinism that is most definitely thrilling.

To those who don't play the game, they can be forgiven for thinking it a tad eccentric.

In a good hard winter, Britain has great number of icefalls that form, particularly in Wales, the Lake District and Scotland. However, they are far less reliable than their continental cousins.

Another art form of climbing with axes and crampons that has developed over the same period, is 'dry tooling' or 'mixed climbing'. As the name suggests, *dry tooling*, is a style where a climber uses features in the rock to gain height using strategic placements of the hardware.

When a specific route up a cliff face or mountain has a combination of snow, ice and rock, the ascent description would be termed a *mixed line of ascent*.

Mixed climbing connoisseurs at the top end of the game, have reached incredible elevations of difficulty, leading to extremely impressive achievements even in the biggest of mountain ranges.

There have been many exhilarating mid-grade classic routes my mates and I have ventured onto. I thought some of them worthy of a mention here.

France, Chamonix Area

My first venture into icefall climbing was on the large ice-covered granite steps close to the Argentiere glacier. Two years on the trot from 1992 and I still hadn't truly come to terms with the sheer wonder of those vertical icefalls.

It was a scary initiation, the things were bloody steep and access, via abseiling in or negotiating the glacier, could be tricky, depending what routes we were after. Not only that, risk of avalanches from the slopes above, or the unnerving collapse of huge chunks of ice from the glacier, certainly focussed the mind.

One of those years, we hired a caravan (Martin, Rob, his pregnant wife Ann and myself) on a caravan park in Chamonix. The site was plastered in 3ft of snow. After an eventful battle in locating the thing, and then obtaining access to it, we eventually opened the door to find snow piled high inside it.

France, Briançon Area

Many visits to this area took place for us in the early years from 2000. The Vallon du Fournel, Ceillac, the Freissinères Valley and best of the bunch for me was La Grave.

La Grave village lies at the foot of the majestic north face of La Meije, a mountain in the Massif des Ècrins range with an elevation of 3,984m.

Icefalls are easy to reach and almost always in good condition.

France, Cirque du Gavarnie

Gavarnie in the French Pyrénées must also be mentioned here. A glacial cirque presents a paradise for ice climbing, albeit an area with good mountaineering experience to fully justify the visit.

Gavarnie is part of the Pyrénées National Park and a UNESCO world heritage site.

It is certainly the domain holding long icefalls, one of them called *Overdose* has a drop that is the longest in Europe.

A week spent there by four of us, climbing and ski touring to a high alpine hut, was another great winter experience.

Italy, Dolomites Area

Italy, particularly regions of the Dolomites, have some of the most concentrated and fabulous icefalls in Europe.

Sottoguda has an easy access with a ten-minute walk into the canyon.

There we find many icefalls of different grades and difficulties. It is a historical area for ice climbing and probably the most frequented spot in the north-east of the region.

To add to the popularity a great little café serves coffee and cake.

Then there are the longer valleys such as, Val di Fassa and Val Gardena that are reachable from the lovely alpine town of Canazei.

Val Gardena holds fond memories for me with a stupendous four star route called Bullaccia.

Aosta and the Cogne valleys are among the most frequented areas for ice climbers in Europe. Here we find a high concentration of fantastic icefalls of every grade of difficulty and length. To add to the ambience, the area is part of the Grand Paradiso National Park, a very special place indeed.

Norway, Rjukan

Well known for its severe winters and mountainous landscape, Norway is also a wonderful playground for ice climbing.

Hemsedal and Romsdal are well known areas for year-round mountaineering, whereas places like Rjukan, fit into the ice climbing paradise category.

Situated a short distance out of Oslo, in the centre of southern Norway, Rjukan has over 150 icefalls that give guaranteed ice climbing for long periods of winter. Most of the ice climbs are easily accessible, even when there has been heavy snowfall.

The valley sees little sun during the main winter months apart from a sun trap created by a large reflector, strategically placed high up on the northern hillside. It cleverly projects a warming beam of sun onto the local seating area down in the valley.

Other than that, take plenty of warm clothing.

20 April—Covid 19 Update:

Lockdown eventually managed to bring the runaway number of cases and deaths under some sort of control. This was most certainly helped by the continual number of people getting vaccinated.

A road-map out of lockdown was published (see Government list). These 4 steps would not be brought forward any earlier, and could, if targets were not met, be taken out further.

Step 1—8 March and 29 March
Step 2—12 April
Step 3—17 May
Step 4—21 June (but no earlier)

So far Steps 1 and 2 have been met, enabling some freedom of movement and return of non-essential shops to re-open under strict Covid guidelines.

As of this date the current figures now look like:

Number of new daily cases = 2,524
Number of deaths in the latest twenty four hour period = 33
Total number of deaths to date = 127,307
Number of 1st dose vaccinations given = 33+ million
Number of 2nd dose vaccinations given = 10.5 million

New variants are popping up across the world, a new one has recently been found in India.

Covid cases across the world to date:

Number of cases = 142+ million
Number of deaths = 3.04 million

Many countries have been added to the UK's travel ban 'Red list' with ten day quarantine requirements still in place.

Chapter Twenty-Five
Piz Badile, North East Face

It was Martin's idea.

"About time we tried a scary North face."

"Really! I thought we had only just got off one the other day, on the Ben."

I couldn't find any excuses this time, I had all the time in the world having just retired from Biomet and full time working in 2010.

Three years previously, we had successfully climbed the North Face of Les Courtes via the Swiss route. This is described in Gaston Rébuffat marvellous book *The Mont Blanc Massif—The 100 finest Routes* as one of the greatest routes of the range. At around 800m of climbing from the bergschrund, it is about the same length as the Piz Badile.

The Piz Badile, however, seemed a different ball game in my mind. It is regarded as one of the six classic North Faces of the Alps, and our line of choice was the legendary route put up by Riccardo Cassin and his team in 1937.

As with all of Cassin's routes, it was a fantastic first ascent. It had had many attempts by different teams over the years, and was finally climbed by him and his team after three bivvies and fifty-two hours on the face.

It was, however, unfortunately marred by tragedy. Not with any of Cassin's team, but another pair of Italians from their home town who were attempting the same line.

The pairing of Mario Molteni and Giuseppe Valsecchi got into trouble and succumbed to the terrible conditions experienced on the face, despite the efforts of the Cassin team to help.

Martin and I arrived in the Bregaglia valley late August to fine, sunny weather, having driven down by car from the UK. It was rather late by the time we descended from the Maloja pass and eventually bivvyed beside a cable car station, close to the Swiss/Italian border.

The following morning, we booked into the *Aquafraggio* campsite with great views of the mountains.

Most of the next day was spent sizing up the face of the Badile (noting rather more snow towards the summit than we anticipated), as well as climbing a couple of short routes on a local crag.

The inevitable 'law of sod' arrived overnight with heavy rain in the valley and higher up over the Pizzo's Cengalo and Badile. It was at least an opportunity to sample the local coffee and cake situation and explore the lovely town of Chiavenna.

Fortunately, the weather had picked up within a couple of days, and although another dusting of snow had been put down on the Badile face, we decided to head off to *Bondo* village and pick up the track leading to the *Sasc Fura* hut.

Within two hours we had reached the hut, but carried on to locate a strategic bivvy spot to spend the night below the north ridge. A good site was found with water supplied from a large patch snow melt. After several brews and an instant supper meal, we made a quick recce of the col that gave access to the start of our route.

By 20.30, it was close to freezing and time to get into the sleeping bags. Our alarm was set for 04.30 and I dozed off beneath a clear sky and billions of stars with a little trepidation.

I was woken, not by the alarm but by chatter and foot-fall. Head torches were passing not far from us; the penny dropped that we were in danger of not being first to the route.

Fortunately, it didn't take long for us to get going (climbing with Martin never does). We soon arrived at the col and then climbed down ledges, then behind a bergschrund, to gain the 'Cassin boss' and start of the route.

There were three parties ahead and with only a litre of water each for Martin and I, we knew it needed to be a fast ascent, by whatever it took!

I have chosen not write up our route description in detail here, but the fact that it felt more like a winter ascent on snowed up rock, added to the excitement of being a big undertaking.

The climbing was some of the most enjoyable, difficult (due to conditions), amazing and memorable I had done on a big face. It took us approximately twelve hours and twenty-four pitches of climbing to get to the summit ridge via slabs and diedre's[50] and another six pitches to reach the summit bivvy shelter.

Due to the parties ahead of us, it ultimately became necessary to take a line off the original route to keep up our steady progress. It may have been climbed before, it may not have, who knows!

Although we chose not to climb with bivvy gear, we had reached the Redaelli bivvy shelter knowing we had enough gear to survive. It was certainly a better option in my mind, than to abseil down the north ridge in the dark, whilst being very dehydrated.

Having made that decision we were delighted to find blankets inside the shelter that made for a decadent night's stay.

In the morning, Martin and I discussed our two options of descent. Should we abseil the ridge or descend the south side to the Gianetti hut? I was concerned the ridge could have been busy, given the numbers on the face, making it potentially very time consuming.

In the end, we descended to the south via abseils and scrambling, taking every opportunity to soak up any rivulets of snow melt to fend off our growing thirst. We rested a while at the Gianetti before taking the very long hike back to the Sasc Fura hut via Passo Porcellizzo.

After retrieving our possessions we had left at our bivvy site, we spent the next two days drinking beer and coffee whilst reliving another of the best climbing days I had ever done.

---

[50] A diedre is a French term in rock climbing for a corner, usually near vertical, that splits a rock face.

Chapter Twenty-Six
Cycling in the Alps and Andalusia

Tour of Mont Blanc

Lynne and I have always been keen cyclists, even more so having moved to Oxfordshire.

These days we probably spend more time off road than on road, as going back a couple of decades, it wasn't so bloody confrontational or dangerous.

If we do end up cycling a route on the roads today, it can occasionally end up with Lynne sticking two fingers up to some 'careless idiot'. Leaving us with the restraint of how to deal with the moron when he or she tries hurling abuse at us.

Anyhow, in 2007 we were comfortably fit bikers and decided to take on the challenge of the Tour of Mont Blanc. I had spent many happy years climbing in the Alps and thought it would be a great way of us seeing them together.

Our start point for the circuit was going to be Chamonix. We had looked at different ways of getting over to the continent, deciding in the end to drive our old VW Golf, bikes included.

First, I needed to knock up a bike rack that held both front forks firmly inside the car. With the rear seats down, wheels taken off, they were a snug fit, but certainly left enough room for the rest of our gear.

I had seen one or two nasty incidences on motorways where external racks had given way under the load, and deposited bikes all over the carriageway.

We had a good run down to Chamonix taking advantage of one quiet service area off the motorway, equipped with toilets and washing facilities, for our only overnight bivvy!

A friendly first night in Le Dahu hotel and restaurant in Argentière enabled us to recover from the long drive and get both sets of panniers organised. The usual basic needs of clothing, camping gear, nutrition, bike spares and medical kit, just about fitted into bulging bags. The hotel offered us a spot in their carpark to leave the car while we were away, for which we were very grateful.

Our route followed the classic tour of five days round the Mont Blanc massif, and covered 341km with an overall height gain of 7631m.

Chamonix to Beaufort 82km1526m
Beaufort to Bourg St Maurice 46km1407m
Bourg St Maurice to Aosta 86km1375m
Aosta to Martigny 84km1889m
Martigny to Chamonix 44km1434m

Totals 341km7631m

Our itinerary kept us off the main tourist routes and gave breath-taking views of the mountains, glaciers and higher snowfields.

We travelled through three countries, France, Italy and Switzerland, negotiating six major passes, which I must admit to being a little apprehensive about to start with, panniers and all.

Our first stage to Beaufort took us via Sallanches and Megève.

The road to Sallanches gave great views of the Chamonix Aiguilles, which for me, always offers up profound climbing memories. It was then onwards up steep gradients to the posh ski resort of Megève. The road descended for a fair distance, giving us a breather before tackling our first major pass over the Col des Saisies at 1650m. We took it steady and then enjoyed the run down to Beaufort.

It is a lovely alpine town, famous for its cheeses, the best of which for me is Beaufort d'alpage.

The second stage took us south to Bourg St Maurice, a short but interesting hop via Areches!

There are in fact two Col's on this stage. Col du Pré (which isn't recognised as a Col) got us warmed up for the second and main climb to the Cormet de Roseland.

Descent from Col du Pré took us past the picturesque Roseland Reservoir, and over the dam onto the steep incline up to the Roseland. It is obviously a training ground for 'Grand Tour' cyclists, as we witnessed, when a peloton of a well-known tour team pissed past us as if we were standing still.

Fair play, they did offer us encouragement and patted Lynne on the shoulder, which made her day, while I shouted, "vous n'iriez pas si vite si vous aviez ces sacoches sanglantes." which roughly translates to; "you wouldn't go so fast if you had these bloody panniers".

The Col is at 1967m and the surrounding area attracts one of the largest amounts of snowfall in the Alps. It still hung around down to road level in places and certainly made us delve in the panniers for a fleece before stopping for a quick lunch.

A long, effortless ride down the lovely valley led us into the town of Bourg St Maurice.

Bourg is a hub for skiers and cyclists alike; it also has nice clean campsites, one of which we soon settled into.

Day three took us through the towns of La Thuile and Pré-St-Didier to Aosta and into Italy.

It focussed our minds for tackling the second highest pass we would encounter on the tour, the Col du Petit St Bernard, an elevation of 2188m.

Saint Bernard's Day (20 August) is not a time to tackle the pass, as every mother and her brother gathers at the summit to celebrate the famous day. Fortunately, we were a month early.

There is an enormous amount of history associated with the pass particularly linked to the Romans and consequent events after the fall of their empire.

We, however, had enough to concentrate on, which was getting up and over the thing.

With endless push-pulling of the pedals, and a couple of pit stops thrown in, we made good progress. We were beginning to acclimatise, which must have added to us feeling stronger on the hills. If we were not careful, we would soon be enjoying it!

Lynne coped brilliantly as I whinged constantly about a sore arse. Soon enough we were over the top where it crossed the border into Italy, and started winging our way down the long valley to the city Aosta.

Aosta is a very pleasant city with a huge amount to explore. Unfortunately, our timescales didn't allow for a great deal of sight-seeing. All too soon the following day we were back on the bikes bound for the Swiss city of Martigny.

Our fourth day took us from Aosta to Martigny via Bour-St-Pierre and Sembrancher.

This was our hardest day of the tour, for not only was it another 80km+ day in the saddle, it took us over the highest pass, the Col du Grand St Bernard at 2469m.

This pass, like most of the others, has been used by travellers over millennia. Julius Caesar is known to have travelled over the pass, when he and his army conquered the pagans of Martigny.

The two passes are named after Bernard of Menthon, who was an Italian canon, founder of the Great St Bernard Hospice that gave shelter and safe-haven to travelling merchants. It is now used as kennels, caring and breeding of the famous St Bernard dogs.

It was certainly a test of our strength and determination by the time we arrived at the seemingly endless journey to the top. As we passed the statue of St Bernard and neared the top of the pass with its abundance of summer souvenir stalls, we both bore huge smiles and took a long welcome rest.

Then a long leisurely ride north down the valley into Switzerland towards the sprawling city of Martigny, was only interrupted once by a very inviting coffee and cake pit stop.

Our tent was soon up in a spacious campsite, followed by numerous brews and wallowing in the late afternoon sun.

The last leg of our tour took us from Martigny to Argentière via two final Cols.

We had learnt our lesson in having light breakfasts (I'll say no more) as no sooner had we got on the bikes, we were onto steep inclines all the way to Col de la Forclaz at 1562m.

From there, our journey led us on a road through fragrant pine woodlands and back to the border with France.

A rather inviting spot in the sun beside a small river, was too much temptation to have a quick brew, before crossing the border. Our brilliant journey was soon to end, we wanted to suck up as much of the ambience as possible.

Stunning views of the Aiguille Verte, Chamonix Aiguilles and Mont Blanc in near cloudless skies, greeted us from the Col des Montets 1461m.

It was then downhill all the way back to Argentière and Hotel Dahu. The following day was spent in Chamonix, and of course drinking coffee and eating cake, reflecting on the test we gave ourselves and the enjoyment it brought.

Cycling in France and Andalusia

In 2012, my cycling buddies Michael and Moby (Maureen) O'Connor, who were to join me and Martin the following year to South America, decided a cycling extravaganza in France and Spain would be fun. I was keen, but from its inception, I have no manly guilt in admitting, I saw it more likely to be extreme physical torture than fun!

After all, it was to be around 1000km of cycling with over 9150m (30,000ft) of ascent.

As it turned out, it was a remarkable journey. However, I also admit to being completely buggered for the 'Piece de resistance' of the trip, a circular route over Alpe d'Huez.

I didn't join them, making excuses I was missing climbing crags and needing to go off and find one to boulder on. That was not a total falsehood, as I did search for a wee while, before succumbing to my main inner impulse, a quiet spot in the sun with a nice café close by.

We used my VW T4 van to get us there and back and for links in between cycling.

Rather than write reams of similar material, I thought it was worth adding Michael's itinerary below, which we pretty much kept to, for anyone who might be slightly interested.

June 24—Ferry from Plymouth (VW van plus 3 adults).

June 25—Arrive Santander. Drive to Jerez de la Frontera (920km, 10 hours driving).

One overnight stop in Seville.

June 26—Sherry tasting at Bodegas in Jerez. Drive to Ronda through white town of Arcos de la Frontera. Cork Oak forest of the Parque Natural de la Sierra Grazalema. Overnight in Ronda campsite.

June 27—Ronda to El Chorro, **62km** *(Cycle touring in Spain, page 98 and 101)* with via ferrata of the Camino del Rey in the Garganta del Chorro.

June 28—El Chorro to Alfamatejo, **70km.**

June 29—Alfamatejo to Alhama de Granada to Granada, **101km** *(Cycle touring in Spain, page 98 and 101)*.

June 30—Sight-seeing: Alahambra Palace and Gardens.

July 1—Granada to Pitres, **90km** *(Cycle touring in Spain, page 93)*.

July 2—Pitres to Laroles, **63km** *(Cycle touring of Spain, page 90)*.

July 3—Laroles to Alhama de Almeria, **82km** *(Cycle touring of Spain, page 88)*.

July 4—Drive from Almeria to Châteauneuf-du-Pape, France (1260km, 12 hours).

July 5—Wine tasting: tried some Rhone wines, then drive to Vaison-la-Romaine. Cycle from Vaison-la-Romaine to Sault, **59km** over Mont Ventoux *(Lonely Planet Cycling France, page 359 and cycle touring in France, page 153)*.

July 6—Drive from Sault to Valensole, **84km**, Lavender route and the Lavender fields.

July 7—Valensole to Comps-sur-Artuby, **79km** through the Grand Canyon du Verdun *(Lonely Planet Cycling France, page 348)*.

July 8—Drive from Comps-sur-Artuby to Puget-Thénieres, **65km**. Cycle form Puget-Thénieres to Isola, **65km** *(Cycling in the French Alps, page 158)*.

July 9—Isola to Jausiers, **65km** *(Cycling in the French Alps, page 194)*.

July 10—Jausiers to Guillestre to Briançon, **96km** *(Cycling in the French Alps, pages 191 and 192)*.

July 11—Briançon to St-Jean-de-Maurienne, **86km** *(Cycling in the French Alps, page 130)*.

July 12—St-Jean-de-Maurienne to Bourg d'Oisans, **70km** *(Cycling in the French Alps, page 142)*.

July 13—Circular route over Alp d'Huez, Col de Sarenne and back to Bourg d'Oisans, **58km** *(Cycling in the French Alps, page 140)*.

July 14—Coffee and cake all day!

July 15—Drive to Calais (910km).

July 16—Ferry to England.

Chapter Twenty-Seven
The Beautiful Lofoten Isles

I hadn't the remotest idea where the Lofoten Islands were when Nick Walmsley suggested we should visit them. But as soon as he showed Dave, Martin and myself a few photographs, we were soon on the case.

The Islands form a peninsula stretching south west into the Norwegian Sea near to the mainland town of Narvik, northern Norway. They lie approximately 100 miles inside the Arctic Circle, but are somewhat protected from the severest weather by the Gulf Stream.

The diverse landscape is not too dissimilar to that of the Scottish Highlands. However, the rugged peaks and ridges of majestic mountains that rise directly from an azure sea are much sharper and jagged than those of the more weathered eroded Highlands.

The area is steeped in Viking history. Today, though, it is famous for cod fishing, with the unmistakeable air-drying lattices full of cod scattered around the islands. Norway, and indeed Lofoten, is also famous for the undeniably elegant bridges that now link its islands. So much so that the impulse is to walk or cycle across every one.

In February 2005, we chose to make a winter climbing adventure of the islands, rather than a summer rock climbing one. Our research appeared to show it was much less popular for winter climbing, which helped focus our thoughts for some first ascent opportunities.

The flights took us from Heathrow to Oslo, then onwards to Bodo and eventually to a very snow covered Svolvaer. The town of Svolvaer is around the mid-point of the Lofoten peninsula.

Having landed and weighed up the conditions, landscape and time available, it was clear we wouldn't be exploring its entire length.

Nick had found us a very cosy cabin nestled amongst snow drifts on the outskirts of town.

It was basic but well equipped and spacious; best of all it was warm, as the temperature outside was bloody freezing.

We wasted no time the following day driving to Henningsvaer, a small fishing village, in the hope of finding their café open, whilst recceing the local climbing scene, from information the café was supposed to be the keepers of.

Not surprisingly it was closed, as was most of the village, nevertheless, armed with a little UK climbing info, we set off to climb ice!

It took a while to come to terms with the driving conditions, for like the Alps, there was no rock-salt used, only grit spread on a compacted snow base.

After a few hours of playing on ice and 'feeding the rat', we arrived back at our cabin having completed a fine 8 pitch route on 'Rea' crag.

The following day we drove to 'Eggum' on the northern tip of 'Vestvagoy'. Beautiful scenery of snow-clad monoliths, reaching skyward straight out of an ice crusted sea, were incredibly inspiring, this was similar scenery for most of the coastal areas we visited.

We picked out impressive, obvious lines on mountains in the area, but they looked too heavily loaded with snow for imminent climbing.

A big icefall at Nordfjellett left an impression on us, a possible project for the following day, as did the double peaks of Himmalstinden and Nordtinden.

'Hot toddies' became a favourite habit in the evenings, but made it a bugger of a job to get up at 06.30 each morning to get those vital brews going.

We did manage a good 5 pitch route on Nordfjellett (two of which were Scottish grade 5), before snow and sleet abandoned, play (see new route list).

Bad weather forced a day and a half off climbing, all the excuses necessary for coffee and cake in Svolvaer and a bit of snow shoeing around our local frozen lake.

The following day improved and enabled us to put up what we believed to be, a new line on Sundklaak icefall (see new route list). A good 350m route with 2 good lower pitches, some dead ground in the middle, and a final 3 pitches up a great line (Scottish grade 5), with a finish through a cornice to the top.

Nearly a week had passed, when we were forced into another rest day. As it turned out it was hardly a rest day!

Dave, whose turn it was to drive, ploughed us straight into a huge snow drift. Bless him, he won't mind me taking the piss here, as well we all did on the day.

In fairness, the road edges could be quite indistinguishable. Going slightly off right with the front wheel merely nudging the snow boundary, was enough for the snow to grab it.

Then, like some waiting troll pulling you to its lair, not letting you escape for all your struggles and cussing, there was only one inevitable conclusion.

We were stuck!

Snow reached almost to roof level, it was certainly at window height, and none of us could open the doors. Two of us got out of a window to start clearing a door, followed by us all spending a good couple of hours uncovering the vehicle.

We were in the middle of nowhere, save for a lonely farmer and a tractor. He was soon on the case, as if he'd done it many times before. It enabled us to limp into Leknes (the capitol town of Lofoten) and the Hertz showroom to beg a replacement.

After much less hassle and admin than we expected (it must be a regularity), we finished the afternoon eyeing up new route potential for the following day.

I should add here, having forgotten to mention it, that daylight climbing hours inside the Arctic Circle in February, is limited to around seven hours.

If the previous day's event was more about adolescent amusement than serious climbing, we were about to get the latter by the bucket load.

Nick, while suffering with a heavy cold, had decided not to join the three of us on a quality line on the east face of Svartinden. Our assault on the 1st pitch via a direct line up a steep icefall, was met with a 2nd pitch that looked extremely thin and dodgy.

We decided to rappel off and take another line to the right. It was the correct decision as our new line offered up some sensational, varied climbing.

The first pitch was again steep. That led to a couple of pitches of easier ground, which in turn led curiously, to a bergschrund. That was negotiated before two more very steep pitches were tackled. Further easier ground was followed by a technical chimney, which in turn led to a final three rope lengths to the top.

We arrived on a complex summit around 17.00, just as it was getting dark. We had climbed 12 pitches (600m) and now needed to make a swift decision on the best way off before total darkness was upon us. It was not straight forward by any means.

There were complex ridges with huge cornices the size of buses, and steep alternative gullies, that didn't look particularly inviting either. There was only one sensible option, which was to reverse our ascent line.

Numerous abseils off rock spikes and the odd Abalakov, using our own 'tat', bore witness to our ascent and descent. The final 50m abseil anchor back to terra firma, proved to be the most difficult to find. I exaggerate not, that a tiny Juniper sapling, poking out of the snow, and no bigger in diameter than my forefinger, was what we ended up nervously trusting.

We arrived back at the car knackered, but obviously exhilarated, as we were confident it was a first ascent (see new route list). It had been a long, seventeen hour day. We arrived back to our warm cabin, at ten minutes past midnight, to a much-relieved Nick, who was about to send out a search party.

The weather had been kind to us up to then, but took a turn for the worse with heavy snow and strong winds. It gave us chance to relax a little longer in the mornings, drink coffee and research more of the area. Between breaks in the weather, we did manage one or two short routes, believing them to be new lines (see new route list).

A final outing before heading home, was a brilliant line up an icefall on Presten crag near Henningsvaer. We started up a thinly iced corner to a ramp line that led to the foot of a main icefall. That led to steep icy steps and a chock-stone and 3 further pitches to the top ridge. All in all, approximately 450m (5 pitches) of excellent climbing (see new route list).

Hot toddies drew the evening to a close, but not before the Aurora Borealis showed itself. Dave was quick off the mark to catch the display on camera, a glorious finale to end yet another fine adventure.

Chapter Twenty-Eight
Les Courtes—North Face

The Argentière glacier sits high above the Chamonix valley and stretches for some ten kilometres south east from the village of Argentière. On its right flank lie four of the most famous snow and ice routes in the area if not the Alps, the Triolet, the Droites, the Courtes and the Verte.

Their imposing walls of snow, ice and mixed ground, can still get the hairs aroused on the back of a climber's neck looking to climb one of them.

What it must have been like for the first ascensionists of these iconic routes back in the late 1930s to late 1950s, as they step cut their way up the faces with rudimentary protection, one can barely imagine.

It is still very much a challenge for the mid-grade alpinist who today like me, use state-of-the-art, light-weight gear such as axes, crampons as well as tubular titanium ice-screws.

Back in May 2007 Martin and I decided to take on the challenge of the North Face of Les Courtes (3856m) via the Swiss route to the summit. Considered a desirable prize even now, and is still considered one of the best ice routes in the Alps. It was sure to 'feed the rat'.

The route is approximately 800m long and takes a direct line up the centre of the face, is reasonably sustained throughout, with one main crux pitch at around one third height. In good conditions the objective dangers are minimal and together with frequent opportunities for solid belays, it makes for a challenging climb without too much of the scare factor or for being scared shitless.

Today there are dozens of routes that take more claim to fame, but the 'fab three' should not be underestimated by those seeking a challenge (the fourth 'the Triolet', has now developed serious serac collapse and is considered too dangerous to climb).

After travelling to Chamonix and using a couple of days for acclimatising, we headed up to the top station of the Grandes Montets téléférique adjacent to the Glacier des Rognons.

In true Brit style with no skis or snowshoes, we headed down the Rognons glacier to meet up with the Argentière glacier way below with nothing more on our feet than big boots and crampons—this always brings a smirk on the faces of our French Alpinist comrades who are always so slick and bloody expert.

Within an hour, we were on the Argentière glacier followed by a further hour up and across to the Refuge d'Argentière, situated on rocks above the glaciers left flank.

It would have been too easy to book ourselves into the nice warm hut like everybody else, but no, we yet again showed our true British grit (or frigging stupidity) and set about sorting a bivvy spot a hundred metres above the hut in the snow and a temperature of minus twelve degrees centigrade.

After a good few brews and some food, we packed our sacks for a slick start in the morning. It was then time to hunker down into our sleeping bags as darkness fell and the temperature dropped like a stone. We made plans to be away from our warm pits and onto the face by 04.00 in the hope of beating any early starters from the hut. As is always the case, it makes for a safer, speedier ascent to be first on the route.

If there are any doubters out there as to why anyone should want to bivvy, especially in the snow and at altitude, all I can say is you must try it!

Open water swimming, or walking in the woods may be good for the soul, (I know it's each to their own), but choose a clear night any time of the year in the wilderness or at altitude, preferably in the autumn or winter when the sky is clear and crisp, it will not disappoint.

From a cosy warm pit, gaze up to the heavens, study the stars, the milky way and if you're lucky, the comets. If you are far enough north, you may even get a fleeting visit from the Aurora Borealis. I guarantee it will take you a while to nod off to sleep, your soul will be enriched and you will want another dose.

It took me ages to nod off, if the clear sky and all that goes with it wasn't enough of an attraction, the full moon shining on the north face picking out our line of ascent certainly was. Martin on the other hand, was snoring his bloody block off.

The alarm sounded at 02.30, it was frigging freezing. It took a while to gear up, put on frozen boots and get a brew on, but we managed to get away for 03.00.

It was then down onto the glacier and across to the bergschrund, which we crossed via a small snow bridge just left of our proposed start point on the face. We had made good timing and the correct decision as head torches were beginning to flicker outside the hut.

It was 04.00 as we geared up at the foot of the face in preparation for the 50degree snow and ice couloir, the first third of the route. It was absorbing climbing on wonderful squeaky névé as the faint glow of dawn began to show. Good progress got us to the narrows forming the crux of the route (Scottish winter grade IV) culminating in a steep exit of around 70 degrees. There was sound protection and belays that we found on the walls of the couloir throughout, which added to the pleasure rather than the concern.

We were going well and soon on the broad ice wall above, alternating leads as we went. Tiredness was beginning to set in and my calves were now screaming as I had been on front points most of the time. With few technical problems to deal with, and pulling on last dregs of energy, we were on the upper slopes of the Courtes. Finally, a short diagonal line joined the WNW spur which led us wearily to the summit after 8hrs of climbing.

It was in the bag and both of us were chuffed to bits albeit a tad knackered, me more so than Martin I think. Our descent took us along the WNW ridge to a point where the NE slope joined it. The slope looked ok but seemed to take an age to descend purely because I was buggered.

We eventually arrived back at our bivvy site and succumbed to endless brews and grub before packing gear away for the long plod down to Argentière.

This again, I can only imagine, would have been sheer pleasure if we had skis to run the glacier and the skill to avoid the crevasses. I was rather glad we didn't as it would have taken a good level of ski touring ability to negotiate one or two of them.

I for one, was happy to carry the 'stupid Brit' badge and walk down, knowing full well it could have ended in tears if I was on skis.

Canada – The Weeping Wall (Icefields Parkway)

Canada – Johnson Canyon icefalls near Banff

Piz Badile – The N.E face *Piz Badile – On the 1st pitch*

On the face feeling more like winter

Piz Badile – On the summit at the Redaelli bivvy hut

Lofoton Isles – Svolvaer in winter

Lofoton Isles – One of many pink skies and glorious views

Lofoton Isles – Sweeping, elegant bridges abound

Lofoton Isles – Drying gear, getting a brew in the warm

Chamonix Mt Blanc – Les Courtes North Face

Part 7: UK Playground

<u>*Determination*</u>
If you think you're beaten, you are,
If you think you dare not, you don't,
If you think you'll lose, you've lost.
For success begins with a persons will
and state of mind.

Walter D. Wintle

Chapter Twenty-Nine
Circuit of the Lairig Ghru

Adventures with family are just as important and fun for me as the more serious ones I've undertaken in my mountaineering career.

The UK and Eire, with its 6000+ islands, offers such a diverse landscape for limitless playtime, exploration and adventuring. So much so, there is little need to automatically think of heading off to Europe and beyond, we just need to search for them here.

One such adventure occurred in early summer 2004.

I had winter climbed a lot in the Cairngorms and occasionally skied, but it had always been in the depths of an arctic-alpine winter. A spring/summer trip was required, to soak up some of the sub-arctic flora, diverse landscapes, running streams and clear pools, instead of a frozen, frigid wilderness.

Lynne didn't need too much persuading to join me on a circuit of the Cairngorm massif via the Lairig Ghru and Strath Nethy.

The Lairig Ghru (Làirig Dhrù in Gaelic) is a mountain pass in the Cairngorms historically used as a route between the districts of Strathspey in the north to Deeside in the south. It was once used as an old 'Drove Road' in the late eighteenth century, but also for a variety of reasons well before then. The word Lairig means hill pass, but the origin of Ghru or Dhru remains a bit of a mystery.

The Cairngorms consist of a range of rolling mountain slopes and peaks with summits between 1000m to 1200m. Cairngorm mountain summit itself sits at 1245m on a large high plateau. The highest point in the range is Ben Macdui at 1309m. They cover the highest, most extensive and wildest upland found anywhere in Britain. The mountains were once much higher, but were modified by glacial ice during the Quaternary period that started some 2.5 million years ago.

Those glacial ice sheets eroded the highest peak of Ben Macdui and gouged great troughs and corries into the landscape, one of which was the Lairig Ghru.

In late spring of 2004, we travelled up from Wantage to our place in Kendal, followed by a good journey the following morning to the town of Aviemore in the Cairngorms National Park.

We wasted little time gathering provisions for our four day (three nights) leisurely camping and hiking trip, in contrast to the little more time we gave ourselves sorting gear and packing the sacks.

The weather forecast was reasonable. However, it was important for me to know we each had the appropriate gear packed should it change, as it so often can, very quickly!

From Aviemore, we parked the car at Coylumbridge and started our trek through the privately owned Rothiemurchus estate. The area is one of the most treasured in the Cairngorms. Not only for its history of early settlements dating back to the eighth century, but also for being the hub of the great Caledonian Pine Forest.

One got a true sense of its significance walking slowly through it, even in the twenty-first century.

As we ground out the footsteps, gaining height under the heavy loads towards the Chalamain Gap, the views behind us were fantastic. A further 5km got us to our first wild camp near the Pools of Dee (source of the river Dee). It had been a long day, the sky was clear, the air was chilled and the mountains were high above us on either side. We were in a different world soaking up the atmosphere with a brew and meal in a bag!

We didn't hurry the following morning, still blessed with good weather of broken cloud and occasional sunny periods. We even donned our shorts as we headed south down the Ghru, passing Ben Macdui high to our left and Cairn Toul (1293m) to our right.

The trail south following the River Dee was pleasing and reasonably flat at the 600m contour level. We skirted round Carn a' Mhaim heading east for 5km or 6km until coming across Derry Lodge. It was a great opportunity to sit and relax a while on the bank of the Derry Burn with a brew on the go, absorbing the atmosphere.

It was difficult to get going again, having lingered longer than planned. We now headed north up Glen Derry for another 6km or 7km until the trail split, with a north-west track that led up to the Hutchison Memorial Hut. Although tempted to have a recce for a place to sleep, we needed to keep on the trail due north. Besides the late afternoon weather was too nice not put up the tent where we stood, for our 2nd nights wild camp.

Onward the next day, following the Lairig an Laoigh track, until we came to the Fords of Avon (pronounced Arrn) Refuge. The wind had picked up, there was a threat of rain, it seemed a good opportunity to put a brew on, tuck ourselves out of the wind in the refuge and see what developed.

The weather cheered up and once again we soon got on the move. Here we headed due west following the Loch Avon burn in a valley between A' Choinneach summit to the north and Beinn Mheadhoin to the south.

After 2km, we started a rising traverse of the hillside to the north of Loch Avon at a point known as 'The Saddle'.

The views were gob-smacking, everything I could have hoped for in doing the trek at that time of the year.

Loch Avon was clear and stunning, instead of being the iced over whiteness I had only ever seen. The infamous Shelter Stone crag to the south-west had a streak of snow still running down the gully between it and Carn Etchachan. Cairngorm Mountain and the plateau to the north-west were still nurturing large amounts of spring snow.

To cap it all, two mottled Ptarmigan were croaking a short distance away, slowly shedding their white winter coat.

We sat for five minutes, soaking up the atmosphere once again; even Lynne, a seasoned trekker, slightly less emotional in the mountains than myself (I'm sure she would agree), was pretty gob struck.

We knew from the map the next leg north was going to be long and tough.

It was a gradual, downhill 10km stretch along Strath Nethy, following the charming River Nethy, wild spring flowers were popping up everywhere. The trail led to the small pool of An Lochan Uaine. Here it turned south-west towards Glenmore Lodge, a further 3km through an open forest.

By the time we reached Loch Morlich, we were buggered, it had been a long day. Although only another 4km to reach our car, there seemed little point in rushing back.

The sun was shining as we considered options. It took only a few seconds to decide the tent was going up at the first opportunity.

And so, we relaxed in the evening sun, drinking brews and eating the few crumbs we had left.

We reflected on the journey we had undertaken, like you do when you have achieved something special. Lynne had once again been stoical in carrying a heavy pack; I knew she would enjoy it, and I was really pleased we had made the effort. For me, it was another spiritual journey in the mountains.

Our thoughts moved on to Gary and Nicky, the journey home and the return to work in a couple of days.

'Determination' is so important in our lives. It gives us 'purpose' and 'resolve' to do stuff, rather than sit on our backsides taking easy options or living in the status quo.

Chapter Thirty
Three Ridges

The British Isles are also hugely endowed with ridge lines, traverses that range in difficulty from moderate hikes to challenging Alpine adventures.

The three that I shall mention briefly here have left special memories with me, but there are others that come a very close second. Those include the A'Chir Ridge on the Isle of Arran, Aonach Eagach Ridge, Crib Goch, Striding Edge, Sharp edge and of course Tower Ridge on 'The Ben'.

All done with members of the family or with friends.

Cuillin Ridge of Skye

This is, without doubt, the most famous expedition in the British Isles, often quoted as being equivalent to an Alpine adventure in Europe. It is probably the greatest single outing to be had in Britain.

It involves over 3000m of ascent spread over a horizontal distance of 12km. The technical standard of summer rock climbing is never more than Very Difficult, but due to the sustained nature throughout its length, it is wise to be able to lead Severe.

Fitness, time and weather are the common barriers that prevent a successful traverse. A combined time of eighteen hours from the Glen Brittle campsite, onto the ridge, followed by a full traverse to the Sligachan Hotel is pretty good going.

A winter traverse is common nowadays, although conditions are very fickle. Given a Scottish climbing grade V, it is a mighty tick on any climber's CV.

I have attempted a full traverse of the Cuillin on three occasions, not being successful on any of them, time being the critical factor on all three.

In May 2010, Gary and I found a few days to give it a bash. I had just retired from full-time employment with Biomet Ltd, and Gary had justified a few days off from growing his security business. It was an opportunity to have some precious time together.

We made it to the Isle of Skye and the Glen Brittle campsite after a long journey from 'down south' and an overnight bivvy somewhere in the southern highlands. The campsite is in a glorious position by the shore of Loch Brittle. This is a very popular base for rock climbing, kayaking, walking and the start for a traverse of the ridge from south to north.

The weather was not playing ball, in fact it was pissing down, but time was not on our side.

Our first objective was the high point of Gars-bheinn (895m), the start of the ridge proper.

It can be gained one of two ways: a long, soul destroying slog for around 3 hours up the fell-side, crossing Alt Coire nan Lagan, or a more 'interesting' approach via Coir' a' Ghrunnda.

As we couldn't see much more than a hand in front of our face, we decided on the former.

Soaked and a little disorientated in the clag, we knew roughly where we were, having followed the compass for most of the time. An altimeter reading gave us our elevation and a fortunate break in the cloud enabled a bearing off the island of Soay. That enabled a fix on our position and an aim point for the ridge.

It was pure luck that we crested the ridge to find a convenient bivvy spot in lee of the wind and rain. By now it was dark, we were soaked, but in our relatively sheltered space it was indeed fun getting a brew and some grub on the go. Like me, Gaz (I have various uneducated names for both Gary and Nicola) felt he had 'fed the rat' a little.

I didn't let on that there were certainly going to be more opportunities for that along the route.

Gary had wormed his way into an alcove all snug in his bivvy bag and sleeping bag. It left me a little more exposed to the elements and by the time I woke up in the morning, I had a good few millimetres of wet snow laying on my bivvy bag.

"So much for you hard-core Paras," I shouted, as I wriggled out of my crusty cocoon attempting to get a brew on.

Visibility had improved a little, and although it was windy and raining we decided to press on.

We were going well, passing Loch Coir' a' Ghrunnda down to our left. Soon the ridge steepened ominously as we made it to the infamous Thearlaich-Dubh Gap. The gap is a chasm with almost sheer vertical walls. It necessitates abseiling down to a huge jammed boulder, where a belay is taken for the impending thrutch up the wall in front of us.

It was here that Gary and I met a trio who had become stranded and stuck.

The 25m north-west wall facing us was the most technical section of the ridge. It involves climbing a very polished chimney crack, V. Diff standard in the dry, bloody diabolical when wet. Eventually we all made it to the top and carried on along the ridge.

However, the weather was getting worse. Gary and I decided to escape down the huge scree slope to Loch Coire Lagan while we could, and see if the weather improved the following day. The three also decided to join us down and head back to Glen Brittle camp site, clearly still a little shocked but none the worse for wear.

After another cosy bivvy, the morning was upon us with less wind and rain; it heralded another bash at the ridge. Essential brews were followed with a bacon and scrambled egg boil in a bag. It got us mobile and helped with the slog of some 250m back up the scree to the ridge, determined to at least tick the east ridge of the Inaccessible Pinnacle, if nothing else.

Not surprised by the lack of anyone on the arête, as the weather was closing in again, we got straight on it. G had no problem seconding my lead, and made light work of abseiling the west ridge down to terra firma.

Descent down to Sgurr a' Mhadaidh was reasonably straight forward, but fog was closing in rapidly. By the time we got to Sgurr Thormaid, it was a pea soup and inevitably made for a wrong turn. We lost a fair bit of time sorting out the correct line, but knew we were back on it when faced with another impending wall with a large amount of exposure below it.

We took a line climbing solo, the holds were ok but soaked yet again, adding a whole new dimension to it. In hindsight, I was perhaps irresponsible (as a father) not pitching it with a rope. The fog and awareness of the void below, certainly focussed the mind.

We made it to the top and carried on.

"That was the scariest effing thing I've done for quite a while," G said to me.

It obviously stuck in his mind, as he remembers it vividly to this day. He jokingly reminds me every so often that I was a terribly irresponsible parent, whilst wryly grinning and admitting, it was another 'rat fed'.

We were running out of time, it was inevitable the full traverse was not going to be possible.

Next up was the exposed narrow ridge of Sgurr a' Ghreadaidh. Once more the conditions focussed the minds but slowed our pace.

As we finally approached Sgurr a' Mhadaidh, we made a decision to escape down the easy Bealach na Glaic Moire before the complex tops and the rest of the technical ridge were taken.

Another inevitability as we headed back to Glen Brittle campsite round the slopes of Sgurr nan Gobhar, was that the bloody sun came out!

It was the correct decision to bail when we did, a short window of opportunity for us both and we took it. Had we had more time or the weather wasn't so awful, it would have been in the bag.

More importantly, it was about the time, the experience and the mutual enjoyment of being in a wild environment together. Working together in difficult situations, sometimes close to the edge!

'Carpe Diem' we certainly did.

Bosigran (Commando) Ridge, West Cornwall

There are climbs in the country that must be done, purely for their history and sheer ambience. Bosigran Ridge is one of them, and at a grade of Very Difficult (V.Diff) is quite easy, in fact there are only two grades easier (Moderate and Difficult) on the British Traditional (Trad) climbing scale.

Arthur Westlake Andrews was born in 1868 and followed a typical middle-class upbringing. At Oxford University, he was an exceptional sportsman and was introduced to mountaineering, as it was in Victorian Britain, by Revd W A B Coolidge. Although visits to the Alps and Norway were regular 'mountaineering' trips, it took a few years before his lifelong involvement with rock climbing at West Penwith and Bosigran took hold.

North Wales was the favoured training ground for the Alps, but the Atlantic coast of Cornwall offered a lot too. In 1902, Andrews and his companions climbed a *remarkable serrated ridge of granite* as he called it, a multi pitch route of some 700ft, Bosigran Ridge was thus named.

That was only the start of wild adventurism he and his formidable wife, Elsie, undertook on the cliffs of the Atlantic. Only complete eccentrics would have thought of traversing the entire coastal cliffs of Britain, Tyrolean traverses included!

...Now there's an extreme thought for someone?

There is a myriad of pre-war climbing history to the area, but a famous one refers to 1940–45 and the cliff assault wing of the Royal Marine Commandos. The area became an extensive training ground for the Commandos in World War 2. It also saw many new routes put up by hardened physical training instructors on their more leisurely outings to the cliffs.

Bosigran Ridge is now more commonly known amongst climbers as 'Commando Ridge' and is certainly worth the adventure. Particularly so in an Atlantic swell, no matter what grade one climbs at, V. Diff or E9.

Once again in 2010, having retired from fulltime employment, an opportunity arose to get away with Nicky for a few days. It was for something challenging, but within her capabilities for us to enjoy some quality time together. She knew about Commando Ridge from my exploits and wanted to try it.

We have always been exceptionally close as a family, keen to involve ourselves in each other's activities. Although never wanting to take up the climbing baton like her old man, Nicky had been on climbing days together in the Lake District, North Devon and North Wales.

She was going through uncertainty in her life both in a career path and in her personal life. It was an opportunity to get away, forget about issues, to focus on something completely different and absorbing, as climbing adventures so often do.

We arrived at our West Penwith campsite in need of a brew and some breakfast. The weather was on our side, and a lazy, or should I say relaxing, start outside the tent ensued.

The ritual of packing sacks and going through plans, starts the process of de-cluttering the mind of other unnecessary worries in life.

I parked the car on the small off road 'pull in' next to a ruined building of an old tin mine, a short distance from the Counts House, now a climbing hut owned by the Climbers Club.

From the old mine, a track runs down to Porthmoina Cove until another small ruin is met. There, a track runs west and leads to a 'notch' high in the finishing part of Commando Ridge.

At this point, a Commando commemorative plaque has been strategically fixed, on the rock above.

The weather was beautiful as we geared up, putting harnesses on and sorting a small rack of gear. Negotiating the notch, and the subsequent scramble down beside the ridge, soon set the scene and the heart beating a little faster. I sensed a little hesitation from Nicky at mid-height, but after attaching the rope to her, it soon gave her the confidence to continue down to the slabs at sea level.

Unfortunately, the sea swell had made the first pitch too wet to climb. It required a scramble to gain the ridge above it, but soon we were both on the ridge proper with no one else in sight. Blue skies and a crystal-clear sea was more than I could have hoped for, enabling her to fully appreciate the atmosphere. I could tell she was thoroughly absorbed in the climbing too.

Friction on the granite rock was fantastic, so often it can be the opposite when wet.

We climbed the next six pitches of slabs, cracks and pinnacles on beautiful dry, weathered granite. Nicky seconded my lead and took most of the problems the ridge presented direct. Others she skirted round, all at her own discretion without input from me.

At the end of the ridge, she was beaming with a broad smile, it was another poignant moment for me, knowing we had both achieved something special again.

Coffee and cake were the order of the day, along with a quick dip in the Atlantic.

Surfing at Sennen Cove, followed by a walk to Land's End and back to Sennen the following day, rounded off our weekend together.

A simple weekend of fun and pleasure between father and daughter, on a truly enjoyable, historical piece of traditional climbing.

Skeleton Ridge (HVS 5a), The Needles, Isle of Wight

The UK abounds with such diversity and quality of rock it surely is enough to satiate a lifetime of climbing.

Included in that, is our unique coastline that offers umpteen opportunities for exploration and new routing. According to the Ordnance Survey, the British Isles has more than 11,000 miles of coastline. Granted, many sea cliffs have been developed, but for the explorers to come, there must be scope for heaps more.

One veteran explorer found a route on a coastal ridge in 1984 that is one of quirkiest of them all.

Who else, other than Mick Fowler, would have put up one of the most ridiculous, yet visionary routes in the country, on a lump of chalk that is The Needles. It is not just a quirky route, it is a whole bloody Alpine adventure. Of all the ridges in the UK, this would certainly be in my top ten. Anyone taking a conventional rack of rock gear is in for a shock!

We arrived on the Island in the year 2000 and headed straight for the 'Old Battery' on the extreme western-tip of the isle. The Battery is an old cliff top fort in a spectacular position looked after by the National Trust. It was built in 1862 and has a fascinating military history. Originally built as a Victorian coastal defence fort on the orders of Lord Palmerston to protect the naval dockyards at Portsmouth from attack by the French.

The Needles are three stacks in the English Channel that take their name from a fourth, that was shaped like a pillar or needle. It collapsed into the sea during a huge storm in 1764.

Martin and I signed the register at reception having pre-booked our climbing visit. I was amazed at the ease of which climbing was accommodated and accepted back then, I hope it remains like that today. The warden was very hospitable and offered us a ladder to negotiate a flat roof(s) of the battery that gave access to the top of the cliff.

An abseil was set-up with two 50m ropes tied together, followed by a launch down to Scratchell's Bay in the hope we had got the ebbing tide correct. Further excitement came half-way down using our 'prussik knots' (used in those days) in conjunction with an abseil devices to negotiate the knot.

In no time at all, we had left the busy fort, and were stood on the wet sand of Scratchell's Bay below. The instant isolation and atmosphere was quite foreboding, but the half hour waiting for the tide to go out further accustomed me to the unnerving environment.

The tide had retreated enough not to be a problem off the abseil, but needed that time for shoes to come off, and the short wade along the cliff to the start of the route.

"This is some frigging adventure you've got me into again mate," were my words to him.

"Aye," he said.

"And if I remember correctly from our last trip, it's your lead."

The chalk was a little green and slimy to start with, which made getting to the col between the two pinnacles interesting. The exposure on both sides of the ridge was instant.

The excitement and adrenalin rush, accompanied me throughout the 6 pitches of climbing, as it has done for most of my climbing life.

I guess the feeling may be akin to a drug like craving (not that I have ever been tempted by drugs) needed to feed a gnawing rat, that hadn't been fed for a while.

With care and common sense, the chalk ridge was solid and dry, which gave absorbing climbing and belaying throughout. Occasionally, belay protection became a little more reliant on faith rather than soundness, as it usually relied on slings round a chalk spike, warthogs driven in half way, or the occasional ice-screw, screwed into an existing hole.

We had chosen (or were lucky) a fine day, with glorious views across the Channel.

The final, often photographed pitch astride the knife edge ridge 'Au Cheval', was a fitting end to a wonderful adventure.

Chapter Thirty-One
The West Highland Way

Not many medium length hikes, in the UK's playground, can match the diversity and sheer magnificence of Scotland's West Highland Way.

We've hiked some multi-day ventures between us, from the Lyke Wake walk in the north, to the South West coastal path and Ridgeway ancient trackway in the south. But for Lynne and myself the West Highland Way (WHW) stands head and shoulders above them all.

In 2009, with both of us approaching the big sixty, a couple of challenges needed tacking while we felt capable.

The WHW is 95 miles (152km) long. It runs from Glasgow to Fort William and links Scotland's largest city to the foot of its highest mountain, along its largest freshwater loch.

It was to be a tough challenge as we elected to camp most of the pit stops, carrying everything we needed on our backs.

The journey from Wantage to Oxford, to London, then to Glasgow central railway station took most of the day. A wander round Glasgow's interesting and clean central square, was enough to get us fully pooped and in need of a comfy hotel bedroom, the last for a while.

A good catch up on some sleep was needed, before setting off on the trail to Fort William.

Fully fit in the morning, we caught a short train ride to the town of Milngavie, a northern suburb of greater Glasgow. The WHW was well signposted and very soon we were on our way.

The trail quickly became rural, and soon we were walking through woods carpeted with late spring Bluebells. It was a pleasant flat, easy start to the trip as we crossed Strath Blane water and headed north to our planned campsite at Drumquhassle, 2km south of Drymen. It was good to be on the trail, then setting up camp after a 19km hike. More specifically to relax around the tent, not pestered by those dreaded Scottish midge beasties.

We were up and away early, with a hike of 26km to our next pit stop at Rowardennan. As we did so, through Garadhban Forest an even greater carpet of spring Bluebells was on show. The waters of Loch Lomond came into view at Balmaha. From there, the interesting ups and downs along the east bank of the Loch got us to the small campsite (no facilities) just north of Rowardennan Lodge.

It had started to drizzle by early afternoon, but undeterred although pooped once again, we set up camp and enjoyed the ambience whilst drinking a glass of wine and tucking into a well-deserved meal in a bag.

The next leg to Beinglas farm campsite just north of Inverarnan was around the same distance. We found this leg tougher than expected with the continuous ups and downs along the loch. However, it was also beautiful and gave us plenty of excuses to take short breaks on small sandy beaches. It was a bloody joy to take off our boots and socks then paddle in the refreshing waters of the loch.

Another excuse was to seek out Rob Roy's Cave, shown on our map just south of Sroin Uaidh. Eventually, we arrived at the north end of the Loch, by the famous Grey Mares Tail waterfall of the Ben Glas Burn, and then the campsite.

It was raining, but it mattered not as we went into automatic mode erecting the tent and getting a brew on the go. The campsite utilities were great and clean, another fine end to a day.

Tyndrum was the next destination on the plan, a distance of 20km. It was a height gain through tranquil Glen Falloch as the trail followed serenely beside River Falloch. There was a definite feeling of being in the Highlands by that time, as is so often the case with the numerous climbing trips over the decades. Once again it was too enticing not to stop and absorb the ambience and views of the glens.

The trail dropped down the hillside, but turned a sharp left before the town of Crianlarich.

It would have been so easy to justify, or come up with a feeble excuse for tea and cake or even an ice-cream, if only Lynne had succumbed. That's the problem with accompanying a hardened hiker!

Onwards towards Tyndrum through 3km of forest until crossing the A82 to the north and following the river flats, cum flood plain of the River Fillan. The trail crossed the A82 once more to the west following the River Cononish before finally delivering us at Tyndrum campsite.

"God, I love camping and hiking, particularly that trail and would do it all over again, but it was bloody hard work."

At that point, I needed to have a word with myself. Funny as it is though, by the morning, as it always is, I was good to go. Just a little bit of mind control over a knackered, unwilling body.

A slightly shorter leg of 16km, would see us passing through Bridge of Orchy to Inveroran.

I looked forward to this leg, as so often we travelled north at night when on a climbing mission, one hardly got chance to take in the scenery.

On leaving Tyndrum, the trail follows the A82 and the Highland railway, all of which go through the Glen under the great bulks of Beinn Odhar (901m), Beinn Dorain (1074m) and Beinn an Dothaidh (1002m) before reaching the Bridge of Orchy Hotel and a must have tea and cake.

It is another beautiful part of the Highland way, even the road and railway add to the attraction as they make their way towards Rannoch Moor. Whilst admiring the natural landscape, we also admired the man-made elegance of the 'Horseshoe Viaduct' as it curves round Auch Gleann following the Old Military Road.

I had been on two railway journeys to the Highlands during climbing trips, both from Oxford with one taking the west coast line to Fort William, the other to the east via the Cairngorms and the town of Aviemore. Great train journey's I would recommend to anyone.

As lovely as it was sitting in the sun at the Bridge of Orchy scoffing cake, we needed to get a move on, the next 0m over the steep hillside of Mam Carraigh, down to the campsite beside the Inveroran Hotel was going to be a slow plod.

Arriving at the hotel, I wondered if they had a room available, I think I could have been very tempted!

As it was they didn't, so it was the tent for the 5th night in their neat campsite. We pitched camp beside a small stream that ran into the nearby Loch Tulla, a rather nice spot with grand views once again.

Our next leg was going to be the toughest, although I hadn't really planned in getting as far as we eventually did. Lynne was going well and the initial idea was to get to the Kingshouse Hotel, a stretch of 16km, then see how we felt.

The trail gained height reasonably steady around Beinn Toaig (834m), and headed due north across the western fringes of Rannoch Moor. An amazing solid trail that eventually picked up the Old Military Road that took a line through seemingly endless peat bogs either side of the trail. During one or two short pit stops it was amazing to just sit and watch an abundance of Dragonfly's hovering and darting close by, unperturbed by our presence.

Eventually, we passed east of the Glencoe ski lifts high on Meall a' Bhùiridh (1108m), then a short distance to cross the A82 once more. As we headed to the Kingshouse Hotel, and a welcome break, it was hard not to take eyes off the magnificent sight of Buachaille Etive Mór (1022m).

The Kingshouse lured us in for a welcome brew and lunch, as we discussed our options.

As both of us were going well, the decision was to try and make it to Kinlochleven, a further 13km and a total of 29km for the day. If we had had enough before then, we at least packed the gear to fly camp somewhere. So we set off following the A82 westwards for 5km, consumed by the view of 'The Buachaille' until Altnafeadh. There we left the road and headed north up the steep slopes of *The Devils Staircase.*

The terrain is rugged and famous for the deaths of many a labourer who, having picked up their wages from working on the KInlochleven dam, would hike all the way to the Kingshouse to get 'plastered' only to succumb to hypothermia (especially in winter) on the way back.

The dam was built in the early 1900s for the British Aluminium Company, by 'navvies' using nothing but hand tools for smelting aluminium. It was a huge undertaking in the remotest of spots, without the help of any mechanical powered machinery and in squalid conditions. It is believed to be the last creation of the true 'navvy' whose labours included many canals and railways across the countryside.

We made it into town completely buggered but to a very convenient campsite in the grounds of the local Pub. Needless to say, the first pints didn't touch the sides and the fish and chips tasted the best in the world. There was one leg of the trail to go!

What makes the trail so special is its diversity, a word I'm in danger of over using, but which I cannot use enough. The last leg of the journey to Fort William is truly 'Alpine'.

After gaining several hundred feet out of Kinlochleven, the trail follows a valley of watercourses westwards. Great hulks on either side especially to the north, still held spring snow high up. Peaks of Am Bodach (1032m), Stob Bàn (999m) and Mullach nan Coirean looked amazing, without even mentioning much of the 'must climb' ridges.

As we headed north around Meall a' Chaorainn and gained a little more height, Ben Nevis (1344m) came in and out of view amongst great faces and slopes.

Once in Nevis Forest the landscape changed again and again until popping out into Glen Nevis and into Fort William.

Justifying a hotel bed for the night was a 'no brainer' and we made the most of a hot shower, plenty of wine and lots to eat, whilst re-living what we had done.

A relaxing train journey to Mallaig and a brief visit to southern Skye, rounded up the couple of days that remained, before returning home with memories that will last a lifetime.

Chapter Thirty-Two
Maesglasau Falls

I couldn't leave this little beauty out of my short list of UK playground adventures.

It took sixteen long years of waiting for the requisite winter conditions to turn the 650ft (200m) thundering waterfall into 6 pitches of solid climbable ice.

Maesglasau Falls lie in a small valley in the Dyfi Hills off the A470, between the village of Dinas Mawddwy and the town of Dollgellau. The area also makes it into the southern boundary of Snowdonia National Park.

The impressive falls tumble through a massive escarpment which can be clearly seen from the road. In full spate during wet months, it's hard to imagine they could ever freeze.

However, freeze they certainly do, but they require severe sub-zero temperatures with prolonged bitterly cold easterly winds, to bring them into condition. A good dose of snow is also useful to coagulate the fast running water.

It is the sheer ephemeral nature of the thing, which combines with its magnificence and local scenery that should make it a 4 star tick for any ice-climber to look out for.

I visited the falls for the first time with New Zealander, Rob Blackburne back in 1994.

The weather forecast seemed to favour our chances. After a quick phone call, followed by a gathering of gear, I was soon on my way to Birmingham to pick up Rob.

We travelled there overnight, slept in a layby and made an early start for the base of the escarpment. It was too dark to get a true idea of the ice build-up from our vantage point, but as we neared the falls, the ominous sound of running water dampened our optimism.

True enough it was unconsolidated ice and pissing with water underneath. A meagre attempt of climbing a few feet gave little solace, before a reluctant abandon back to the car.

Two more unsuccessful attempts during years leading up to 2010 were made, but it was in the first week of that year a large dump of snow hit Wales and the South of England.

On the 5 January, ten inches of snow fell overnight in Wantage, prompting me to uncover the skis once again and head onto the Ridgeway. Better still, temperatures were plummeting.

I was certain conditions were more favourable this time, however, as Rob had gone back to live in New Zealand and Martin was unavailable, I was buggered for a partner at short notice.

A phone call to Pete, my brother on Anglesey, had him convinced it was worth the challenge.

Pete is not a regular climber, but has followed me up a few rock routes. He is a competent Paraglider and as such, is used to a 'little risk', I certainly had faith in him belaying me and seconding me up the route if it was in nick!

It was Saturday, 9 January, I had to be in work for several hours, but agreed to meet up with Pete at Dinas Mawddwy early Sunday morning.

At 06.00 we met up, Pete coming directly from home and me having spent the night in the car. By 06.30, we were on our way.

It was bitterly cold and felt promising, I had fingers crossed all the way. The silence of the morning was deafening, but not a sound of running water could be heard.

And there it was, a beautiful frozen steep column of ice rising from the frozen stream bed. Frozen further than we could see, and not another soul around.

We wasted no time, gearing up with plenty of ice-screws, slings, a few wires and pegs (pitons). I led off up the steep section, then onto easier ground and fixed a belay. Pete seconded the pitch easily as I knew he would.

The second and third pitches had steep ice walls, were more technical and fun, with each stance and belay set up with ice screws.

The fourth pitch was again on steep ice leading to a ledge and tree belay.

The atmosphere was fantastic, Pete was climbing confidently, I felt he was enjoying it as much as I was.

Pitch five was interesting as it followed a frozen stream channel between side walls of iced up rock. Not technically demanding, although intricate placements of axes and front points required concentration to the penultimate short steep wall and screw belay.

The final pitch of short, steep ice led to the top of the escarpment.

We waded amongst knee high heather and snow as we made our way off the hill, grinning like Cheshire cats all the way back to the cars.

It couldn't have been a better day, I was so grateful for Pete's partnership. As I sit writing this chapter in 2021, it could easily have been an opportunity of a lifetime lost.

There has not been another spell of weather to bring the falls into condition since.

Global warming is having such an impact, it is very conceivable they may never freeze again.

Note

I should make a point here, on the off chance of someone ever reading this account that, access to the falls has no public right of way! The farmer was a friendly guy, but understandably would be pissed off if a car blocked access or litter was left around.

Chapter Thirty-Three
Land's End to John O'groats (LEJOG)

I had decided to write only one of our cycle trips in this chapter, but there were two on my mind!

It was difficult to exclude our south to north cycle ride link-up of the Outer Hebrides, during a particularly beautiful spell of weather. However, there was really no contest, it had to be *LEJOG*.

Nevertheless, a quick paragraph on the former follows for anyone interested.

Our start point was a ferry from Oban to the southern tip of Barra at Castlebay. A short circuit of the island on the bikes was followed by a ferry to Eriskay. From Eriskay our ride north on the A865 and over the interesting causeway, led to South Uist.

It was then onwards through South Uist to Benbecula via another short causeway, stopping at one of the many beautiful beaches that abound on the west coast of both islands.

Next up was North Uist, which has two main cycling options, one longer than the other. Either one leads to the north of the island, and yes, another causeway linking it to Berneray and the ferry to the Isle of Harris.

Harris is a wonderful island, with amazing beaches and interest on the west, in contrast to more remoteness on the east. We included a circumnavigation of the island which, on the east side, had an almost alpine feel to it, and shouldn't be left out.

Our final ride onto the Isle of Lewis and up to Stornoway had plenty of wild alternative cycling options. Given more time, a fitting finale to end the trip would have been a cycle to the northern tip of the island and the Butt of Lewis.

Land's End to John O'Groats (LEJOG for short) had been on my mind for a few years. Lynne and I were leisure cyclists, nothing more, but we were a fit old couple.

Given some extra leg work, and some bum training (that's my weak point), I felt we could manage the challenge. It needed to happen soon though, neither of us were spring chickens anymore.

Brave or stupid, we (*it was me*) decided to take panniers, in the hope we might get a few nights 'under canvas'.

In 2011, we were as cycling fit as we were going to be, so with laden bikes we set off from Wantage to Didcot railway station and a GWR train to Penzance.

We were certainly not going to break any records. I had initially planned the flattest most direct route possible, and we were certainly not looking to be heroes, by taking in the likes of Snowdonia, the Lake District Fells or excesses of the Highlands.

However, some bright spark we bumped into on the train, suggested and convinced us, we *must* take a route across Dartmoor!

The traditional route by road is 874 miles long (which we had planned) but our plans changed on the Scots border, from a westward direction via Fort William to an easterly direction via Aviemore due to weather. Our eventual LEJOG cycle distance was 912 miles, with an overall cycle distance, inclusive of travelling to and from train stations, of 960 miles.

As for records, the current record for cycling the route is an incredible 41 hours, 4 mins, and 22 seconds, held by Andy Wilkinson.

Over the decades, the route has been covered by just about every conceivable means, from a Lawnmower to unicycle, on foot to walking backwards, even on a bed and motorised bar-stool.

Having arrived at Penzance, we cycled 10 miles to our B and B at Sennen Cove, immediately realising the enormity of the challenge, obviously not helped by the weight on the bikes.

"Perhaps our training should have included hefty panniers," I shouted to Lynne!

After a quick brew at the B and B, we cycled to Land's End and back to the B and B (minus panniers of course) to relax before the off the following day.

We were keen and away the next morning, with the aim of getting somewhere near St Austell. As with most of the legs on the trip, we did not bother to pre-arrange our overnight stays. Our first leg of the journey ended at Par, after 56 miles and six and a half hours of riding.

Par is a small village east of St Austell, with not too many options for B and B's. However, we found the Royal Inn to be very friendly and comfortable to rest our weary legs. The first leg in Cornwall was unexpectedly hilly, but worse was to come.

Driving a car doesn't really register the true steepness, or undulating relentless of roads, unless of course you're driving a Reliant Robin, a Citroen 2 CV or it's blindingly bloody obvious.

I suppose by trying to stay off the main 'A roads' and Dual Carriageways as much as possible was always setting ourselves up for a harder time. The next day from Par started in that vein, getting progressively worse through Liskeard and Tavistock to the edge of Dartmoor.

Then it all turned bestial across the moors, until we had covered another 55 miles to Moretonhampstead, and in need of a second night's pit stop.

Although knackered, we were loving it really, in a masochistic sort of way.

This chapter could turn into a book of its own if I were not careful. It was such a great challenge, with plenty of stories to tell. I felt it best to include an extremely abbreviated spread sheet of our journey instead.

Land's End to John O'Groats, June 2011						
Leg	Day	Mls	Guide Time	Actual (incl breaks)	Accommodation	Notes
Land's End to Par	1	56	4h 30m	6h 30m	Sunnybank Hotel / The Royal Inn	B & B at Sennen / Unexpectedly hilly
Par to More'hstead	2	55	5h 10m	8h 30m	B and B Plus	Dartmoor and 25% hills were good to do early in the trip
More'hstead to Bridgwater	3	59	4h 35m	6h 15m	Crossways Inn	
Bridgwater to Stroud	4	65	5h	7h	Railway Hotel	Grand hotel with low cost rooms
Stroud to Ironbridge	5	74	6h	8h 15m	Tontine Hotel	Grand countryside
Ironbridge to Warrington	6	62	4h 40m	6h 45m	Premier Inn	Great cake shop in Bridgenorth
Warrington to Kendal	7	79	6h	8h 30m	Collincroft	Our 2nd home
Kendal to Canonbie	8	65	4h 45m	6h 30m	Cross Keys Hotel	Opened for us, closed 'coz wife was ill and he couldn't cope!
Canonbie to Edinburgh	9	78	6h 30m	7h 30m	Cameron B and B	wild orchids on roadside, spent day in Edinburgh
Edinburgh to Dunkeld	10	58	4h 45m	6h	Royal Dunkeld Hotel	Scary on the bridge
Dunkeld to Aviemore	11	71	6h 40m	7h 45m	Cairngorm Guest House	Only real wet day, on the Highlands
Aviemore to Alness	12	54	5h 40m	6h 30m	Morven House	Owners from Cornwall
Alness to Helmsdale	13	57	5h	7h 15m	The Ship Inn	Museum of Geology / Herrings and The Silver Darlings
Helmsdale to John O'Groats	14	58	4h 15m	6h 30m	The John O'Groats Guest House	Arrived on the longest day
Guide Book Total		891				
Actual LEJOG Total		912				
Actual Overall Total		960	Includes, Grove to Didcot, John O'Groats to Thurso, Oxford to Grove			
Average /day		64				

Cycling LEJOG as we did, showed us many things, two however, stick in my mind.

Firstly, a reminder to me (as if I ever needed it) of the wonderful diversity this tiny island of ours has. From world heritage landscapes and beaches to majestic flora and fauna.

Secondly, is the abomination and total disregard we show of our surroundings, by the way many of us litter just about bloody everywhere. Most of the time it has proven to come out of vehicle windows, yet we seemingly tolerate it like an irritating rash.

The LEJOG challenge we gave ourselves took us fourteen days, arriving at John O'Groats on the longest day. It would be impossible to choose a favourite day, place or time. However, we did ensure we fitted in places of interest wherever possible.

The tent was not used once, favouring instead a shower and cheap comfortable bed for our sweaty, dirty, knackered bodies. Our stove on the other hand came into its own on every stage of the journey for those very welcome brews.

A final leg of the journey was the 20 miles to Thurso to catch a train for the start of the long journey home.

****

A few months after our successful LEJOG adventure, Nicky dropped a bombshell that for Lynne and myself, was indeed a shock. A shock not for her news, but despair for Lynne and I that we had not picked up on it a lot sooner.

Like me, Nicky was not a great academic at school, but always achieved well at sporting disciplines. They helped carry her through into an initial and successful working environment as a gym instructor after leaving school.

She was well respected in her role as a personal trainer at various gym locations and gained a Diploma in Personal Training and Sports Therapy from a world recognised training body, *Premier Global.* Unfortunately, salaries in that sector were never rewarding enough.

She took time out like her brother, and grasped an opportunity for a spell visiting several countries around the world with a friend, perhaps to seek her next direction in life, or escape something underlying.

On her return, Nicky was still undecided on a career path, but again, like me, she turned to immersing herself in sport as a replacement.

An enormous amount of self-discipline went into her training for a dozen or so Triathlons, an Ironman as well as the London Marathon.

Her fitness and early childhood kicking ability (gained at Grove Challengers FC), also enabled a first team placement for Reading Ladies Rugby Club.

Nicky had given a variety of jobs a go, even moving away from Wantage to find a way forward in her life. However, none of them truly defined or satisfied a direction for her future.

New office administration skills and qualifications were building with a lean towards Human Resources, but a move back to Wantage was not really what she wanted.

Around the same time, Gary had left full-time engagement with the Army and was building his security business, initially based in Guildford, Surrey.

His staff were growing, which prompted him to make a generous offer to his 'Sis' to go and work for him. It was an extremely kind and noble thing to do. It was not only an opportunity for Nicky to expand her skills but also move from Town life to City life with more freedom.

Gary's motivation, energy and entrepreneurial skills drove his business forward in such a way that eventually led him to move the business into Central London. It was where he thought his business needed to be placed, to be most effective in a competitive market.

He also looked to expand a business opportunity in Kenya, East Africa. It was certainly a busy period for him and no doubt Nicky, who had continued her support in the Human Resources department.

In the paragraphs (a précis of the years) above, I have condensed, simplified, or left out so many events that occurred, that are not appropriate for me to write. It does not do justice to the tremendous hard-work, sheer determination and stressful times both Gary and Nicky went through during that period for independent reasons. But typically, it would have been battling the 'ups and downs' of business, to move it ever forward, or dealing with their own personal difficulties that were a constant challenge and distraction.

And so…a telephone call from Nicky with a subsequent meeting in London, set the scene to discuss with the four of us, that she now had the courage to explain that she was 'coming out' as gay, to explain the life she had been living and dealing with for nearly twenty years, and to make us aware of her move to Sale, Cheshire. The move was to be immediate to join her partner Becki, who had lived there all her life.

It was also an opportunity to apologise to her brother for the various consequences of leaving the business so suddenly.

It was a genuine shock for Lynne and I, we didn't give a toss about the sexual orientation bit, just deeply, deeply sorry we were not more aware to help when she needed it most. Her happiness and well-being all that mattered and always will be.

In hindsight, events that happened during that period seemed to interlink with one another the more we chatted. Were we just stupid, or unable as parents, to see the signs?

Or was Nicky's façade which, no doubt many like her, are forced to display, so convincing?

Lynne on the Lairig Ghru trail passing Loch Avon (A'an)

Nicky on Bosigran ridge (Commando ridge)

Martin approaching Skeleton ridge   *LEJOG – on our* way

Classic 'Au cheval' style

Part 8: Epilogue

When youth departs, may wisdom prove enough.
WC

Chapter Thirty-Four
Past and Present

The Past

In this book of adventure and mountaineering life, I have barely touched on the skill of ski-mountaineering. A skill that for me, truly epitomises the 'complete Alpinist'.

I would love to have acquired the necessary skill, to access the more remote corners of the Alps or greater ranges. Alas, time and money were not available to do that.

Yet corners of the globe my colleagues and I have visited, meant we accessed and extracted ourselves from situations primarily by foot, snowshoe or simple skiing. I do recall a few times however, where skis and skins were used off-piste and on glaciers. On most occasions, it led me to making a complete arse of myself, but more to the point, the worry of gliding headlong into the jaws of a bottomless crevasse.

Looking back, I'm glad I didn't gain that elegant ability, otherwise it may have been one of the crucial skills that could have turned my earlier climbing from a rich and rewarding hobby, into the hard graft of professional guiding.

In this book of my climbing life, I have also by-passed 'Big wall climbing'[51], 'Aid climbing'[52] and 'Siege style tactics'[53], as well as some of the skills that go with it.

This has been predominantly due to limited time available from work and family life by choice. It was also most certainly down to the unlimited options to scare oneself shitless in other mountain environments, where far less bureaucracy and expenditure was incurred. In all cases, it did not detract from our preferred choice of 'going light' and in 'Alpine style'.

I made a statement at the start of this book that should my number be up early, I would go with a smile on my face; and nothing has changed. I have pursued my dreams, whilst enjoying my beautiful family. I would not wish for anything else, or to change a thing.

The various crossroads one comes across in life, obviously leads to anxiety, stress and decision making. In considering benefits not just for oneself, but those close to us, and involving ourselves in the synergy of each other, makes success tick. It does for me anyway.

That does not mean it was easy or came without hard work!

The Present

The most wonderful recent news I've saved for this chapter is the birth of our grandson, Chester Hope-Powell, born on the 23 July 2017 at Wythenshawe Hospital, south Manchester.

Nicola and her partner, Becki Powell, decided to try and have a child via IVF treatment, with Nicky being the biological mother. On the 4th attempt, after it had taken up three years of their lives, it was successful.

---

[51] Big wall climbing, is the art of climbing sheer walls and faces of great height, which often require multi-day climbing. A vast range of skills, techniques and equipment would have been acquired to be successful.

[52] Aid climbing is best described as the 'direct use' of inserted devices (bolts, pitons, ice screws, cams, etc) to assist progress up a climb, by pulling on, or stepping into, instead of using them for protection only.

[53] Siege style tactics was the traditional method of 'high altitude' climbing. Involving the establishment of several well stocked camps, often connected with fixed ropes, and the rate of progress very slow.

Chester was born a *Downs Syndrome* baby, and although it was an initial shock to them and us all, he has grown into a most wonderful, happy, cheeky and loving little boy.

Although there maybe difficulties ahead, the three of them and the families and friends they have supporting them, are sure to overcome any obstacles that stand in their path.

****

Like our climate, climbing is undergoing gradual but certain change.

As I write this in August 2021, the Olympic Games (2020) have gone ahead in Japan, albeit a year later than planned due to Covid 19.

'Sport climbing' has been included in the Games for the first time, with Speed climbing, Bouldering and Lead climbing the three disciplines in the competition.

There is no doubt competitors are at the top of their game in these fields, showing great gymnastic ability and skills. The competition must be entertaining for many watching.

Not all top Sport climbers favour the competition side however, there are many out there equally as talented, pushing sport grades on bolted routes ever higher on outdoor crags around the world.

It is understandable that this tangent to the world of climbing, is attracting more and more young guns coming into the sport. It is safe, sociable, and an opportunity for expression. *However, it is predictable and unadventurous.*

There has been a massive increase in bespoke Sport climbing walls throughout the country and worldwide, with a growing number of outdoor cliffs (predominantly quarries) now supporting bolted sport routes too.

In one sense, it's great to see more of our youth being attracted to Sport climbing, but sad that there appears to be only a small contingent that transition to the noble, traditional form of climbing on rock and ice outdoors.

It is all too clear to see on our rock faces and mountains today, the huge decline in 'Trad' climbing. Climbing that imparts greater challenges in a pure form, such as honing mental power, acquisition of technical skills, and gaining all round physical strength.

Let us not forget other positive acquisitions that 'Trad' climbing can deliver, such as dealing with risk, taking one's own responsibility for safety and above all, acquiring a degree in common sense of when, or when not to push the boundaries.

So aptly described in Audrey Salkeld's book 'World Mountaineering' and my introduction.

****

Covid 19 update

From my last update on the 20 April 2021, the UK continued to battle against the moving target and changing face (variants) of an enemy, it continues to cause many deaths and hospitalisations around the world.

For the UK, there was continued lifting of restrictions on Step 3 (17 May 2021) of the Governments plans following the lifting of steps 1 and 2 (March and April 2021). However, step 4 (21 June), the removal of all restrictions, was moved forward to the 19 July 2021.

The large uptake of vaccinations during early spring to July helped enormously, leading to Government's ability in lifting most of the restrictions after the 19 July.

Holiday travel restrictions have increasingly been opened using the *traffic light system*, but the moving target means changes could occur overnight.

A number of countries are still experiencing falls followed by large rises in infections. Many countries are still having to be on the UK's *Red and Amber lists*.

This will be the case in the UK for a long while yet, as Covid 19 is not going away in a hurry.

Current statistics for the UK are as follows:
Total of population vaccinated (1st dose) = 47 million = 88.7%
Total of population vaccinated (2nd dose) = 39 million = 73.5%
Current testing +ve/day = 30,000+ (going down)
Current deaths/day = 86 (going up slightly)

****

Gary continues to be successful as "Founder and Chief Executive" of his security business based in Kenya, whilst establishing and growing Skydive Zanzibar, Tanzania.

He has unlimited enthusiasm and strength for taking on business challenges as well as possessing a quality of 'never giving up'. I know both businesses under his wing will go from strength to strength.

It is pleasing for Lynne and I to know Izzy, his partner, has now joined him after giving up her teaching role in Dubai. I'm sure they will try and *live the dream* together taking time out to relax wherever possible.

A downside to that, is not being able to meet up. We have not seen them both for two years. It is unlikely to change in the short term as Tanzania remains on the UK's Red list.

As the world begins to slowly open once more after Covid 19 and we flock to our open spaces, let us realise how much we depend on them for our well-being and spiritual uplifting. We really do need to look after them.

If ever there was a time the Earth needed our respect and help for the future of humanity it is now.

For me, the underlying motive in heading for the mountains is to pit my wit against the challenges and sometimes difficult situations that are put before me. The rewards are a huge amount of pleasure, and give enormous stimulus for health and living.

Winning or losing against rock or ice is irrelevant. It is dealing with the challenges ethically and aesthetically that gives me the greatest reward and spiritual uplift.

It is certainly not about material rewards.

It would please me enormously to know that by reading this book, even just one person, may have been inspired to 'Step Out of the Ordinary'

Now, at the wrong side of seventy years old, I'm hoping further battles are still in my capability, it's certainly still in the mind, it's whether the body is willing to play ball.

As the desire and capability to do less training diminishes for reason of 'pushing the grades', it opens the door for other opportunities like seeking out first ascents possibilities. This has been the case over the last few years with Martin from the Lakes and Peter Williams, 'Pedro' to us all, at our local limestone crags of the Wye Valley.

Most importantly, I will remain eternally grateful to Lynne, Gary and Nicky for their love, mutual respect for the outdoors and total support and encouragement.

It has enabled us all to enjoy this wonderful world together in parallel with my climbing passage in life.

A special thanks to Martin who, after spending forty years of climbing together and escaping with in the mountains, remains a close friend and companion. His enthusiasm for the hills and natural instinctive ability in the mountains continues to rub off on me.

We share a similar passion for the environment which is in desperate need of change, having witnessed so much abuse first-hand, through our journeys around the world.

I'm sure Martin will continue to persuade me into new challenges (he is four years younger mind), as I'm sure Lynne will be as equally keen to see the back of me from time to time!

Meanwhile our lives in Wantage on the edge of the North Wessex Downs, sandwiched between the Cotswolds to the north-west and Chilterns to the east (all Areas of Outstanding Natural Beauty, AONB) will continue to keep us active and our souls fulfilled.

We need mountains for a variety of reasons, for one, it helped me rediscover myself.

I'm glad I know who I am and what I want, as what I have is all I want.

I think I can already hear those next vague wild calls of the mountains!

Nicky, Chester & Becki 2021

*Nicky & Chester 2021
(picture by Becki Powell)*

Gary & Izzy 2021 (picture by Gary)

Gary – Doing what he does (picture by unknown)

Wintours Leap – A 2nd home

First Ascents

Lofoton Isles, Ice and Mixed climbs

Nordfjellett	Thing Fish	5/IV
Sundklaak	Sundklakk Couloir	4/IV`
Svartinden	The Long Trawl	5/V
Preston	Fissure of Men	6/V
Storbenken	Storbenken Icefalls	

Wye Valley

Wyndcliff Quarry

Three Amigos	F6a
ApostropheS	F6a+
Dog Face	F6b/6b+

Wintours Leap, Fly Wall

Flies undone	VS 4b
Fly in the Ivy	E2 5b
Alphafly	E3 6a
Fly Havoc (2nd pitch variation)	E2 5c

Wintours Leap, Great Wall, Small Wall

One for Button	E2 5c

Woodcroft Quarry

Thingfrith	F6a+
CornerCrackEliminate	F6b
Between The Lines	F6a+

Bolivia, Quimsa Cruz

Korichuma	TD+

(SE wall with North wall traverse to summit)

Lake District
Raven crag, Langdale
Endever	E1 5b
Demeter	HVS 5a

Upper Scout Crag, Langdale
Something Fishy	MVS 4b

Duddon Valley, Wallowbarrow crag
Placoderm (2nd pitch)	VS

Adventures & Climbing Record – Mike Hope

1982 – 1st Abingdon Peoples Marathon – 3hrs 22mins

1983 – 2nd Abingdon Peoples Marathon – 3hrs 30mins

1985 – Cycled Grove (Oxon) to Land's End
24 hour cycle ride to raise money for The Sue Ryder Foundation

1986 – Austria – Glockner region (June/July)
Grossglockner (3,798m) – (terminated due to weather)
Sassois rock
Fontenbleau bouldering

1987 – France – Chamonix (Sept)
Aig du Pouce (3,792m) – South Face with summit
Aig du Chardonnet (3,824m) – North Spur with summit, descent via Forbes Arete
Aig du Midi (3,842m) via Frendo Spur
Envers rock climbs

1988 – France – Chamonix (July)
Tour Ronde (3792m) – North Face with summit
Buoux rock climbs

1990 – Canada – British Columbia (May)
Mt Robson (3,954m) – North Face (terminated due to conditions)
Mt Athabasca (3,491m) – North Face (terminated due to conditions)

Mt Colin – rock climbs

1992 – France – Chamonix (Feb)
Winter icefall climbing

1993 – Alaska (May)
Mt Hunter (4,442m) – North West Spur (terminated due to snow conditions)
Mt McKinley (6,190m) – via upper section of the West Rib with summit, descent via West Buttress

1993 – Scotland – Ben Nevis fell race – 2hrs 4mins

1994 – France – Chamonix (Jan)
Winter icefall climbing

1994 – Switzerland (July)
Grindelwald – rock climbs
Leysin – rock climbs

1994 – Lakes – Langdale Horseshoe fell race – 2hrs 47mins

1994 – Welsh 1000m peaks fell race – 5hrs 43min

1995 – Peru – HuayHuash (May)
Mt Jirishanca (6,125m) – West Face (aborted due to storms)

1997 – Italy – Aosta Valley (Mar)
Winter icefall climbing
Lillaz
Val du Valnontey

1997 – Canada – British Columbia (July/Aug)
Mt Robson (3,954m) – Kain Face with summit, descent by same
Mt Edith Cavell (3,363m) – East Ridge with summit, descent by same

1998 – California – Yosemite (July/Aug)
50 miles section of the John Muir trail with Lynne.

1999 – Baffin Island (July/Aug)
Mt Asgard (2,015m) – North Peak via South East face with summit

2000 – France – Briancon (Feb)
Winter icefall climbing
Valle du Fournel
Ceillac
Valle du Freissineres
La Grave

2000 – Corsica (June)
GR20 high level traverse with Lynne

2000 – Isle of Wight
Skeleton Ridge (HVS 5a)

2001 – Italy – Canazei (Feb)
Winter icefall climbing
Sottoguda
Sella
Val Gardena
Val di Fassa

2001 – Lakes – Langdale Half Marathon
Lynne – 2hrs 7mins
Nicky – 2hrs 10mins
Mike – 1hr 57mins

2002 – Italy – Canazei (Feb)
Winter icefall climbing
Sottoguda
Val di Fassa (Fontanazzi)
Val Gardena (Orteisi)

2002 – Alaska – Ruth Gorge (May)
Mooses Tooth (3,150m) – West Face via Ham & Eggs Couloir

2003 – Canada – Rockies (Mar)
Winter icefall climbing
Grotto Canyon
Lake Louise
Haffner creek
Bow Lake
Icefields Parkway

2003 – Spain – Picos du Europa (Sept)
High level traverse with Lynne

2004 – France – Cirque du Gavarnie (Feb)
Winter icefall climbing on the Cirque

2004 – Spain – Sierra Nevada (June)
High level walking with Lynne

2004 – Scotland – Cairngorms (May)
Circuit of the Lairig Ghru & Strath Nethy with Lynne

2005 – Norway – Lofoton Isles (Feb)
Winter icefall climbing
5 new routes & exploration
Henningsvaer
Nordfjellett
Sundlaak
Svartinden
Kongtindan

2005 – Scotland – Orkney / Hoy (July)
Old Man of Hoy (137m) via East Face

2005 – Lakes – Langdale Horseshoe fell race – 3hrs 22mins

2006 – France winter – La Grave (Feb)
Winter icefall climbing

2006 – Scotland – Isle of Arran
A'Chir Ridge Traverse with Gary

2006 – Africa – Morocco High Atlas (July/Aug)
High level circuit – Lynne, Carol, Martin with Toubkal (4,167m) summit

2007 – France – Chamonix (May)
Les Courtes (3,856m) N.Face via Swiss route with summit, descent via west ridge.
Cosmiques arête.

2007 – France – Chamonix (July)
Tour du Mt Blanc – cycle tour circuit with Lynne – 350km/7500m

2007 – Scotland – Assynt (over Christmas)
Ben More Assynt (998m) & Quinag (808m)

2008 – Scotland – Isle of Skye (May)
Cuillin ridge traverse with Mo including 'Inn Pin'(not full traverse)

2008 – France – Ecrins Region (Sept)
Ailefroide – Granite rock
Buis les Baronnies – Limestone rock

2009 – Oxfordshire – North Wessex Downs (Feb)
Cross country ski via 'The Ridgeway' home to work (Grove to Swindon) 20 miles in heavy snow. Believe it was the first to be done.

2009 – Scotland (May/June)
West Highland Way camping with Lynne – 96 miles (7days)
2009 – France – Chamonix (Aug)

Rock climbing
Vallorcine
Clocher du Brevant
Gendarme de droite
Brevant
The Blatiere – Red Pillar
Aig du Midi South Face – Eperon des Cosmiques
Aig Crochures
Chezery

2010 – Mid-Wales – Dinas Mawddwy (Jan)
Winter climbing
Maesglasau Falls with Pete

2010 – Scotland – Isle of Skye (June)
Cuillin ridge including 'Inn Pin' with Gary (not full traverse)

2010 – Cornwall – West Penwith (July)
Bosigran (Commando) Ridge with Nicky

2010 – Switzerland / Italy (Aug/Sept)
Piz Badile (3,308m) – North East Face via Cassin route with summit, descent via South face

2011 – Scotland – Orkney / Hoy (May)
Old Man of Hoy (137m) – East Face
(Chris and sponsorship for Gloucester House)

2011 – Lands End to John O'Groats (June)
Cycle ride with Lynne – 960 miles (14 days)

2011 – France – Chamonix (July)
Tour du Mt Blanc
Cycle circuit tour with Michael & Mo – 350km / 7500m

2012 – Spain / France (June/July)
Cycle tour west to east across Andalusia & Southern Alps with Michael & Mo
Approx 1000 miles (15days) over 30,000 feet of ascent

2012 – Kenya – East Africa
3 day Safari to the Masai Mara reserve

2013/14 – Patagonia (Nov>Jan)
2 months+ adventure – Martin, Michael & Mo
Central Tower of Paine – (did not summit due to weather)
Kayak the Grey & Serrano river systems with wild camping.
Visit Tierra del Fuego & Navarino Island.
Rafting on the Futaleufu River.
Travel North 1000km from Punta Arenas to Puerto Montt via the Carretera Austral.

2014 – Morocco – Anti Atlas (Oct)
11 days rock climbing around Jebel al-kest / Ida Oudnidif area

2015 – Norway – Rjukan (Feb)
Winter icefall climbing

2015 – Kenya – East Africa (Dec)
10 day visit with Lynne to visit Gary.
Lake Naivasha & Hells Gate National Parks – cycle tour of the areas
Diani beach – Tandem skydives
PADI Scuba diving basic training with open water dives.

2016 – France – Ecrins region (Feb)
Winter icefall climbing
La Grave & Vallon du Salle area

2016 – Scotland (June)
Sandwood Bay & Highlands with Lynne & van

2016 – France – Ecrins region (July)
Aiguille Dibona (3,130m) via Madier route with summit
Chemin Du Roy – Limestone rock climbing
Croix Du Toulouse – Limestone rock climbing

2017 – Italy – San Martino Valley (July)
Pizzo Cengalo (3,369m) ridge via Vinci route with summit

2019 – Bolivia – South American Andes (June)
Quimsa Cruz range
Korichuma (5,312m) – new route via S.E wall & North wall traverse with summit

2020 – Italy – Cogne Valley (Feb/Mar)
Winter icefall climbing
Lillaz, Val di Grauson, Valsavarenche, Valnontey

2022 – Scotland – N.W Sutherland (May)
Hike & summit Ben Hope (927m) – furthest latitude Munro
Explore parts of the NC500

Bibliography

Relevant Books and Articles

World Mountaineering, Audrey Salkeld, published by Mitchell Beazley.

The Mont Blanc massif, Gaston Rébufatt, published by Bâton Wicks.

50 Years of Alpinism, Riccardo Cassin, published by Diadem Books Ltd.

Personal diaries of Mike Hope.

The Internet and Google.